940.53                          73415
L933w

Lucas, James Sidney
World War Two through German eyes

| DATE DUE | | | |
|---|---|---|---|
| | | | |
| | | | |
| | | | |
| | | | |
| | | | |
| | | | |
| | | | |
| | | | |
| | | | |
| | | | |
| | | | |

James Lucas

ARMS AND **a&ap** ARMOUR PRESS

# WORLD WAR TWO

### BASIC PROGRAMME OF THE
### NATIONAL SOCIALIST GERMAN WORKERS' PARTY

The programme of the German Workers' Party is a fixed one. The leaders reject the idea of setting new goals once the initial aims laid down in the programme have been achieved, simply in order to prolong the life of the Party by artificially creating unrest among the masses.

1.    On the basis of a people's right to self-determination we demand the uniting of the Germans within a Greater Germany.

2.    We demand equal status for Germany, vis-à-vis other nations, and the annulling of the Peace Treaties drawn up in Versailles and St Germain.

3.    We demand land and property (colonies) to provide food for our nation and settlement areas for our surplus population.

4.    Only a German can have the right of citizenship. A Volksgenosse can only be a person who has German parents, irrespective of religion. THEREFORE NO JEW CAN BE CONSIDERED TO BE A VOLKSGENOSSE.

5.    Those people who have no citizenship rights can only be considered as guests in Germany and must be subject to laws concerning foreigners.

6.    Only citizens should have the right to decide the leadership and laws of the state. Therefore, we demand that only those with citizenship rights should be eligible to serve in a public office, whether this be at national, Länder or local level. We oppose the corrupt parliamentary system in which people are employed only on the basis of the political party to which they belong and not according to their character or ability.

7.    We demand that the first priority of the state should be to ensure that its citizens have work and decent living conditions. Where it is not possible to feed all the citizens of the state, foreign nationals (who have no citizenship rights) should be repatriated.

8.    Further immigration of non-Germans must be halted. We demand that all non-Germans who have entered the Reich since 2 August 1914, be forced to leave the country immediately.

9.    All citizens must have the same rights and obligations.

10.    The first duty of all Volksgenossen must be to work, either manually or with the mind. The actions of an individual must not be against the general good but must be in accord with it.

THEREFORE, WE DEMAND

11.    The abolition of unearned income.

THE DESTRUCTION OF THE DOMINANCE OF INVESTED CAPITAL

12.    Because wars demand of the people great physical and personal sacrifice, any personal gain through war must be considered as a crime against the nation. WE DEMAND, THEREFORE, THE CONFISCATION OF ALL WAR PROFITS.

13.    We demand the nationalization of all publicly owned companies (Trusts).

14.    We demand profit sharing by all large companies

# CONTENTS

# AUTHOR'S
## ACKNOWLEDGEMENTS

ONE summer evening in 1943, I sat around the camp fire of a German field hospital near Sousse. The campaign in Africa had ended, and men of this medical unit were waiting to be shipped off to a prison camp in America.

We soldiers talked easily, and the discussion ranged across a great number of topics, passing eventually from warfare and weapons to politics. I was astounded at the naïvety of the points my companions advanced. Their arguments I thought to be simplistic and hopelessly biased – it was obvious they had been brainwashed. They, for their part, considered me to be the brainwashed victim of a fettered press, which would not allow me to see the positive aspects of the dynamic new Germany they represented.

During the years of the war and since the end of hostilities I have met and have corresponded with a great many Germans. These were usually former soldiers, but my contacts have also included a great many civilians – men and women; laymen and priests; many who had been politically active; those who despised politicians; a few who had been fanatical Nazis; and also implacable opponents of that regime. To all of them I am grateful for the answers they gave to the questions I asked. To those institutions in this country, in Germany and in Austria whose resources were so freely given and whose officers were invariably helpful and obliging I am also indebted. To those who supported me in the initial writing and in the subsequent rewriting of a difficult text that sets out to show the viewpoint of a former enemy country, go my especial thanks.

To my dear wife Traude, our daughter Barbara who typed the text, to Terry Charman who read the typescript and offered so many useful suggestions I am particularly grateful. In conclusion my thanks go to David and Beryl Gibbons and to Tony Evans, who produced this book from my typescript as well as to Sheila, Mandy and Fiona, my agents.

James Lucas, 1987

# PREFACE

THE Third Reich was proclaimed in 1933 and those who created it forecast that it would live for a thousand years. Only twelve years later, the Thousand Year Reich perished and passed into history.

Those twelve years were a period of high drama. When Hitler, the chief architect of the Reich, came to power Germany was a weak nation crippled by inflation and burdened with millions of unemployed. By 1939 Germany was once again a major military power in Europe. By 1940, after a series of short but successful campaigns, she dominated that continent. In the autumn of that year Hitler, unable to invade Great Britain, directed his attention eastwards. During June 1941 he produced the conditions for Germany's eventual military defeat by invading Soviet Russia and in December compounded his blunder by declaring war against the USA. The Third Reich was thus faced by an alliance of the three most powerful nations on earth.

Against such a coalition it was doomed to fail. No firm, well-thought out, long-term strategy had been formulated at any level; military, political or social. No effort had been made by the Nazi leaders to prepare the nation for the war to come, nor to conduct the war with the ruthlessness required. Despite a chronic labour shortage there was no immediate conscription of German women either into the armed services or the armaments industry. There was no central control of industry and there was a complete misjudgement of how the war would develop and of the weapons required to fight a global conflict.

The perspective which the leaders of the Third Reich had of countries and peoples outside Germany was as faulty as our own perspective of Hitler's Germany. Our perspective had been influenced by media sources that were hostile to the National Socialist regime even before it came to power, which retained that hostility throughout the years of the Reich and which have maintained the same attitude since the war's end.

It is my intention to show in this book only the German perspective. The view of the German people vis-à-vis their leaders. The way those leaders saw the masses and, in particular, their attitudes towards German women. The perspective the Germans had of enemy nations as well as of those allied to the Fatherland. Of importance, too, are the viewpoints of the service leaders faced with professional problems they were either unwilling or unable to resolve.

The rationale for this book is the need, as I see it, to dispel the ignorance regarding the National Socialist regime. I came to the idea of seeing the world through German eyes from an awareness that there is a bias in our knowledge of modern European history. A very literate graduate friend of mine saw a showing of Leni Riefenstahl's film, *Triumph des Willens*, and declared it to be a brilliant piece of Nazi propaganda because from the film it appeared that Hitler had been popular with the German people. My friend could not accept that Hitler *had* been supported by the German masses almost to a point of adulation. Another friend had believed that the extermination camp at Auschwitz had been operating since 1933. The fact that Auschwitz was not in pre-war Germany was dismissed as nonsense.

Much has been written about the destructive features of the National Socialist state, but very little has been published about those aspects of it which the German people felt to be beneficial. The dimensions and content of the picture are unfamiliar because it is the German perspective of people and events which is depicted in the pages of this book.

The misery of the 1920s. Above: German women rake through a coal refuse tip to find fuel. Left: the curse of inflation. Civil servants burn the worthless paper notes.

# INTRODUCTION

IN Flanders, in Artois, in Picardy, in the Vosges and along the whole length of the battle-line on the Western Front; at Vittorio Veneto and in the high Alps of Italy as well as in the deserts of the Middle East, the guns fell silent obedient to the order that a ceasefire would take effect from 11 a.m. on 11 November 1918. An armistice had been signed between Germany and the Allies. By definition an armistice is only a truce, a suspension of, not the end of hostilities, but the Allied nations believed firmly and as it transpired, correctly, that the Great War was over.

The horror and the bloodletting had ended. The Allies' cause, the Good, had triumphed over that of the Central Powers, the Evil. Now the task that faced the victor nations was to convert the uniformed hosts of their armies back to factory workforces, to resume Trade and to return, politically, to the pre-war system of balances of power. In Europe that political intention might not be easy, for a revolution had been raging in Russia since 1917. The Bolshevik government was anti-capitalist and, therefore, an enemy of the Allies. It proved necessary to send expeditionary forces to destroy the Communist madness in Russia before it could escape and infect other nations. The Allies did not succeed in that interdiction. Trouble in Russia apart, a happy future for the victors seemed assured. Their defeated enemies, the nations of the Central Powers – Germany, Austria–Hungary and Turkey – would have a more difficult future but that was their fault. Everybody knew that they had started the war. The Central Powers had brought upon themselves the hardships which they were now enduring and which they would have to suffer until things got back to normal.

The peoples of the Allied nations, influenced by their political leaders, expected that the terms of any peace treaty would include demands for the defeated nations to make reparation. It had become the custom that the losing side in a war paid the victor's costs and although the bill for the Great War would be abnormally high, the principle would still apply. The Allies and their leaders were determined to make the recent enemies pay for their aggressions. 'The German orange', Lloyd George had declared in his election manifesto, 'must be squeezed until the pips squeak.'

The British and French governments, both of which had had to borrow extensively from foreign sources to finance their war efforts, demanded that Germany be required to pay ALL the costs that the Allies had incurred in fighting that war. Conferences were convened to discuss this unrealistic demand and out of them emerged a compromise. Germany would pay five billion dollars in gold or its equivalent, as a down payment on the final bill for the war – a bill whose sum was of such magnitude that it had not yet been possible to calculate it so soon after the Armistice. In the first six months of peace three things occurred which were to influence in a negative way the future course of European politics. First was the Allied demand for financial compensation referred to above. Secondly, there was the inclusion in the Peace Treaty of an Article under which Germany acknowledged her guilt in having started the war. Thirdly, there was a speech by the republican Chancellor of Germany, Friedrich Ebert. In an address to troops from the Western Front who had paraded through Berlin's Bradenburg Gate, Ebert proclaimed, 'I salute you who have returned unvanquished from the battlefield.' Out of Ebert's rhetoric was born a myth; the myth that the German Army had not been defeated in the field. The German Chancellor may not have realized the significance of his words. Others before him may have expressed that same conviction. What was important was that he spoke as Chancellor of Germany, the political leader of the nation, and that gave his words a tragic power. His statement begs the question; if the German Army had not been beaten militarily, why had its leaders sought an armistice? Nationalist politicians answered this question by saying that the German Home Front, weakly led, demoralized and seduced by Left-Wing, front-dodging politicians, had stabbed the Army in the back. The statement that Germany had not been beaten in the field was not a salve to diminish the pain of defeat, but was to become an article of faith; a dogma to be accepted and believed without question by all right-minded Germans.

The Great War is at an end and there are two perspectives of Germany. The Allies see her as a defeated aggressor which, having engineered a world conflict, must admit her guilt and pay heavily for the ruin she had caused. The German perspective of herself was that she had been forced into war by a ring of hostile enemies. That she had taken up the sword out of treaty obligations and in defence of her honour. To add to the humiliation of having to ask for an armistice she must accept a dictated peace treaty in which she was branded a war criminal and she was to be ruined by monetary debts that would enslave her forever.

Two points of view; two differing interpretations. Allied vindictiveness and Germany self-pity would have but one result. The seeds of a new war were planted. These would be fertilized and grow during the years of financial, economic and moral misery Germany would suffer as a result of hostile Allied policies. These poisoned plants would come to fruition during the years of Adolf Hitler's Third Reich.

What the German people longed for during that time of misery was a strong man to lead the nation; until such a one came to power she would continue to be humiliated in the way that the French humiliated her in January 1923. On the pretext that Germany had defaulted on her reparations debt the French Army occupied the Ruhr, the industrial heart of western Germany. The default? A quarter of a million telegraph poles which had not been delivered on a certain day. The Reichs government in Berlin, furious at this invasion over so trifling an infringement, ordered passive resistance by the workers of the Ruhr

against the occupying forces. To pay the wages and salaries of the Ruhr workers who were receiving nothing because of their passive resistance, the presses in Germany printed paper money. Inflation was the inevitable result. The mark crashed and the savings of the thrifty German middle class, accumulated over the years, were wiped out in days. What followed was nearly a decade of humiliation.

Throughout the years of National Socialist power it was those terrible years of inflation, misery and degradation to which the Nazi propagandists returned time and again, contrasting the weakness of the Weimar republic with the power of the Third Reich. The Nazi perspective of that republic contrasted with the view of the German way of life as seen by Western 'liberals'. That 'liberal' perspective was of a Germany without censorship; where the arts in all their forms, even the most sexually advanced, could be found, where liberal attitudes to homosexuality, drug taking, abortion and contraception were encouraged and where there was a *laissez-faire* attitude towards free enterprise.

The Nazi view of those years of national humiliation – the 1920s and 1930s – was that inflation ran riot and the old men of Weimar were impotent to act as Germany was infiltrated and taken over by 'aliens from the East'. An alien, with a supply of strong currency, could buy almost anything in Germany. These 'Eastern aliens', the accepted euphemism for foreign Jews, bought up theatres, factories, property and newspapers. Nazi statistics showed that Jewish control of the legal and medical professions, to give just two examples, had given the 'aliens' a virtual monopoly. According to Nazi reports all the media sources were in 'alien' hands and only news which favoured their interests was printed.

The 'alien' control of the German theatre, film and art worlds meant, according to the Nazis, not only that decadence was allowed to flourish but that it was positively encouraged by those who were determined to destroy German culture. Great play was made in the most virulent Nazi propaganda of the seduction of young German girls by 'alien' doctors, stage producers and film directors. These 'aliens' were destroying the moral fibre of Germany by forcing girls into the vice rings of Berlin and Hamburg, by propagating decadent art and by mocking the efforts of honest, upright, patriotic Germans in the recent war.

Above: The national humiliation of 1923 as French troops enter the Rhineland following the German default on a reparations payment. The oppressive French occupation produced a wave of resistance.

This Nazi view was shared by many millions of Germans, who thought that the Fatherland was being poisoned by 'alien' influences and needed somebody to save her. There was little point in seeking help from the politicians of the left for they encouraged the moral decline of Germany, believing that out of the chaos that would be produced would come the proletarian revolution. The hopes of Germany lay, therefore, in the other parties. Among the grey mass of mediocre politicians of the German Right, one man began to emerge – Adolf Hitler. He, they felt, had the right ideas. Germany must reject the Diktat of Versailles. Germany was not to blame for the war. She was being ruined by international financiers – and we all know in whose interests they are working, don't we? The moral decline of the nation was evidenced in open drug addiction, pornography of

the basest sort, transvestites, lesbians and other freaks. The National Socialists demanded the removal of drug dealers, filth peddlers and sexual perverts from German life.

The Nazis demanded that Germany be saved socially as well as politically. Unemployment must be cured. Living conditions for the masses were a scandal; Germany must rebuild. The slums must be torn down and decent houses built for German families. These rebuilding projects would employ men. In order that the rebuilding advanced as quickly as possible there could be no submission to the wild excesses of the trades unions, those political traitors who spent more time protecting the interests of the Soviet Union than in fighting for the German working class. Then, too, the widows and orphans of the heroes who had fallen for Germany would be properly looked after and

In grösster Not
Adolf Hitler zum
wählt auch

wählte Hindenbur
Reichskanzle
Jhr Liste 1.

given generous pensions. There would be increases in other pensions, too. There was something for everybody in the programme of the Nazi Party.

Hitler was projected to the German people as a strong man leading a united party. This won support. Years earlier he had written in his book, *Mein Kampf*, 'The psychology of the masses as a whole is not susceptible to anything hesitant or weak . . . their feelings are not swayed so much by abstract reason as by a longing after strength . . . and thus (they) would sooner be dominated than supplicated. The masses, in fact, feel themselves to have been abandoned by a weak government and prefer one which brooks no rival to one which gives them a liberal choice.' The masses needed a strong man with a firm hand. He was that man.

He had learned from his failure to overthrow the Bavarian government in November 1923, that revolutions do not always succeed. The Party policy after that failure was to gain power through legitimate means; through the ballot box. By September 1930, through pursuing the legal line, the Nazis had won 107 seats in the Reichstag and had become a serious rival to the Social Democratic Party.

Little more than ten years had elapsed since Hitler had joined the German Workers' Party. By 1930, it was one of the largest parties in the Reichstag, but he had not yet achieved full national recognition. In 1932, in a brilliant political ploy, he stood as a candidate for the presidency of Germany against the incumbent, the veteran soldier, Field Marshal Paul von Hindenburg. It is unlikely that Hitler expected to win the presidential election, but he did gain eleven million votes against Hindenburg's eighteen million. What Hitler did achieve by his candidacy was national recognition as a politician and, thereby, his claim to be a serious contender for high political office.

His time was about to come. In 1932 the need of the German people was more than ever before for a strong man. There were now six million Germans unemployed. Farms were being foreclosed, businesses lost through bankruptcy. Active young people were emigrating to the Americas, to Africa, to wherever their skills and abilities would bring them work and a fair reward for that work. If this emigration of the youngest and the most capable could not be halted Germany would become a land of old people, weak and defenceless against the enemies who surrounded her.

To the ordinary Germans it was obvious that the old political parties had failed. Their leaders – the Eberts, the Stresemanns, the Bruenings – the weak democrats, had not succeeded in mastering the crises which afflicted the Fatherland. In November 1932, the results of a new general election increased the power of the Nazi Party in the Reichstag. It won 230 seats out of the total of 608, making it the largest of the political blocs of the Right. Without the Nazis the Right could have no overall majority in the Reichstag. President von Hindenburg, unwilling to entrust the Chancellorship to a 'Bohemian corporal', made two attempts to form a coalition government of right wing parties. He failed in both attempts. There remained only one option for the President. He sent for Hitler and charged him with the task of forming a national government, but added the provisos that only three cabinet posts were to be held by members of the Nazi Party and that Franz von Papen was to be appointed Vice-Chancellor. Hitler accepted the conditions which Hindenburg had imposed in an effort to confine the Nazi leader and his Party within the limitations of a Conservative coalition. Of course, Hitler agreed. He had his own plans to gain power. President von Hindenburg appointed Hitler as Chancellor of Germany.

Late in the afternoon of that day, 30 January 1933, the former down-and-out of the Vienna dosshouses, the failed artist and ex-soldier, Adolf Hitler, walked into the Reichskanzlei.

Left: Hindenburg and Hitler – the Grand Old Man of the German Army, seen by many Germans as a rock of stability in the crisis-torn 1920s, endorses Hitler at the 1933 election. The caption reads: 'At the time of greatest need Hindenburg chose Adolf Hitler as Reichschancellor. Vote List 1'. (Imperial War Museum).

# I. POLITICAL AND SOCIAL PI

## THE GENESIS OF THE NAZI PARTY

FOR the greatest part of the lifetime of the Third Reich Adolf Hitler was the Chancellor of Germany. He also became the Supreme Commander of the Wehrmacht (the German Armed Forces). But above everything else he was, and this he never forgot, the Führer of the Nazi Party. The Party dominated his thoughts. His actions were influenced by, and his decisions made for, party political reasons.

Before the assumption of power by the National Socialist German Workers' Party (the Nazis), it was little understood by the German people or by those outside Germany, that Hitler was a revolutionary leading a revolutionary Party. Thus the social, economic and political policies which were introduced during the lifetime of the Reich were the products of a German national and socialist revolution at work. That it was not possible to fulfill all the policies outlined in the Party's manifesto during the short years of the Reich, is understandable, for its creators were working on a period of government of a thousand years. Measured against such a time-scale all the manifesto promises not immediately accomplished would be made good; in due time. It was a question of priorities and the first, most important and urgently pressing of all needs was to build a National Socialist Volksgemeinschaft. That noun can be translated as 'a people's or a national commonwealth', but such a bare translation cannot convey the emotional impact of that word upon the German soul. Nor can a mere translation show the depth, the strength and the longing which it evokes. Upon the basis of that Volksgemeinschaft the revolutionary policies of National Socialism would eventually be constructed, but before the Volksgemeinschaft could be created a unified Germany was necessary. Germany had never been one nation in the sense that Great Britain has been united for centuries. Even when the German Empire had been proclaimed in 1871, Prussia, whose King was created Emperor, was only *primus inter pares*, the other equals being the kings of Saxony, Bavaria and Württemberg. The Nazi Party intended first to unify the now republican States and Provinces of Germany into a single nation and then to go on to unite all Germans within one Fatherland. With a Germany unified and with its people all brought Home, the Party could then go on to its long-term policy.

Reduced to a simple proposition, the long-term strategy of the National Socialist government was to gain for Germany primacy among the world's powers and for her to retain that eminence for a thousand years. Primacy would bring with it dominion over other races, a dominion whose considerable privileges and advantages would be shared by all those loyal, pure-blooded comrades within the Volksgemeinschaft. The German people could not hope to attain such primacy without sacrifices. It would be naïve to think that the other nations of the world would surrender their own privileged position to give the highest station to Nazi Germany. No! Such eminence would have to be fought for and, in this context,

# RSPECTIVES

Hitler's words are an illustration of the future he projected for Germany. 'If anyone would live then let him accordingly fight. And if anyone in this world of perpetual strife is loath to struggle, he does not deserve to live.' The nation had been warned. The perspective as envisaged by the Führer was a series of wars which the Fatherland must win or else go down in defeat and ruin. The Nazi Party had laid upon the German people a do-or-die situation.

These wars were not, however, immediate policies but lay in the future. What was needed immediately was to establish the Volksgemein-schaft. This would be accomplished by imposing the Nazi Party's political structure upon the nation and by that close control organizing the nation for eventual war. The Party had prepared for power by appointing Party officials in a 'shadow' capacity at provincial, rural district and local council levels. With the assumption of power the 'shadow' officials took up post and the Party was in full control of the political life of the country. The structure of the Party, the leadership principle – the Führerprinzip – was then applied to the nation. This system extended from Hitler and filtered through each level of command, down to the most humble Party official. Each stratum of the hierarchy had a leader to whom his subordinates were answerable for their actions, just as that leader has a superior officer to whom he was responsible. Since every order was issued by the Party of which Adolf Hitler was the Führer, each recipient of the order had to see it as if the Führer had issued it direct and in person. There was no room for discussion or argument. 'It is the Führer's order', became the standard method of terminating opposition, for against that qualifica-tion there could be no appeal. This dictum was to be used as a defence by the accused in War Crimes Trials. 'I was only carrying out orders,' was advanced as a valid and incontrovertible defence. The people who used it had been schooled in the belief that the man in authority accepts the responsibility and that Hitler, as the highest authority, accepted the ultimate responsibility and thereby exonerated his subordinates.

The Führerprinzip was the policy and the Nazi Party was the instrument that would create the National Socialist state. At the most senior level was the Party Leader and Chancellor of Germany, Adolf Hitler. He ruled through a Party Chancery which also ran a cabinet of government ministers. This, the highest of the hierarchical structure, we shall call the Reichsleitung level throughout this book. The next senior level was that of the Gauleitung, the provincial governor stratum.

Hitler had been well served by his Party com-rades and as Chancellor rewarded them by con-firming them in the post of Gauleiter (provincial governor). Before 1938 there were thirty-six Gauleiters, but that number was increased as a consequence of Hitler's political gains, notably the Anschluss with Austria, the restoration of the Sudetenland and the creation of other Gaus in the territories of the East which were conquered during the war.

The Gauleitung was the most important stratum of the whole Party political system for the Gau-leiter was the party's senior representative in the province or, in some cases, a major city. Within his Gau he had supreme political authority, a situation which some officers abused by inter-preting the orders which they received from Party Chancery as they saw fit. A great many of the Gauleiters saw the Gau to which they had been appointed as a sort of feudal fiefdom. Josef Goebbels, the Gauleiter of Berlin, ruled very firmly and demonstrated his control in a case of

The beginnings of the Nazi Party in Bavaria. The people chiefly attracted to the new party were ex-soldiers, nationalists and the unemployed. The flag in the first photograph bears the Nationalist colours of black, white and red, in contrast to the black, white and gold of the Weimar republic. Local costume is evident in the top left photograph of an early march; at this stage, uniform consisted of little more than armbands. Those at the top of the party structure were the first to be able to afford complete uniforms; the followers gradually took on a cohesive appearance. Meanwhile, the Communists, the Nazi's opponents in many street battles to come, were also displaying a marked uniformity of dress (bottom right). On the left of this photograph is Ernst Thaelmann, leader of the German Communist Party.

looting from a bread shop in the last weeks of the war. Two of the three ringleaders were condemned to death and were beheaded.

In peacetime this system of Gauleiters, based upon and backed by a strong foundation of established bodies such as the national or regional civil services and local government, worked well enough. Under the strains of wartime and the need to make fast, binding decisions, the touch of the provincial governor was often less sure. Some, indeed, abdicated their authority and abandoned their people. We shall come across some who did well. Few Gauleiters were capable administrators and in most cases these untrained men, who had been original members of the Party or among the first to join, were put into positions of almost unchallenged authority as a reward for Party loyalty rather than for competence and ability. SS Obergruppenführer Wolff, a confidant of Himmler and *persona grata* in the highest political circles of the Reich, was contemptuous of the unsophisticated roughnecks he encountered among the Gauleiters and found that 'Hitler surrounded himself with followers . . . some of whom were definitely inferior'.

Below the Gauleitung level were the Kreise (districts) into which each Gau was divided. A Kreis was ruled by a Kreisleiter. Subordinate to

the Kreisleitung level of the hierarchy were the Ortsgruppen (district councils). Below these were the Cells, each of which contained a number of Blocks. A Block was made up of a group of Party comrades and the local leader, the Blockwart, was the lowest strata of the Nazi political system.

From the perspective of the ordinary German this chain of command reaching downward from and upwards to the leaders of the Reich, gave him a feeling of security and the assurance that he, the humble Party comrade, was of interest to and could have the ear of the highest in the land. Even towards the end of the war, Goebbels' diaries recorded how members of the public wrote to

Reichsleitung officers in the conviction that they would resolve their difficulties or deal with their problems.

The Party which ruled Germany from 1933 onwards, had begun in a small way and Hitler had joined it as Member No. 7. It was typical of other parties which had sprung up all over Germany, many of them made up of ex-servicemen who could not accept what had happened to their world. Thirteen years after he joined, Adolf Hitler stood in the windows of the Reichskanzlei in Berlin, taking the salute as the brown-shirted army of his Party, the SA (Sturm Abteilung or Storm Troops) marched past him, their blazing

Left: Hitler speaking at an open-air meeting during the winter of 1922 surrounded by a cordon of SA members. Above: The defendants and their lawyers pose for a photograph during the trial following the Nazis' abortive 1923 putsch in Bavaria. They include General Erich Ludendorff, the famous general, Hitler, the future Führer, Ernst Roehm, the leader of the SA, and Dr Wilhelm Frick, who was to become the Nazi Minister of the Interior. The publicity resulting from the trial, which was reported throughout Germany, and Hitler's very political speech during its course helped to lift the Nazis from local politics to the national arena.

torches forming a river of light flooding through the Brandenburg Gate.

In the early days, when the Party had been small, its members realized that their policies and dogma would be challenged and would meet physical violence from political opponents. Those parties of the Left, whose sympathies were with Soviet Russia, would seek to destroy a party which believed in Germany; a party that was national in outlook and programme. The Left, they argued, would use its traditional methods of brutality and intimidation to stop the meetings of the infant Nazi Party. To meet violence with violence the Nazis formed the SA. Wearing uniforms and

organized along military lines, the task of these early units was to protect the Party's meetings. As the Nazis grew in power and strength a new task was given to the SA. They were now to go over to the attack and to smash the meetings of their political opponents; Left, Right or Centre. In Goebbels' opinion 'Whoever can conquer the streets will, one day, rule the State, for every type of power politics has its roots in the streets.' The task which the SA had been given was clear and they swept the streets clear of the other parties. SA man, Horst Wessel, did not write an empty boast in the second verse of the Nazi anthem when he claimed that the streets were free for the

By the mid-1920s the Nazi movement had spread throughout Germany and started to be organized formally on a regional basis. Top left: A rally c.1926 in Berlin. Below left: A rally by a district battalion of the SA, c.1926–8. The sticks were wielded by the public speaking defence squads. Right: A 1927 rally at Nuremberg. (Imperial War Museum)

brown battalions, for the SA men. They confronted Red violence. Hitler had forecast in *Mein Kampf* that victory could be won over the Left by using methods as brutal as they used. They were used and power was won, but it was not an easy victory. It was a hard fight and to protect the Party's leaders from the train loads of thugs which the Reds brought in, a new and special unit of the Party was formed, the SS (Schützstaffeln or Defence Squads). The duty of this small group, its first establishment was only 26 men, was to guard the Nazi speakers and each man had sworn to lay down his own life if need be, to defend Adolf Hitler.

These years of street fighting were known as the Kampfzeit (the time of struggle) and their memory was deeply impressed upon the psyche of the 'Old Guard' warriors, each of whom felt bound by strong bonds of comradeship born out of the Kampfzeit. Each year in November the 'Old Guard' met in Munich to commemorate the anniversary of a failed *putsch* in 1923. Ten years after that failure, Hitler had the political power of Germany in his hands. In that time of triumph Hitler must have reflected that it was the Party's beliefs, the Party's will to victory and his own political genius that had brought him out of obscurity to lead a great nation.

On the streets of Germany's cities, the Nazis dealt with their opponents in savage fighting. Left: SS and SA men pose around some of the banners captured from the Communists during the street fighting of the Kampfzeit. One of the red banners reads 'Defend Soviet Russia!'. Above: Nazi thugs on the streets, here implementing a boycott of Jewish businesses. (Imperial War Museum) On the whole, despite the ugliness and brutality of the conflict, Germans approved of the resulting suppression of 'undesirables' such as the Communists, who were seen as a real menace to the well-being of the country, anti-Christian as well as anti-social. The battles on the streets continued until after the Nazi assumption of power, when Hindenburg's enabling act gave legal authority to the Nazi street squads. Below right: the first legal round-up of suspects by Nazi para-police units, 1933.

Above: Nazi election poster of 1932. It reads: 'We construct. Our bricks are Work, Freedom, Bread. The construction plans of the other parties are Promises, Unemployment, Emergency Regulations, Social Decline, Corruption, Terror, Lies.' (Imperial War Museum)

Above: Nazi election poster of 1932. It reads: 'Those who work with the mind or with their hands vote for the front-line soldier Hitler.' (Imperial War Museum)

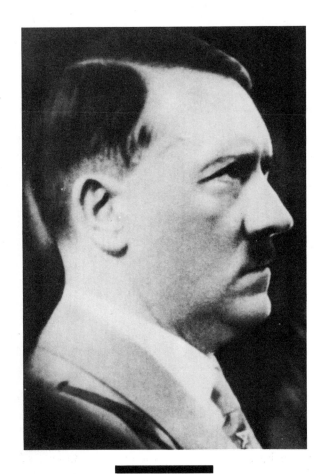

Adolf Hitler, the Führer.

# THE GERMAN FÜHRER: ADOLF HITLER

'The Party is Adolf Hitler, but Adolf Hitler is Germany and Germany is Adolf Hitler.' With those extravagant phrases Rudolf Hess, the Führer's Deputy, closed the Party rally at Nuremberg in September 1934. That hysterical declaration loses its impact when seen in cold print, but delivered as it was, to an audience which had been electrified by Hitler's powerful oratory, Hess's words contained an emotion and a fervour which brought his hearers to a frenzy of excitement.

At senior Party level it had been feared that the 1934 rally might be overshadowed by the events of the June of that year. At that time Hitler, fearing a counter-revolution by the SA, had had its leaders shot. During the Nuremberg Rally the Nazi leaders had by skilful and emotional oratory restored harmony to the Party, had rebuilt the confidence of the SA and had set the Party the goal of forming a National Socialist State whose finest comrades from the mass of the people (the Volksgenossen) would be, so the Führer claimed, his Party comrades (Partei Genossen). They would lead the State; they would set the example to be followed.

A great many books have been written about Hitler and it is not my intention to repeat the details of his life except to say that he was a skilful politician who had a flair for detecting and exploiting an opponent's weaknesses. A good poker player has the same capabilities. Hitler was a 'chancer', a gambler whose chips were the lives of his soldiers, the civilian population and the Reich itself.

The Third Reich, was directed and swayed by him and it was his ideas, his concepts, his philosophies and his hatreds which formed the dogma that was followed. His word was law; his fantasies were acted out. At his command divisions of soldiers moved into battle. At his direction fleets of aircraft bombed targets and at his orders millions were put to death. Yet politically Hitler was a pragmatist. As a revolutionary he was prepared to compromise his political beliefs if such a move would gain the Party an advantage, just as he was prepared to sacrifice Party comrades in pursuit of a wider goal. This he demonstrated in the execution of the SA commanders mentioned earlier in this chapter. Military leaders had promised assistance to help one Party formation, the SS, crush its rival Party formation, the SA. That assistance had not been necessary and Hitler's way of thanking the Army for its offer of support was to unleash upon it the SS Intelligence Service, the SD, charged with uncovering or inventing scandals involving service leaders. The most senior of the victims of that persecution was General von Fritsch, Commander-in-Chief of the Army. His retirement was soon followed by that of Field Marshal von Blomberg, the Minister for War. Into the vacant posts were placed the Führer's compliant tools; officers who would offer no opposition to his demands. Walter von Brauchitsch took over the Army and Wilhelm Keitel the post of Chief of the General Staff of the Armed Forces (OKW). This was the first step by which the Party intended to gain political control of the Army, and was to lead to the raising, during 1944–45, of several Party-inspired military bodies in addition to the existing political, military force, the Waffen SS.

Hitler was a paradox. On the one hand he allowed his political appointees, the Gauleiters, almost unlimited power despite proof that many abused that power; on the other his growing suspicion of the Generals led to his increased meddling in military affairs. His orders halted the drive on Moscow in the autumn of 1941 and gave the Soviets time to prepare the defences of the Russian capital and to bring up reinforcements. In 1942, the Führer intervened and ordered that the Army Group South offensive should divide and that one thrust should strike eastwards towards Stalingrad while the other drove into the Caucasus. He countered the criticisms which his advisers made to this division of military strength with the dismissive comment, 'My Generals know nothing of economic warfare.' By inference – he did.

Towards the end of the war his need to be involved in military matters became an obsession and he was so deeply immersed in pettifogging detail and bureaucratic procedures that the real objective was lost to sight. Examples of this meddling can be seen in the December 1944 offensive in the Ardennes. At that critical stage of the war when he should have been concentrating on strategic problems, Hitler spent hours poring over maps working out the roads along which the spearhead units were to travel. Then, too, in 1945, when the Red Army's winter offensive was about to strike for Berlin, the Führer's principal concern was not the defence of the Reich's capital, but the working out in detail of the routes, flying heights and aircraft escorts for a pointless special Luftwaffe bombing operation against power-stations around Moscow.

A story which circulated during the first months of the Russian campaign may be apocryphal but serves to illustrate the point of the Führer's interference. At a concert in Berlin the Commander-in-Chief of the Army, von Brauchitsch, was asked by Furtwangler, the world-famous conductor, 'Why do you allow a man who did not rise above the rank of corporal to tell you how to fight a war?' Brauchitsch's reply encapsulates Adolf Hitler in Nazi Germany. 'My dear Furtwangler,' replied the Field Marshal, 'if the Führer could play the harmonica you would not be conducting the Berlin Philharmonic.'

As a result of the SD persecution campaign the Army High Command had been purged and it was clear that the eventual objective would be to politicize all three services. For the last years of peace and then throughout the long years of war, Germany was able to produce commanders for all the services and at every level of command; men who must have been aware that a Nazi victory would destroy the traditional role of those services. Yet there was never any shortage of competent commanders. How was that possible?

As the source of supreme authority Hitler had the gift of patronage and any person with that gift will attract those who are ambitious. This is no less true of the military forces of a dictatorship than it is of a religious body in a democratic country. To hold high rank and to exercise power are potent attractions and ones which produced the men who led the military and political forces of the Reich. Together with the natural feelings of ambition there was another, emotional factor. These men were the inheritors of centuries of tradition; of an almost mystic belief in the omnipotence of a Supreme War Lord. Inhibited by that concept it had not been until the last weeks of the Great War that Field Marshal von Hindenburg, the Commander-in-Chief, had had the courage to advise the Kaiser that the army could no longer be relied upon to support the throne. It was the army that must be preserved as an instrument of state. It was the Supreme War Lord who must go. Hitler, the new Supreme War Lord had no Hindenburg, nor would he have accepted any suggestion that the mass of the army could be disloyal to him. How could it be? Each and every soldier had taken an oath of personal allegiance and a soldier's sworn word laid upon him a sacred obligation. And, if the inconceivable happened and the soldiers were to break their oath, the dedicated and totally loyal legions of the Party; the SS, the SA, the political leaders and the Gauleiters would deal with the dissident elements. There would be no spectre of 1918, with its mutinies to haunt Adolf Hitler and to destroy the Third Reich.

The Party's dominance of the military and civil services can be traced to the training and upbringing of the officers and officials. Such men and women are, by nature, conservative in their approach, are meticulous, hard-working and impartial in serving the government in power. This latter benefit had been enjoyed by all the German governments from the Imperial to the National Socialist. The bourgeois concepts of loyalty and devotion to duty were two of the pillars which supported the revolutionary Third Reich; both were exploited by the Nazi leaders.

The army had seen the Nazi rise to power with repugnance and alarm, but was then bolstered against the Party's wilder elements by Hitler's growing fear of the SA. In his closing speech at Nuremberg in 1934, Hitler had declared the army to be the weapon-bearer of the State. Placated by that promise the military accepted Hitler as the New War Lord and swore the oath he had demanded. Soon he had them convinced of his ability. His political flair showed that the fearful attitudes of the Generals, born of their military appreciations of political events, were hopelessly at fault. Hitler's decisions had been shown to be right in the case of the Rhineland, Austria, the Sudetenland and the rump of Czechoslovakia. His support for Manstein's unconventional plan to strike through the Ardennes in 1940, had led to a campaign which had won the war in the West in six weeks. During the summer and autumn of 1941 his switching of the German point of maximum effort in Russia, had produced great tactical victories and had brought in millions of prisoners. His firmness in the face of all conventional opinion had gained victories for Germany, and his iron resolve, his rejection of orthodox military advice and his decision not to retreat during the first terrible winter in Russia, had proved to be the correct course to follow. His will had triumphed. He, a corporal in a provincial infantry regiment during the Great War, had shown more ability in military matters than Generals with a lifetime of experience. In view of his run of successes, starting as early as 1935, the perspective of the professional military officers, *vis-à-vis* Hitler, was that he was a leader whose touch was sure and whose genius was undoubted. A deterioration in the Führer's handling of military affairs was noticed after that first winter campaign in Russia, but the belief that he was

Hitler takes control of the military. Right: Field Marshal Werner von Blomberg, the German War Minister who was removed from office in order that Hitler could appoint a more pliant commander. Below: The Führer 'in his element', directing military operations in detail, with Field Marshal Walter von Brauchitsch (centre), Commander in Chief of the Army, and Field Marshal Wilhelm Keitel, head of the Oberkommando der Wehrmacht.

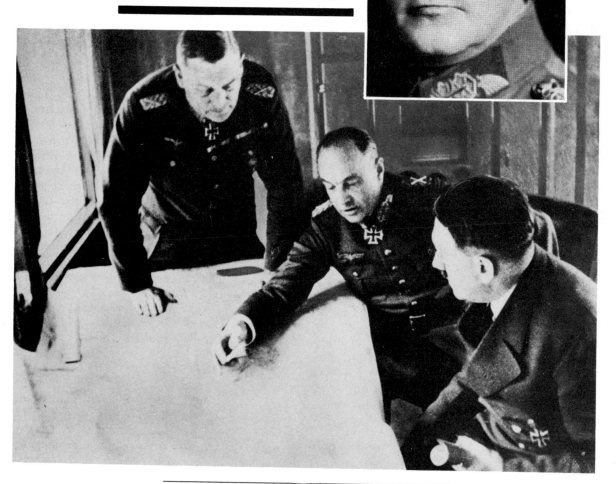

Oaths of loyalty to the Führer. Above: a ceremony of the SS, the voluntary élite of the Nazi forces, at the Feldherrnhalle in Munich, a place of emotional significance in Nazi Party history: it was here that the Nazi 'martyrs' fell to the bullets of the Bavarian Government during the putsch attempt of 1923. (Imperial War Museum) Left: Army recruits take the oath of allegiance during a parade in Brunswick on 11 January 1936, following the introduction of conscription the pervious year. Right: The military genius and his ally. Adolf Hitler and Italian dictator Benito Mussolini at manoeuvres in 1937.

infallible was now so deeply ingrained in the thinking of the military that disagreement with his directives was minimal. Those who did disagree were retired and the new commander to a post felt himself capable of carrying out even the most pointless orders, convinced that Hitler saw the complete picture and that the orders he issued must be correct.

There was in addition to the compulsions of ambition and the natural loyal desire to serve the Fatherland, the factor of Hitler's ability to sway people at a personal level. That ability has been ascribed to many things. Yet how could this man have achieved control over those of greater intellect than himself? One can accept that his closest Party comrades were in awe of him and that, according to Rudolf Semler, Goebbels' chief collaborator, even the cynical Propaganda Minister was affected by the Führer. Yet how could skilled, trained and dedicated service officers be influenced? That Hitler could exert charm, could produce or withdraw it at will, is undoubted, but charm alone is not sufficient to cause professional officers to change their minds on fundamental issues, nor can this loss of will power on the part of service commanders be put down to Hitler's blue eyes.

To advance the excuse of the hypnotic influence of his eyes is to evade responsibility. It is significant that nobody in the doss-houses of Vienna in which Hitler lived before 1914, seemed to have been influenced by his eyes. His military superiors between 1914 and 1936, including Ludendorff, Hindenburg and a great number of other military commanders seem not to have noticed this effect and yet it is a recurring theme in the post-war interrogations of German service leaders. One reads of officers determined to lay before the Führer the truth about military operations, to demand solutions on the problems of supplies, to question the direction of his strategy or to point out the senselessness of his plans. They each go in to see him and then leave his room refreshed, invigorated, confident of victory and assured of his genius. Colonel Goettschling, Chief-of-Staff of the Luftwaffe in Italy at the end of the war, declared under interrogation, 'I have seen the most brilliant and decisive men of my acquaintance go to see Hitler determined not to acquiesce with his whims. Those intellectual and critical men returned fascinated and for weeks remained under the spell of Hitler's charm . . .'

These are incredible pictures. The scions of noble houses, with centuries of service to Germany and to the army, holding firm views on what should be happening, armed with files, statistics, maps and documents to back their arguments, meet and are confounded by an unqualified, Austrian builder's labourer. Among the ordinary people Hitler aroused almost Messianic devotion and his accessibility in the years leading up to the outbreak of the Second World War played a great part in that phenomenon. He retained the common touch and had been, in the pre-war years, approachable by the ordinary people, particularly when he was in Berchtesgaden, his country retreat. Only in the later years of the war did restrictions upon access to the Führer imposed by Martin Bormann, turn Hitler into a recluse who saw only those who had been selected or authorized by Bormann.

An example of the attitude of those pre-war days is shown in this account by a woman who had been only 18 years old when she met Hitler. 'In the autumn of 1938, I went on a visit with a ladies' choir group to a festival in Munich. After our Saturday evening performance some of us learned that Hitler was in Berchtesgaden and was in the habit of meeting people, informally, after Sunday lunch. A few of our group decided to go out to see him. It rained quite heavily as we walked up the road but by the time that we reached the Führer's home the clouds had gone, the sun was shining and the view was breathtaking.

'At about 3 in the afternoon a door in the side of the house opened and Hitler came out on to the lawn. He was wearing a grey, chalk-striped civilian suit and was wearing a grey felt hat which he took off and waved in response to our cheers. One of his staff approached us and asked who we were. We told him that we were members of a Styrian singing group and after he had reported this he came back and asked if we would like to meet the Führer. As Hitler came towards the road he passed too close to a tree and the left side of his jacket was sprinkled with raindrops from the branches. He talked to us for a few minutes and seeing that I had a camera offered to have his photograph taken with us. The disappointment must have shown in my face that I would not be in the picture and he told one of his adjutants to take the photograph. The raindrops on the Führer's lapel and shoulder can be clearly seen in that picture. When I see the security which these days surrounds politicians I think back to when the Führer of Germany came out and mixed with ordinary people on that Sunday afternoon.'

Although he seldom visited his soldiers in the field and not once went round a bombed city to talk to the survivors of a raid, Hitler commanded the loyalty of the great mass of the German people. They trusted him to produce even at the eleventh hour some wonder weapon, some political miracle which would win the war and justify the losses which had been endured and the sufferings which they had had to undergo. He had been so successful since 1933. He would be successful and win the war. He could not fail. The Führer would achieve victory.

Hitler, like every other dictator, would not delegate authority to those whose loyalty he doubted. He trusted the Gauleiters because they were Party comrades. He trusted Speer, because he was an architect and the Führer had always wanted to be accepted as an equal by a successful architect. The Generals he did not trust, considering them to be a pack of traitors, particularly after the bomb plot of July 1944. Refusing to trust his senior commanders and determined to take military control from their hands, he then appointed Party leaders to positions for which they had had no training. Himmler became Commander-in-Chief of Army Group Vistula and, despite his poor showing while in command, was then promoted to become Head of Replacement Armies. Sepp Dietrich, the first commander of Hitler's Leibstandarte SS (his SS bodyguard formation), rose to lead Sixth SS Panzer Army, although his military contemporaries judged him as about adequate to command a regiment. As the war drew to its close Hitler had fewer and fewer direct personal contacts with his field commanders, usually limiting this to a series of operational directives from which no deviation was permitted. No unit could be moved without his knowledge or approval, a situation which led to Field Marshal von Rundstedt's bitter comment, 'I cannot even have the guard changed outside my room without referring the matter to the Führer.'

Those Generals who were in the Führerbunker with him at the end had as little idea as Hitler of the true military situation. Buoyed up by the confidence he exuded they believed that the divisions and corps marked on the wall maps in the bunker were at full fighting strength and not, as they in fact were, the shattered remnants of front-line formations. When late in April Hitler ordered General Wenck's Twelfth Army to join Busse's Ninth Army and relieve Berlin, those in the Führerbunker could not understand why the relief force had not broken through the Red Army ring around the Reichskanzlei area of Berlin within a matter of days. It was all so easy, seen from their viewpoint. Two massive armies needing only to join up and then advance. The reality was different. Those armies, exhausted and bled white by battle, were fighting against an enemy superior in numbers and equipment. In an effort to spur what was obviously considered to be the laggard approach of the relief force, General Burgdorff and Martin Bormann signed a dispatch and ordered it to be carried to Wenck's headquarters near Potsdam. The text of the message read, 'Wenck, it is about time.' The grasp of those in the bunker on the true situation of the battle for Berlin was so wrong that they were prepared to hazard the lives of two dispatch-riders to deliver a message which had no purpose.

Hitler, according to many who met him, lacked humility. He knew that he was a genius, that he had always been a genius. It had been arrogant stupidity on the part of the Vienna Establishment to deny him the chance to study at the Academy when he was a young and poor artist. From this awareness of his own genius as an artist it was only a short step to arrogate to himself the title of the greatest military genius of all time. This tied in very neatly with his own awareness that he was a statesman of unusual powers and unique gifts. The line is a fine one across which one passes from self-confidence to self-delusion and, eventually, into the engulfing swamp of megalomania. Most dictators cross it at some point in their career. The Führer was no exception.

There was the inability of the megalomaniac to see the logic of any point of view other than his own. Hitler's demand for large numbers of short-range, light bombers when Germany's need was for long-range heavy machines, and the insistence that German women should be denied the opportunity of serving the Fatherland, are evidences of a mind which grasps the immediate, obvious and most attractive solution to a problem without considering the long-term, less obvious and unattractive alternative. A strategic bomber, the direction of labour, a national policy rigidly enforced by central government in place of the rule of Gauleiters intent only upon personal interest – these should have been but were not, Hitler's main considerations.

There must be times even in the life of the most severe megalomaniac when sanity emerges and for that brief interval the sufferer is aware of his tragic condition. There must have been times in the last months of Adolf Hitler's life when a knowledge of the burden he was carrying broke through. At those times, deeply aware of the fact of defeat, no longer the possibility, or even the probability, but now the certainty of defeat, he must have realized that his own attitudes had alienated all those who might and could have helped him. He was alone because he chose to rule alone. When that awareness of his own bitter isolation struck him Hitler retreated into a dream wold of architectural design. Speer reported how Hitler had the most grandiose ideas for the post-

war development and rebuilding of many of the major cities of the Reich. According to Speer Hitler would spend hours doing little more than play with models of buildings which he intended to erect at the end of abnormally long processional routes.

It is the world's good fortune that Hitler's forward planning capabilities were limited to short-term objectives, to tactical targets which were instantly realizable. With his attention drawn to minor preoccupations, his strategic vision extended only as far as plans for post-war development of cities, the construction of buildings in those cities and in the design of memorials to the fallen. Those buildings, that rebuilding; all the components of his glorious dreams would have to wait until the end of the war, which Hitler, in his moments of rationality, must have realized he would never live to see.

Below: Nobody could mistake the Nazis in the Reichstag. This photograph, taken c.1929, shows the members taking their seats, their paramilitary uniforms contrasting with the civilian dress of the other representatives.

# THE DEVELOPMENT OF THE PARTY 1933-1939

In the years of the Third Reich the reasons which swayed great numbers of the German people to vote for the Nazis were widely debated, but chiefly by foreigners outside Germany who condemned the Party for what they saw as its repressive policies. Against that viewpoint most Germans had been attracted by the positive aspects of the National Socialist manifesto and were prepared to give the new men a chance. It was only after May 1945, and the defeat of their Fatherland, that the German people as a whole considered the sequence of events which had brought about the Nazi rise to power and asked themselves why their perception of the Party had been so faulty.

The great mass of the German people during the years of National Socialist government, had certainly not seen Hitler as a tyrant or as a murderer. He was believed in, obeyed and adored and thousands fell in battle believing to the end that he was the salvation of Germany. The charisma of the man who rose to become dictator of one of Europe's great nations was a subject which intrigued the minds of many Germans after 1945. The interrogation of German commanders by Allied officers, and discussions with those commanders on the subject of the Hitler phenomenon released in them a critical faculty which had not been exercised, in public, since 1933. Aware as they were that they had been accessories to the acts of the Nazi Party, many senior commanders sought a justification by concentrating on the positive political and economic achievements which had been gained during the era of the Third Reich. Among those who had time to reflect on the past was General Leyer, Commissioner for German War Production in Italy. During his interrogation by American officers at the end of the war, he reflected that, 'Commencing with just seven men, derided, insulted and at one time imprisoned, this unknown immigrant (Hitler), this son of the lower orders, was able, through his oratory to conquer a nation of seventy millions . . .'

It could not have been oratory alone that inspired a whole nation to death or glory. Nor could a political manifesto have been the spark that ignited and inflamed a nation's soul. What caused the masses to follow their leader was the belief that in some mystic way he was the embodiment of the national spirit and that he could fulill the promises he had made and in which the masses believed wholeheartedly. Hitler's manifesto was nationalist and socialist and it attracted supporters who believed in either, or both of those tenets. Hundreds of thousands of men had joined the Nazi Party in support of its policy of German socialism. They had fought as political soldiers in the ranks of the SA so that when the Party came to power, the vast estates owned by a minority would be distributed among the landless who formed the majority. Their belief was that the army, a reactionary force, would be replaced by a People's Army – the SA. They believed that Hitler's policies would solve the unemployment problem. Other Germans had joined Hitler's party because they saw it as the only one that would break the shackles of the Treaty of Versailles and lead the German Fatherland towards freedom; freedom from foreign interference, from foreign domination of German industry, commerce and capital.

Hitler's manifesto promised each German family its own home and its own car, the Volkswagen, made to run on the splendid autobahns which he would create. For many Germans the promises made in the first years of government were redeemed. Hitler's road building and his programme of slum clearance, did fulfill some of his promises and through them the numbers of unemployed were reduced. Later when he reintroduced conscription for the armed forces and expanded the arms industry, the evil of unemployment was wiped out completely. There was, in fact, from 1937 onwards, a shortage of labour. There was food for all, better social welfare and higher benefits for the old, the sick and the poor. It is no wonder that when Goebbels heard of Britain's Beveridge Plan he remarked sarcastically that Britain was at last approaching the level of social welfare that Germany had attained under Bismarck, some sixty years earlier. By inference, Britain was still decades behind the Third Reich in such matters.

The Third Reich strove towards social equality, too. 'No one', Hitler promised men of the RAD (Reichs Arbeits Dienst, the Labour Corps) when

Above and left: The 'dignity of labour' was a vital tenet of Nazi philosophy; the Germans generally approved of people being taught the value of hard work. Left: Hitler visits workers on an autobahn in 1933. Above: Labour formalized and conscripted. These are members of the RAD (Labour Corps) at the Nazi Party rally of 1936 at Nuremberg.

he addressed them in Nuremberg in 1934, 'will rise to power or achieve influence in Germany except that he has served in your ranks.' What was implied in the Führer's promise was that the days when advancement came as a result of class or social position were over. Every German man would know from personal experience what it meant to have blisters brought about by working with a shovel in his hand or to have a back aching from hard, physical labour. Youth in Hitler's Germany would not be gilded and painted but would be as hard as Krupp steel.

There were many socialist policies which the Nazis were able to initiate and to complete – housing, equal pay for women, marriage loans, increased family allowances and the construction of roads, other than autobahns. Planning for the Volkswagen was begun. Thinking along the lines that self-help produces the finest results and that a

sacrifice by the Volksgemeinschaft had the power to ennoble it, the Party made great efforts in the German version of British flag-days, the various street and house-to-house collections which were organized. This was practical socialism, a common effort to help the less fortunate. Seen from another perspective the charity drives were a form of indirect taxation. The Party's ambitions could not all be realized from the national exchequer but were met as a result of voluntary work carried out by the people. The masses had the desire to help and the Party had the organization that was needed to put men, women and children into the streets with their boxes or on house-to-house collections. The foremost of all these charitable works was the WHW (Winter Hilfs Werk, winter help undertaking) organized to provide extra food and clothes for the poor and elderly. The WHW, in pre-war years, was used by the Nazi leadership as

The caring face of National Socialism. Right and below: Collecting from the public by the WHW organization. Calling upon ordinary Germans to be generous to the underprivileged provided a useful method of 'indirect taxation' as well as a valuable barometer of public opinion.

'Butter will make you fat,' said Goering, 'Guns will make you strong.' Left: The attempt to reduce food and fuel consumption found expression in the Eintopfgericht campaign. Such sacrifice was thought to be in a good cause.

Right: Recycling waste materials. By such means, the ills of Germany might be cured. Preventing waste and obtaining optimum economic results from the resources and materials available were seen as worthwhile policies by the German people.

a barometer of public opinion. If the masses approved a particular action which the government had carried out, the donations were lavish. If there was a general disapproval the offerings were scanty. The WHW was as good as a referendum. These collections were not soup-kitchen charity. The whole of the Volksgemeinschaft worked together either on behalf of the poorer members of the community or else to cope with a crisis, as in the case of the appeal in the winter of 1941 for clothing for the troops on the Russian front. That drive brought in sixty-seven million items of winter clothing. Nor were the street collections just token displays of comradeship. Every Gauleiter, every minister was out on the streets with a collection box – people actually queued to put money into Goering's box, much to the chagrin of less popular government officials.

Looking at their national or regional leaders as they moved among them on charity days, the masses were comforted. These high officials were true sons of the people. They were not drawn from the traditional ruling classes, nor were they professional politicians but were men born out of the masses. Hitler had once laboured on building sites in Vienna and the father of Josef Goebbels had been a railway clerk. The leaders of the Nazi Party, as seen by the German people, were quite ordinary and fairly young men who, with very few exceptions, had been hardened in the front-line trenches of the Great War, who had fought in the skies or on the seas for the Fatherland. Thus, the German people saw that Hitler's Party was not made up of woolly-minded liberals, rigid-minded conservatives, parlour socialists or Communists dedicated to an alien regime, but was one composed of patriotic young working men, with the passion of young men, and with the strength of young men fiercely determined to restore their Fatherland's prestige.

Hitler and Goebbels both lived simple lives. Neither was a gourmet, neither was a wine connoisseur. Indeed, the frugality of the meals and drinks served at the Goebbels' table was notorious. Shortly before the war a campaign was introduced to save fuel and food. On one day of the week, usually Sunday, lunch was to be a one-course meal, a stew, cooked in a single pot (Eintopfgericht). It was a sacrifice which the German people made gladly because Eintopfgericht was a meal which both Hitler and Goebbels were said to enjoy immensely.

The view of the masses was that their leaders were honest, decent men, very much as the people thought they themselves were. 'Michel' is the German equivalent of John Bull or Uncle Sam. He is the national image. Michel is thought of as a simple, rural character, anxious only to be respected, to get on with his work, to smoke his pipe and to drink his beer. That is the view which the great mass of the German people had of themselves. Decent people who only wanted to live their simple, patriotic lives in an atmosphere of beer steins and sausage. All they wanted was to be respected by their neighbours and to have self-respect. That was their view of themselves and of their country.

Although the National Socialist government had a programme of social reform, no government can please all its people, nor indeed all the Party comrades, all the time. Within the SA, which had always contained the most radical, revolutionary Nazis, there was discontent at the failure to introduce and to implement the truly socialist policies for which they had fought. Hitler, in the view of the SA leaders, spent far too much time with the capitalists and the aristocratic leaders of the nation. He had forgotten, or perhaps even worse, he had betrayed the revolution. The men of the SA found that the expected distribution of the great estates and the socializing of industry had not happened. Nor had they been entrusted with the task of being the first defenders of the new Reich. The conservative army still held that post. Discontent from the SA leadership down to the rank and file became so evident that the other Nazi leaders feared it might amount to a counter-revolution and overthrow the Reich. That discontent needed to be stilled. It was stilled. In June 1934, the senior SA officers were arrested and shot to death by the Party's new élite – the SS. Within the Nazi hierarchy the influence of the SA then diminished as that of Himmler's black-and-silver uniformed SS increased. Soon the influence of the SS had penetrated into every sector of German society and extended from the Führer's bodyguard down to the guards in the concentration camps.

While no government can please all its people, during the early years of the government of Adolf Hitler most Germans were pleased. Huge ocean-going liners, of the sort in which capitalists and their doxies had once travelled, were now filled with German factory workers enjoying sea cruises. These German workers were travelling

Dr Joseph Goebbels: propaganda genius, brilliant orator and cynic. Here was the supreme manipulator of public opinion, who orchestrated the Nazi political theatre, organized the rallies and parades and created the dominant image of the Nazi Party in Germany. He claimed to have 'made' Hitler by bringing him out of the provincial political backwoods and turning him into a national figure. His was the task of overcoming German resistance to the political and economic restrictions implicit in the Nazi programme and the war. Left: A formal portrait. Below: At a press conference c.1937/8.

THE DEVELOPMENT OF THE PARTY 1933-1939

Right: The indoctrination of the young began early, with the Jungvolk, the junior organization, and then the Hitler Youth, seen here at a summer camp. Older people could take a longer view of events, remembering the Imperial days and the agonies following the Great War; such people were inclined at the end of the Second World War to surrender quickly to the Western Allies. Not so the indoctrinated Nazis. There were no mutinies in 1945.

with the KDF (Kraft durch Freude, the Strength through Joy organization) of the DAF (Deutscher Arbeits Front – the trades union.) The Party had decreed that there was no need for a great number of separate trades unions. The squabbling and rivalries of those bodies had once nearly ruined German industry. It must not be allowed to happen again. All unions were amalgamated and grouped in the DAF, which alone controlled the hours and conditions of work, pay, promotion and pensions for the workers.

There were of course opponents to the Nazis; those who scoffed, those who in the intimate revue bars of the big cities openly mocked the social advances which Germany had made. But their arguments could be refuted by the very obvious economic and social growth which was occurring in the Reich. Germans asked those who doubted, what other government had ever built cars for its people? Were things really better in the capitalist West? In London and in Paris for example, tens of thousands of homeless people slept on benches along the Thames or the Seine. There were no such unfortunates in the streets of German cities. Slum housing was a feature of the great cities of the Western democracies. In the Third Reich slums had been cleared away.

Germans displayed themselves and their country with pride when the Olympic Games of

1936 were held in Berlin. The cleanness, the orderly crowds, the smart uniforms of the new German Army, the shops filled with consumer goods, all were a mirror of the Germany of Adolf Hitler. Seen from the German viewpoint the Fatherland was prosperous, strong and influential. Within Germany anyone who doubted the evidence of their own eyes was a fool, no, more than that, he was a traitor and deserved to be confined within one of the concentration camps, which had been set up at Dachau, Oranienburg and Sachsenhausen. In these camps the misguided traitors would be held, together with other social, moral or political misfits. Professional criminals, sexual perverts of all sorts, bible-thumpers and Reds of every shade. They and people like them had once nearly brought Germany down. Now they were confined and must be punished. It was the duty of every German to work for the Volksgemeinschaft and if they would not work for that splendid ideal they too would be committed to hard labour in the concentration camps.

Of course, there cannot be a hundred per cent success in any enterprise. Within a few years of coming to power the Party was proclaiming that the world outside the Reich was jealous of her progress and had begun to form coalitions against her. The Fatherland must be strong enough to break the ring of threatening enemies. To build a strong nation would mean great personal sacrifices. Goering had said that what Germany needed was guns not butter. 'Guns', he had declared, 'will make us strong. Butter only makes us fat.' The Reichs Dietician, as he was called in the satirical cabarets of Berlin and Munich, may not have been the ideal politician to make that demand, for he had a reputation as a gourmand, but his words were accepted. The masses prepared themselves for a reduced standard of living in order that they might be well armed against the enemies of the Fatherland. The overweight Goering's call for sacrifices was underlined by the Press and the Propaganda Ministry. Goebbels wrote: 'We must be prepared to suffer poverty if we wish one day to be rich. A policy of self-denial does pay dividends.'

The Fatherland, from the viewpoint of the German people, had progressed and even if the pace had slowed down to meet the challenges of the Reich's enemies, it was still progress towards a finer life. The most obvious advances had been in the areas of social matters and economics. The labour shortage in German factories after 1937, meant that foreign labour had to be brought in and these immigrant workers were astonished to find such amenities as factory baths, higher pay and a legally enforced safety code.

At the political level, too, the people of Germany witnessed a great many examples of the Nazi government's political ability. The results of an election in 1935, reunited the Saar with the Reich. The industrial Saar, which had been torn away from Germany at the end of the war, voted overwhelmingly to be returned to the Fatherland. Then, too, there were areas along the Rhine which had been demilitarized on the orders of the victorious Allies and which had been occupied since the end of the war by soldiers of those nations. When, at long last, those enemy armies

moved out, German troops had still not been allowed to reoccupy the Rhineland. This national humiliation was one which Hitler intended to rectify by marching the army into the Rhineland. He gambled that the governments of the West would not oppose his move and that those in the East could not. The General Staff of the army expressed fears that such a precipitate move would lead to a military confrontation with France. The Führer knew better. The German Army marched and soon in the world's tabloids there were pictures of sentries of that army standing on the battlements of Ehrenbreitstein castle, overlooking Koblenz. Once again the garrison towns in which the Imperial Army had been quartered, echoed to German voices singing German soldiers' songs. The Watch on the Rhine had been recreated. The Third Reich, under the control of Adolf Hitler, had begun its march. He had gambled with the peace of Europe and won.

One of the great emotional themes of National Socialist philosophy had been the demand for all Germans to be united within one Fatherland. To the south and east of Germany lay the rump of the former Austro-Hungarian Empire. Within that rump lived eight million German/Austrians whose military skills, industry and ability had once carved out a vast Central European empire. That empire had been destroyed and fragmented in 1918, leaving German/Austria in a world where she could not survive economically. For Austria to join Germany was the obvious answer, but the union had been forbidden by the victorious powers. Hitler gambled, once again, that the West would not now oppose this reunion of German blood. He opened a political offensive aimed at destroying the opposition of Austrian statesmen to the Anschluss. By 1938, worn down by an increasingly strident campaign, the Austrian government acceded to Hitler's threats. The German Army

The rise of Nazi Germany begins. Left: The military reoccupation of the Rhineland. (Imperial War Museum) Above: The campaign to unite Austria with Germany. The placard reads: 'The same blood belongs in the same land.' The destiny of the Reich was being fulfilled, national pride restored.

marched in. A plebiscite was held and confirmed, as the plebiscites in dictatorships invariably do, the will of the people. In this case the people had voted overwhelmingly for the Anschluss with Germany. German/Austria was back in the Reich.

There followed a new demand from the Führer. In the Sudetenland, the border areas of the republic of Czechoslovakia, lived Germans who had settled in the region during the 13th and 14th centuries. Under Habsburg rule they had been Austrian citizens. When Czechoslovakia was created the Sudeten Germans became part of a Slav land and thus an ethnic minority. They suffered persecution and discrimination – what ethnic minority does not – and cried out to be united with the Reich. The diplomatic crises of 1938 and the political compromises during the autumn of that year had the result that the Sudetenland and its German population were detached from Czechoslovakia and ceded to the Reich. During those months of crisis, when a European war threatened, the hearts of the German people swelled with pride at the realization that it was upon their Chancellor and Führer that the decision depended whether there would be war or peace in Europe. The prime ministers of France and Great Britain had flown to discuss with the German leader those vital questions just as other politicians had had to come to Germany to learn the Führer's will and pleasure. Germany had, once again, the influential voice in Europe that she had had under a former powerful Imperial Chancellor, Otto von Bismarck.

German troops entered the Sudetenland in the autumn of 1938, passing through the modern defensive systems which the Czechs had constructed and which they now had to surrender. More than that; the most efficient armaments industry in Central Europe had passed under Nazi control and the new Reichs frontier with Czechoslovakia now lay just west of Prague. The commanders of the German Army had been fearful during the Sudetenland crisis. They had argued that if the invasion resulted in war, the Western democracies and the small but powerful Czech Army, might defeat Germany in a war for which she was not yet prepared. The Führer knew better. The Munich Agreement ensured that the march of the German Army was unimpeded; its occupation of the Sudetenland bloodless.

Beneš, the Czech President, resigned and went into exile. Hácha, his successor, was a frail, old man, quite incapable of withstanding Hitler's next territorial demand that the remainder of the Czech state be ceded or Prague would be razed by German bombers. On 14 March 1939, German troops drove into the golden city of Prague, into Bohemia and Moravia. Czechoslovakia, in Hitler's words, no longer existed. Along the Baltic, in Lithuania, there was a city, Memel, which had once been an East Prussian port. To Germans that name had an emotional appeal. The words of their national anthem spoke of a Fatherland extending west to east, from the Maas to Memel. Under the peace treaties it had become a Free city; but the Germans did not see that it was free only that it had been torn from the nation, that it was no longer part of the Reich. Hitler's demands that Memel be re-united with Germany were met during March 1939. German 'Michel' saw the developments which had restored his country with a deepening sense of pride. Germany had become a powerful nation and its successes had all been achieved without war – merely by being firm with the Fatherland's enemies and pointing out to them the correctness of Germany's demands. All this the Führer had achieved and in only a few years.

As foreigners saw it, German manoeuvring and posturing had been a direct threat to the peace of Europe. The tactics applied against the politicians of countries which resisted Nazi pressure had been nothing but bullying on the international stage and typical of the Nazis whose Party anthem proclaimed the need to dominate the streets by crushing all opposition. Germany was a power whose Führer and whose armies threatened the peace of Europe.

To 'Michel' there was one little piece of territory which had been stolen from the Fatherland as a result of dictated treaties and which needed to be restored. This was the artificially created Polish 'corridor' at whose exit stood the port of Danzig. The corridor, once part of Prussia, had been cut from that province and bestowed upon the Poles in order that they might have access to the sea. It was a simple matter for the Nazi propagandists to whip up demands from Danzig's German citizens for reunion with the Reich, but the resolute Poles were not minded to surrendered either the city or the corridor. Polish resolution was stiffened when a guarantee was given by a British government determined to maintain the republic's independence. The British guarantee was seen by the

Right: The success story continues. German troops mount guard at Prague's Hradschin Palace (the ancient seat of power in the city) after the occupation of Czechoslovakia in March 1939.

Germans as closing a ring of aggressive nations around the Fatherland. That ring must be broken if Germany were to survive. In order to break that ring it would be necessary to smash its eastern link – Poland. On 23 August 1939, in a complete reversal of their respective Party policies, the Nazi and Soviet governments signed a pact. Poland, which lay between them, was isolated. More than that – she was now under a direct and imminent threat. An outbreak of war could not be long delayed.

The Führer, as Commander-in-Chief of the Armed Forces of the Reich, had already prepared his military commanders by telling them that this political crisis was not one that could be resolved like that of Czechoslovakia. The Western powers could not back down this time. War was inevit-

able. In 1937, at the conclusion of a Führer conference attended by the German political and military leadership, a Major Hossbach of the General Staff, produced a memorandum. This document, which was later used as a principal indictment at the Nuremberg War Crimes Trials, demonstrated that Hitler was determined to use armed conflict as an instrument of policy. His resolve to lead the German people in a war before he became to old to fight it effectively was a theme which he frequently expressed; on one occasion to the British Ambassador. There can be no doubt that Hitler was convinced war was the only way by which Germany could attain a dominant position in the world. He was soon to achieve his ambition.

On Friday, 1 September, Adolf Hitler declared in the Reichstag, that Polish aggression against the

Reich could no longer be tolerated. Polish Regular Army units had been attacking the Reich since the early hours. He had ordered the German forces to retaliate. The Second World War had begun. The Party's propaganda line was that Germany had not started the war. A coalition of nations hostile to Germany had urged Poland to attack her. The Fatherland had retaliated and its just defence of sovereign territory against unprovoked aggression had caused Britain and France to declare war on Germany. It was not Germany that had declared war against the Western Allies. They, not she, were the aggressors. Goebbels admitted, an admission underlined by reports produced by the SD (Sicherheitsdienst, the Intelligence Section of the SS), that war had not been welcomed when it came in 1939, but had been accepted with fateful resignation as having been forced on Germany. Paradoxically, during the war, each new victory gained produced, along with the general rejoicing, a fresh longing for peace and the hope that this new success would be the final victory.

For a nation to prosecute a war and to bring it to a successful conclusion demands an interplay of a great many factors, chief among which are wise and farseeing leadership, the efficient use of human, industrial and economic potential, a united Home Front and well-equipped armed forces. Accepting that these factors are decisive ones, the thesis is valid that the major war upon which Nazi Germany embarked in 1939 was one that she was unlikely to win.

Above: There was ready acceptance of the need for economy and sacrifice for the good of the Fatherland. Here the WHW organization carries out its Eintopfgerigcht role with a military field kitchen and a band to serenade the happy eaters. The slogan reads: 'Today Berlin is eating its one-dish meal.'

# THE PARTY'S PERSPECTIVE OF THE MASSES

In earlier pages we have seen the German peoples' perspective of the Nazi Führer and the Party and have seen how the Nazis made great efforts to win popular approval. Several times in the pre-war years the masses were also asked to take part in referenda to vote whether they approved a particular action which the Party had taken. Referenda were considered by the Party as practical demonstrations of its closeness to the masses and its concern for the opinions of the people.

Let us now see how the Party and its leaders viewed those over whom they ruled. The people as a whole were, in those pre-war days, ready to make sacrifices of any sort in order to maintain the stability which the National Socialist government had brought about. The masses were prepared to support any move that would make Germany strong again. For that reason they welcomed the re-introduction of military conscription which had been a feature of German life for more than a hundred years. Much of the Party's condemnation of Weimar had been that Germany's young men lacked direction; that they had no discipline, because under Weimar there had been no compulsion to join the services.

The Party's pilot schemes for the introduction of food rationing; the guns before butter policy, the Eintopfgericht eaten on Sundays, all these had demonstrated to the Party leaders that if the people thought certain measures to be necessary, the masses would accept and support them. As Hitler had claimed in the 1934 Party Rally, 'Before us lies Germany, behind us comes Germany. With us marches Germany.' It was an intoxicating thought for the Party. Nearly eighty million skilled and disciplined citizens dedicated to the Protestant ethic of hard work. It was an intoxicating thought, but contained within that sentence lay the obstacle which, in the viewpoint of the Nazi leaders, needed to be overcome. This was the influence of religion, the hold of the churches upon the ordinary citizen. The Party's radical and revolutionary leaders realized that Germany had a Christian tradition nearly two thousand years old which taught humility and equality in the eyes of God. That God was, as the Nazis saw it, a Jew. The Catholics in the population also gave obedience to

an alien creed, to the dogmas of the Roman Catholic Church, whose leaders were becoming increasingly critical of the actions of the Reich. All this superstition, this disloyalty must be overcome and replaced by new Nordic beliefs.

If it were just religion, this might be easy enough to eradicate, but there were other liberal traditions which it would be harder to wipe out so quickly. There was a belief in the freedom of the Press to criticise. Accepting, albeit reluctantly, that need but determined to destroy it eventually, the German Press under the Nazis was by no means the docile beast that the Western world believed it to be. This belief in freedom of expression applied equally to radio, and the government's several campaigns to stop the public listening to foreign broadcasts were generally unsuccessful. For one thing many citizens thought that it was not wrong to listen to foreign stations that were playing music and, in addition, many Party members considered that the ban did not apply to them because they were politically reliable and, therefore, proof against enemy propaganda. The German nation, was, as the Nazi leadership saw it, a large, powerful, disciplined nation. On the other hand, it was religious, freedom loving and expected a certain degree of independence in the matter of conscience.

For the Party's long-term strategy to succeed it would be necessary to destroy the negative, Christian influences and replace them by more dynamic concepts, chief among which were those of blood and race. The conviction that the Aryan race and German blood were superior to all others formed the cornerstones of the Nazi creed. Those of the Volksgemeinschaft who accepted these beliefs were, in Nazi eyes, full members of a nation which was racially, and by inference, morally, superior to all others. To eradicate weak Christian beliefs of equality from the German soul might take time, but the Third Reich had time. It had a projected life of ten centuries. The Hitler regime would rule a Reich whose life would be longer than the life spans of former empires. Any mistakes which Germany might make in the first years of the Thousand Year Reich would be excusable. Within ten centuries the system would be made to run so smoothly that similar errors would not occur again and during that time the weaknesses in the German soul could be bred out. The Nazis' belief in racial superiority was neither peculiar to them nor had it first begun with them. For thousands of years the Brahmins have believed that they are twice born and that this makes them superior to everyone else in the world. For thousands of years the Jews have called themselves the Chosen Race. Many nations have had feelings of superiority; racial, political or religious. Germany, that is Nazi Germany, came late to the belief in superiority and it was a creed not accepted by the masses as a whole.

Let us, in the last year of peace, 1938, analyse what had been achieved. The Party had planned to unify Germany politically. That programme had already been achieved. It had planned to unite all Germans in one Fatherland. That part of the programme was in progress. It had planned to reinforce the Volksgemeinschaft through repetition of the creed of racial superiority. This was a long-term ambition, but indoctrination was already in progress. The fourth phase of the plan was to fight a series of lightning wars at the end of which Germany would be the supreme power in Europe. That part of the programme would soon be in train.

At the conclusion of the fourth stage the Party would establish its control over the lands which the Wehrmacht had conquered. The industries and agricultures of those conquered lands would then be integrated with those of the Fatherland. Now enlarged industrially, with food supplies guaranteed and having a reservoir of human material to exploit, the Reich would take time to digest its conquests. Then, made powerful by that increase in strength, Germany would go on to achieve the Party's ambition – a Germany superior to all other nations. Having once gained that place she could then ensure by vigilant policing that there would never be a challenge to her authority, either from external or internal enemies. By the elimination of the weak and the congenitally disabled a Master Race would be created to rule over the subordinate races whom genetic engineering would have bred to work docilely for their German masters.

The people of the Volksgemeinschaft would rule over the lesser breeds and the more important a person's position within the Nazi hierarchy that much greater would be his wealth and eminence

in the administration of these latter-day colonists. The Sicherheitsdienst of the SS, those guardians of National Socialist ethics, would ensure that no member of the hierarchy, at whatever level, set himself up in opposition to the Central government. The Fatherland would be secure for the duration of its forecasted existence.

Even within the concept of a Master Race there are some who are especially gifted. Among comrades of any enterprise, even a Nordic Volksgemeinschaft, there are some who are better comrades, who are more ambitious, dynamic, aggressively thrusting – the natural leaders in a society; an élite within an élite. Thus it was foreseen that there would come a time in the life of the Thousand Year Reich when these aristocrats – that élite within an élite – would need to be grouped into a sort of Teutonic knighthood, a select brotherhood. They would form that very cream of the nation and they would be sound; physically, morally and psychologically. They would be the physical, moral and social élite of the German race and to strengthen them intellectually, the finest minds in Germany would be recruited to instruct them. One day such a proper knightly organization would either have evolved or have been created, but until that time came the best representatives of the Nazi Germany of the 1930s would be grouped within the SS. Himmler's SS were the very best examples of 20th-century German manhood.

So high was the standard of physical excellence in the SS of Hitler's Germany that in pre-war days, it was claimed that a single filled tooth debarred a man. Physically perfect, they were then subjected to an intense programme of Nordic indoctrination to make them racially and politically aware of their special role in the new Reich. Chief among the duties inherent in the role of defenders of the Fatherland, was to ensure that Germany's enemies were neutralized. This process would be accomplished in the camps that had been set up to imprison the enemies of the State. These concentration camps would need to be staffed by guards who were doctrinally sound against the evil, perverted arguments of the politically criminal inmates. Theirs would be a terrible responsibility.

It might be necessary to administer punishment, even capital punishment, but this would have to be carried out with neither remorse nor hesitation, for this well-deserved punishment was being carried out only upon the enemies of the

Reich. The concentration camp prisoners were undesirables, enemies of the Fatherland, and would be treated for what they were, traitors to their race; Germans unworthy of being part of the Vollksgemeinschaft. SS training and indoctrination was a hard and testing process and produced men not so much ruthless as pitiless in their determination to rid the world of the vermin over whom they were placed in authority. Why should they have compassion for vermin? They, the SS, were prepared to fight and die for Hitler. If they, the élite, were prepared to sacrifice everything for Germany, to be so contemptuous of their own lives that they would gladly lay them down for Hitler, how little consideration need be given to the lives of those prisoners who rejected the concepts of the nobility of their race and who were, therefore, unworthy of the distinction of being German? To be hard; rock-hard, against Germany's native enemies meant that the SS had to treat these other Germans – the pre-war concentration camp inmates – very badly. This was not always easy for the prisoners were still Germans. How much easier did the task become, in later years, when it was only alien, sub-humans who had to be guarded – or dealt with. The destruction of racial enemies, like the Jews, that race which Nazi propaganda had claimed had sought to destroy the Fatherland, was an honourable duty. In the war situation and against the racially inferior Slavs, the feeling that one was 'cleansing' Europe made the task so much more bearable. Seen against a time-frame of a thousand years, the decade of racial murder in the concentration camps and the prisoner-of-war camps of Europe, can be seen as a short but brutal introduction to what would have been the policing of the Thousand Year Reich.

Photographs of the wooden barracks of Dachau and Buchenwald might have given the impression that concentration camps were intended to be a temporary feature of the Nazi social fabric. It is necessary to see the stone walls of Mauthausen, metres thick and built to endure for ten centuries, to be made aware that the concentration camps were no passing phenomenon but would be an essential, vital component of the New Order.

Heinrich Himmler, the Reichsführer SS, was anxious that his men should not be seen by the Volksgemeinschaft solely as concentration camp guards. No, his were all-round men belonging to an élite body, a fusion of physical and intellectual perfection. To add lustre to the élite organization, to make the nation aware that this was the cream of Germany, he gave high, honorary rank to the very best representatives of German culture. Richard Strauss, for example, was an honorary General in the SS.

Administration of the Reich's future colonial empire would require fully competent officers and these future SS administrators learned their craft in Germany during the pre-war years. So proficient, so powerful was the penetration of German society by the SS that, in time, its officers controlled every aspect of German social and political life. During the war that penetration extended to the military field and starting in 1939, Waffen SS Divisions were raised. General Lemelsen, commander of Fourteenth Army in Italy during the last months of the war, was only one of the senior officers who expressed the belief that, 'There was absolutely no necessity for the creation of the Waffen SS.' It was clear that Lemelsen had not seen that Force from the viewpoint of the Party; that is that, with final victory, the honour of being the weapon-bearers of the state would be taken from the army and bestowed upon the SS.

Above: Honorary General of the SS Richard Strauss. Conferring high status within the supreme organization of the Party on such celebrities inevitably identified them with the Nazi élite . . . and vice versa.

Within the hierarchy which the Party intended to set up in the new colonies there would be located above the lowest stratum of German managers other strata whose .officers would administer estates. Then there would be those governing regional districts or areas the size of provinces, right up to the final level of men who would be uncrowned monarchs ruling a whole country. During the war years and particularly in the first years of victory and expansion, senior Party men were put into viceregal positions for which they were untrained and for which they were temperamentally and morally unsuited. These men, with their creed of racial superiority, were aware that, so long as tribute flowed from their kingdoms, any brutality on their part would be neither questioned nor criticized by Central government.

From the perspective of these men and of the Party which had appointed them, the occupation policies in Poland, in Russia and in the Balkans, were a pilot scheme for the administration of a Thousand Year Empire. Who were these pro-consuls, the torch-bearers of Teuton civilization? They included Hans Frank, once an undistin-guished lawyer in the days of the Kampfzeit, who was made Governor-General of Poland and lived in viceregal style in Cracow. In November 1941, Hitler ordered the setting up of an administration for the occupied eastern territories of Russia. Alfred Rosenberg, an academic and a Party intel-lectual, was empowered to run that administra-tion and was given one Reichskommissar for the Ukraine and another to administer Belorussia together with the former Baltic republics of Lithuania, Latvia and Estonia.

Erich Koch, Gauleiter of East Prussia, was created Reichskommissar for the Ukraine and his rule was an indictment of the Nazi Party's treat-ment of subject peoples. The Ukraine had fought for years to gain independence from Russia and it had been the region in which the Soviets had committed genocide from 1936 to 1937; a time of repression and murder about which the full story has not yet been told. The Ukraine was the bread-basket of Russia and the Soviet authorities ordered its peasants to amalgamate their small holdings into collective farms. The fiercely inde-pendent Ukrainians refused and to force them to comply with Party orders Nikita Khruschev, acting for Stalin, starved them to death. More than twelve million Ukrainians died in that Soviet-inspired famine. It is not surprising that those who survived welcomed the German Army into their country as liberators. The Ukrainians, a hard-working, willing nation, farming a fertile land, could have provided the Reich with the grain which it needed to make the whole Continent self-sufficient. It was not to be. The sufferings of the people of the Ukraine under the rule of Reichs-kommissar Koch were of so terrible a nature and so wide-ranging that these potential allies for Germany turned away and went back to the tyranny of Moscow where the gaolers were at least Slavs like themselves. The despair felt by those in authority in Germany at the activities of people like Koch, were expressed with great clarity by Goebbels who realised that the fierce resistance put up by the Russian people was due to the fact that they could see no future for themselves in a German victory.

It would have been in Germany's interest to win over to her the great mass of the subject nations of the Soviet Union. Such a policy could only have been achieved by a lenient occupation policy which, accepting the cynical attitude of the Party, would have needed only to be maintained until final victory had been won. Then would come the time to introduce the measures which would reduce the Slavs to the status of unprivileged serfs in the Greater German Empire. But for as long as the Red Army remained in the field and the Soviet Union was undefeated, the attempts should have been made, as Goebbels' appreciated, to win the confidence of the Ukrainians, of the White Russians, of the Balts and of the non-white peoples of the Caucasus. Goebbels realized it but his protests availed him nothing and he lacked the authority to call a halt to the worst excesses of Koch and those criminals like him. They des-troyed any chance of the Nazis' gaining support from the peoples of the Soviet Union. More than that, their activities produced the tide of partisan warfare which destroyed German military opera-tions and the activities of the Party's occupation policies led to the terrible revenge taken upon the peoples of the eastern Gaus by the Red Army. Not a little of the blame for the defeat of Germany can be apportioned to the arrogance of the Party 'Bonzen' and to the complacency of the Party in seeing the war in the East as won when, as a later chapter of this book will show, the Army's Supreme Command had admitted in the autumn of 1941, that Operation 'Barbarossa' had failed.

Above: Hans Frank, Governor General of Poland, receiving a local delegation c.1942. Germans thought him a fair, if tough, administrator of the conquered land; the Poles knew him for a bloody butcher. Next to him in this photograph, and smiling benevolently, is Adolf Eichmann.

Right: Alfred Rosenberg, who was in charge of the German occupation policies in the east. The Nazi Party's philosopher, and editor of Hitler's Party newspaper, he set out to prove that Germany had a 'divine right' to rule.

Above: The propagation of the master race. It was the Nazi ideal for 'racially pure' couples to wed and produce healthy Aryan children. The State paid a dowry (in vouchers) to girls on their wedding. Here a mass SA and SS wedding takes place. These were special non-religious ceremonies. Church weddings, meanwhile, became valid only with the addition of a civil ceremony.

# THE PARTY'S VIEW OF WOMEN

If the perspective we have of the Third Reich as a totalitarian regime, rigid and inflexible but certain of its goals and how these were to be achieved, is distorted, so too is our understanding about the position of women in Nazi Germany. Whereas the men were under conscription for pre-military training and then for service in the armed forces, the same compulsions were not applied to women. Legislation did exist to compel women but this was not enforced until the last stages of the war. This unsure touch was particularly evident in the Party's approach to those women who made up 37 per cent of the pre-war labour force. The problem was that initially women had been encouraged to leave industry, but by 1937 a shortage of labour existed which only a return of women workers could overcome. The Nazi view of women was that they were the domestic partner in a marriage. They should not have to work, but if they did it should not be in heavy industry. National Socialist policy had always been that women should be encouraged to leave industry and return to domesticity. In the first days of Nazi government the principal incentive for that attitude had been the need to give work to men – the natural bread-winners – while they, the women, fulfilled their natural role as homemakers. National Socialist attitudes to the employment of women were thus governed by an economic as well as by a social consideration. Governments before the Nazis' had been unable to conquer the curse of unemployment and, indeed, under Weimar the numbers of those without work had risen to more than six million. On 1 June 1933, within six months of achieving power, the Nazis passed a law designed to reduce unemployment and the preamble in that document reinforced the Party line that women were partners with men and were not in competition with them. That concept was underlined in an article in the Party newspaper, *Der Völkischer Beobachter*, which stated that the task of German women was not to campaign against men but to campaign alongside them. The demand for equality worked both ways. Women did not, in pre-Hitler Germany, receive equal pay for equal work, but gained this right in 1935, in the second year of Nazi government.

Although the Nazi propaganda campaign, which was aimed at taking women out of industry, had stressed the need to give employment to men, there was a deeper, long-term issue which could only be overcome by women returning to their traditional role as mothers. Germany was a land with a declining population and National Socialist policy was aimed at reversing that trend. The production of children was encouraged by every means and to achieve that ambition the Nazi Party needed to eradicate from German society those ideas, trends and attitudes which had been responsible for the low birth rate. Thus the Party opposed, on principle, divorce, birth-control, abortion and homosexuality. The Party programme encouraged the sanctity of marriage, a raising of the health standards of the nation and their visible products: healthy children.

So far as the Nazi leaders were concerned the need to produce children was the most important priority of the Thousand Year Reich and this need could be best, but not exclusively, met within marriage. Analysis of the problem showed that the surplus of women over men had risen from more than three quarters of a million before the Great War to two and three quarter millions in 1935. Research showed that a great many of these surplus women were of child-bearing age. Ideally, to raise the population numbers every woman capable of bearing a child should reproduce. But the Germans were a very moral people and if a woman who had no husband bore a child it would bring upon the baby the stigma of bastardy and against the mother the accusation of immorality. How to overcome these *petit-bourgeois* inhibitions was discussed at the Party's highest levels. Rudolf Hess, the Führer's Deputy, and Heinrich Himmler, responsible for the purity of the Race, not only sought ways to overcome the moral objections of the German people but also strove to improve the lot of the unmarried mother in accordance with the Party line that a woman who had given a child to Germany had performed a patriotic duty. Himmler stated, indeed, that to be an unmarried mother did not debase a woman; rather it raised her to her true level. She was neither a married nor an unmarried woman, but a mother. That was the important thing. To help unmarried mothers who had to go out to work

there were generous tax reliefs, and to remove the social stigma Hess declared that the Fatherland would be responsible for the rearing of their children. The leaders of the Third Reich had their own ideas of what constituted morality and the Party's attitude was that the need for the population to increase was more important than old-fashioned morals which had no place in the revolutionary, National Socialist Volksgemein-schaft.

To encourage the great mass of German women to marry and to reproduce, the Party undertook a massive propaganda campaign and backed it with financial and other incentives. Women who left full-time employment to marry were eligible for marriage vouchers to the value of 1,000 marks. When it is considered that a woman's average weekly wage in 1933 was 27 marks, it can be seen what an incentive the grant was. Within three years more than six hundred thousand marriages had been assisted by such loans, and repayment of the money was spread out over a very long period of time. There were, also, ways in which the size of the debt could be reduced or cancelled totally; for a first child by 25 per cent and for subsequent children by the same percentage of the outstanding sum.

There were other financial inducements for mothers, such as rent rebates, the reduction of electricity and gas bills by 50 per cent and preferential treatment on transport, in queues and in shops. The award of the Mother's Cross was a visible sign that the status of the mother in Nazi Germany had been upgraded. The 1935 Party Rally acknowledged the special and indispensible role of women in society, through the slogans, 'Women have their battlefield, too' and 'Women are the first educators of the new generation'. Motherhood, so the Party said, gave the chance to display their natural qualities of self-sacrifice and sympathy. Women were different from, but the equals of men. Men were productive; women were reproductive – partners in a perfect whole.

To help the German woman fulfil her natural function of motherhood, all influence which might harm the unborn child were to be avoided. Women were advised not to smoke or drink alcohol during their pregnancies and to keep themselves fit through exercise and healthy diet. Ante-natal clinics monitored the health of the expectant mother and her baby. Post-natal clinics ensured the health and well-being of mother and child. Everything that could be done to help was done. In its demand for children the State rejected absolutely and totally birth control and abortion. Both were considered to be crimes against the Volksgemeinschaft and the slogan that abortion was little less than child murder had a dramatic effect. The numbers of girls seeking to terminate pregnancies fell dramatically from nearly a million in 1928 to only a few thousands in the first years of the Reich and remained low. Of course, there were permitted cases where not to abort would have endangered the mother's life, or where the foetus was that of parents with hereditary defects, whose breeding, the Party proclaimed to be an infamy. Considering abortion along racial lines produced the ruling that the termination of pregnancies in Jewish mothers should be encouraged.

In the final months of the war the laws forbidding abortion were relaxed so that those German girls and women who had been raped and made pregnant by soldiers of the Red Army could have their pregnancies terminated. In the interests of the health of the Volksgemeinshcaft such abortions were necessary to destroy babies whose mothers had been infected with the venereal diseases which were thought to be endemic in the Russian forces.

In the days of the 'liberal' Republic, sexual perversions had been tolerated, but in the Third Reich homosexuals were prosecuted and imprisoned in concentration camps. The overt reason for this condemnation was that homosexuality was a sin in the eyes of the Church, but the government was concerned by the low birth rate, and sexual acts between men could not produce children. For that latter reason Jewish homosexuals were encouraged in their perversion. Nor did German lesbians suffer condemnation because it was the Party's conviction that a lesbian might, one day, come to her senses and

Left: Hitler meets women leaders of the RAD (Labour Corps) at the Nuremberg rally of 1935. Behind him is Konstantine Haerl, leader of the RAD.

take up a hetero-sexual relationship from which would come offspring.

The overriding demand was for the German people to bring healthy children into the world because throughout the whole lifetime of the Thousand Year Reich, there would be a need for manpower to serve the Fatherland. In the short term, that is in the first few decades, this need would be greatest. Josef Goebbels, the Propaganda Minister, warned at a staff meeting in October 1941, that although the outcome of the war in Russia had already been decided in Germany's favour, fighting might flicker and break out for more than a decade. During those years Germany would face the same sort of tribal revolt in Russia as that which the British were meeting on the North-West Frontier of India. Thus, for one or perhaps even two generations, there would be a continuing need for warriors to guard the frontiers of the Greater German Empire.

Once the Fatherland had digested its conquests, there would be a demand for administrators, planners, overseers and all the hierarchical structure of a ruling Race. The need for children would remain, therefore, for ten centuries to come. This overriding, national demand could be met only by ensuring that German women did not jeopardize their child-bearing faculties. The result of medical surveys showed that hard manual labour in factories could have a deleterious effect upon their reproductive capacity. Concern that such work could affect the growth of the German nation served to underline the intention expressed during the first years of Nazi rule to take women out of the labour force. Under the influence of National Socialist propaganda there was a slow but continual reduction of the numbers of women employed in industry from 7 million in 1937 to 2.62 million in May 1939, 2.61 million in May 1941 and 2.58 million in May 1942.

To look after the interests of women who did work, the DAF (Deutsche Arbeits Front, the German Labour Front), formed a women's section as early as July 1934. In order that the DAF female shop stewards understood the problems of their members they had to spend a minimum of six months on the factory floor as well as having to graduate in social science. One of the first results of the formation of DAF women's sections was the reduction of the working day and the abolition of night work. By law no female was allowed to work in a factory after 10 p.m.

In one of those contradictions peculiar to the nominally socialist and revolutionary Nazi system, a need was still seen to exist for house-maids and to maintain their numbers, 15-year-old girls could be employed. This move was rationalized on the grounds that such employment would first, safeguard the puberty of very young girls by keeping them out of factories and, secondly, it would teach them domestic skills. They would also learn the hard fact that before one can command one must have learned to obey – and in service they would learn to be obedient.

From 1936 a financial incentive was offered which helped to reduce even further the number of women still in the labour market. The introduction of conscription for the armed forces had taken men from well-paid jobs in industry and in order that soldiers' families should not suffer financial loss the Nazi government issued such generous family allowances that wives did not need to work to maintain a good living standard. For families with children the allowances were sufficiently high to remove completely the burden of financial worry. There was yet another incentive, albeit a negative one, which took women from the factories. The earnings of a working woman counted against her allowances and so far as most women were concerned there was little point in working hard for a small wage.

Within a few years there were policy conflicts within the National Socialist system. There was the Party belief that, for very good reasons, German women should not have to toil in factories. On the other hand, by 1937 the labour shortfall could only be overcome by employing women. Factories needed to be filled if Germany's production was to rise and to meet the demands of a future war. With great reluctance a campaign

Above right and right: Girls of the Bund deutscher Maderln, the League of German Maidens, female equivalent of the Hitler Youth. (Imperial War Museum) Far right: Women members of the RAD tended to fulfil their labour obligations in domestic roles and on farms.

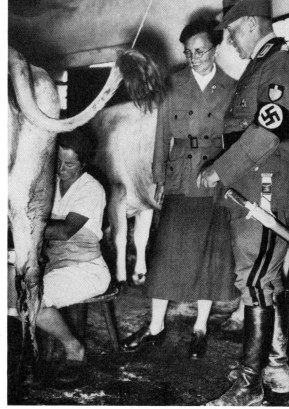

Shortages became more prevalent as the war went on, and the government was forced to respond. This wall poster attempts to ridicule the grumblers. The housewife in the illustration claims that she is starving because there are no bananas in the shops, even though she has plenty of other vegetables and fruits from which to choose. (Imperial War Museum)

was launched to encourage women who had left industry to return to it. As the figures given above show, the campaign did not succeed and there was a decline in numbers of women at work.

Laws enabling the government to conscript women into factories had been on the statute book for years, but had not been implemented, nor would they ever be – in respect of German women. For the great mass of them there was to be no direction of labour. Persuasion rather than coercion was the keynote, for the Party did not wish to offend the people. As late as May 1943, it

was accepted that total war must not, in any way, become a war against women, who represented an enormous power in Germany. Women were not to be compelled to do their duty, but they were expected to see the need and to respond to it.

By a strange and, for the German leadership, undesirable paradox, when war did come the Wehrmacht's military successes served to convince the women of Germany that there was no need for them to enter industry. Each victory had been won after a short campaign, the material losses of which had been made good by the standing labour force. Those military victories had also produced prisoners of war; more than a million of them by the end of 1940, and these could be put into the mines, into agriculture and into steel production. The number of military prisoners would be added to as a result of the Russian campaign, and from Russia too there came a great mass of women who joined the German work force either as volunteers or as forced labour. When the German women learned of the enormous reservoir of workers available to the Fatherland it is not surprising that they felt they were not needed at the factory bench.

The middle and final years of the war were to prove this belief false. A nation of finite resources which is engaged in fighting a war for its very survival must ensure that every able citizen is fully used. A nation in such a situation can afford to reject nobody for the war effort must be a sacrifice made by the whole people. A nation, and particularly one which is fighting an ideological war, cannot afford to risk sabotage by employing large numbers of foreign workers some of whom may be enemy agents, nor can it permit the go-slow tactics of a conscript, foreign work force. There must be no impediment to the flow of weapons and war material from the factories to the armies in the field, but this was the perilous situation the National Socialist leadership was prepared to accept rather than to act in a dictatorial way against the women of the nation.

For the campaigns of 1939 and 1940, factories geared to supply the needs of short campaigns had coped. The plan of attack upon the Soviet Union in June 1941 had, likewise, been planned to be concluded within five months. Had all gone as planned, the German armed forces and the existing work force would once again have been sufficient to bring victory. Despite initial huge successes, it was very soon accepted at OKW level that the war in Russia could not be won in 1941. If it could not be won in that year victory was unlikely in any other year, because the length of the battle line in the east, the overwhelming strength of the Red Army and the constant fight against partisans reduced the numbers of German soldiers who were actually embattled.

The long and growing casualty lists soon brought about a severe shortage of fighting men. The war spread. In 1943 came the Allied invasion of Italy, an intensification of the guerrilla campaign in Yugoslavia and then in 1944 the landings in North-West Europe. The German Army was now seriously understrength, was fighting on several fronts and needed every man for the battle line. What should have happened wss that the Party organizations, the inflated staffs at rear headquarters and industry should have been checked to see where men could be spared. Despite this manpower crisis, the work force in the factories was still predominantly male, and women were neither working in great numbers in industry, nor were they in the armed forces replacing rear echelon male soldiers in vital but non-combatant, basically civilian, clerical duties.

Appeals by the Nazi authorities for women to serve the Fatherland fell upon deaf ears. One government official in the Labour Office complained that those already at work in industry were either women who had always had to work or else the families of service officers who saw factory work as a patriotic duty. That broad stratum of women which did not come forward, the official complained, and whose poor, pre-war living standards had been raised by the Nazi Party, had adopted the 'I'm all right now' mentality; refused to see that the Fatherland was in danger and that it was their duty to give up their coffee mornings or hairdresser's appointments so as to take their place alongside their sisters at the lathes. It was to serve the needs of that type of woman that more than 1.3 million housemaids were still employed, as late as September 1944.

Government threats to enforce the 1935 conscription laws were made in the expectation that such threats would be sufficient to force the women to come forward. It had the opposite effect. The attitude was, 'If we are to be conscripted, why should we volunteer?' The feelings of those other women who had been working for years in war-time conditions can be well appreciated. They had, in addition to their long hours of work, to carry out civil defence duties and to care for their families. Their feelings, already bitter, were further aroused by the knowledge that a great number of girls were evading war work by enrolling as full-time students at universities. The National Socialist regime had always laid great stress on higher education for women, but in the opinion of many working women and not a few Nazi officials, the demand by girls for places at a university was based on a determination to avoid factory work rather than a thirst for knowledge. The fact that so many middle class girls were offered places in higher education seemed to emphasize to the socialist elements in the Party that class attitudes were still to be found in Germany.

In the matter of female education Gauleiter Geisler of Munich was a man not known for a subtleness of expression. He suggested that female students should not fill their heads with learning but that their academic achievement should be to produce a child for the Führer. 'Should any girl', proclaimed the Gauleiter, 'be so unattractive that she cannot find a lover, then I am prepared to assign one of my adjutants to the task of giving her satisfaction.'

In an effort to increase workshop production by a labour force whose numbers remained more or less static, the hours of work in the factories were raised. Despite this there was no corresponding increase in output, rather was there a dramatic rise in the number of women suffering from psychosomatic illnesses. An increase of femine complaints tended to reduce still further the numbers of those who contributed to the national war effort and also of those who should have contributed. In that context Fritz Sauckel, Reichs Minister responsible for the deployment of the labour force, complained that of the 3.6 million women who had been medically examined during 1943, only 1.6 million were fit for work in industry. A further three-quarters of a million were only fit for half-day work and a further half-million had been taken out of industry through health problems. It may well be that the women of Germany had absorbed so deeply the political propaganda to take them out of industry that when they entered the factories they rejected the work subconsciously. The Nazis had been hoist with their own petard.

Efforts were made to overcome the labour shortfall through the employment of women working at home on light assembly tasks. This scheme proved impracticable and wasteful. Then, too, those women who did only a half-day's work in factories soon found that they were required to work 30 hours per week; nearly as many hours as a full-time week in peacetime. Many of these discontented women began to report sick with the usual mysterious, psychosomatic maladies. The manpower shortage was so serious and the problem of recruitment so difficult to resolve that until the middle years of the war only a single shift was worked in many factories.

The situation of the peasant women was even worse than that of urban women. It seems unusual that a political system so closely tied in with the soil, as the Nazis claimed theirs to be, should have been so uncaring of the needs of the workers on the land. Despite the need to produce food, farmers were conscripted into the forces leaving farms to be worked by their womenfolk. The concern of the Nazi Party for the child-bearing capabilities of urban women seemed not to extend to those in rural areas. It is hardly surprising that the birth rate in such areas, already low before 1933, continued to decline.

The employment of prisoners of war alleviated some of the work problems, but emphasized others which the Nazi leadership had obviously not considered. The sexual desires of German soldiers were met in military run brothels. Those same desires in the women left at home went unconsidered and when in rural areas the farmers' wives had young prisoners of war working for them, and these foreigners also had sexual needs, it was obvious that dangerous liaisons could result. Those guilty of such misconduct suffered severe penalties and when a case had racial connotations, that is where the lover was a Russian or a Pole, execution for the male was the standard punishment. The women were usually sent to concentration camps.

When one compares the work undertaken by British and Russian women during the Second World War it becomes abundantly clear that for the greatest number of those years of conflict the majority of German women had no conception of what was implied by the term total war. British women laboured hard and long in factories and in the services. They flew aircraft, served on anti-aircraft batteries and carried out a wide variety of tasks for which they would have been considered unsuitable in pre-war days. In Russia the employment of women on war duties went even farther and they served as fighter pilots, in infantry regiments as snipers, in partisan detachments and in the heaviest industries. In both those countries the conscription of women was accepted as a vital part of the national war effort.

In Germany it was not until quite late in the war that women were encouraged to enlist in the services and then, chiefly into the signals branches of the army and of the Luftwaffe. During the last year of the war more and more women entered the services to replace men on searchlight

Manpower shortages eventually brought German women into military roles. Here women crew part of the anti-aircraft defences. While in uniform they were part of the Luftwaffe; off duty, they were considered civilians.

sites and in flak batteries. The great majority of these 50,000 women were not volunteers, but were RAD members who had been transferred from duties in agriculture to man the guns.

Towards the very end of hostilities great numbers of women entered military service until they numbered more than half a million. by coincidence this influx of women occurred at a time when stories had begun to circulate in the Press of acts of heroism by women in the provinces of the Reich into which the Red Army had thrust. It must be understood that the Russian forces sweeping westwards out of Poland and into eastern Germany were men who had advanced across hundreds of kilometres of their own country which had been destroyed in the war. Ilya Ehrenburg wrote of this time in an article in *Red Star*, the Soviet Army journal, 'We forget nothing. As we march through Pomerania we see before our eyes our destroyed and bleeding Belorussia. The stink of burning on our coats is that from Smolensk and Orel. In Königsberg, Breslau and Scheidemuhl we think of Voronezh or Stalingrad. Men of the Red Army, do not forget how in Leningrad mothers took their dead children away on little sledges. For what Leningrad suffered, Berlin has not yet paid.' The propaganda machine of the Red Army had inflamed the soldiers' minds with stories of German atrocities and underlined those stories with demands for revenge upon the fascists. Whether the Red Army men needed to be encouraged to ravish and destroy, or were ordered by STAVKA to open a reign of terror, as Goebbels claimed, is not important.

What did happen was that stories of rape, murder, arson, looting and senseless destruction of property by Soviet units were soon current. Parallelling those stories of horror were others commending the heroism of young girls who sought revenge upon their despoilers and had gained that revenge using close combat methods. So frequent were these reports that the single-shot, anti-tank rocket projectile, Panzerfaust, became known as 'the woman's weapon'. These stories had a basic theme. Girls would wait in bushes by roadsides, usually singly until the Red armour rolled towards them. Once the 'victim' tank had been chosen the courageous girl of the BDM (Bund deutscher Maderln; the League of German Maidens) would stand up, aim and fire the panzerfaust. A stream of flame would mark the rocket's short flight. A detonation and then, on an isolated road in Prussia, Pomerania or Saxony, a Red Army vehicle would be burning. Sometimes it would be a two-girl team armed with the stove-pipe like, Panzerschreck. The team would 'kill' a succession of Soviet tanks with a series of rockets fired from the launcher. There was also mention of the tank-destroying technique developed by the Hitler Youth and alleged to have been used by some courageous girls of the BDM. In this the tank buster would run towards the enemy machine as it rumbled slowly along and would place an explosive charge on the metal armour. A pull on the detonating cord and nine seconds later, time enough to dive into cover, the grenade would destroy the Red vehicle.

Just how many of these stories were true; whether young girls and women of the BDM, victims of multiple rape or otherwise obscenely maltreated, actually did destroy Soviet armoured fighting vehicles cannot be known or proven. Certainly some accounts of the battle for Berlin reported women fighting in the city. It is a matter of record that they were active in the German partisan organization, Wehrwolf, but they were not able to serve in a woman's battalion 'Adolf Hitler', which was proposed on 4 March 1945. The war ended before the planning was completed.

For those girls who served in military units National Socialist concepts of frugality applied. So far as the services were concerned the women were soldiers only during the hours they were on duty. During that time they wore uniform and were paid for the hours they worked. Off duty, they had to wear civilian clothes and were, for the purposes of administration, considered to be camp-followers. This bizarre interpretation had the most shocking effects upon the women soldiers who were captured by the Red Army. Soviet officers pointed out to them that they could not claim the protection of the Hague Convention, because, 'Even your own army says that you are not service personnel.' The story of one girl is representative of so many who suffered. 'My family was an old Prussian military one, which can trace its service beyond the time of the Great Elector. Such a tradition does not die and although the National Socialists were only marginally better than the left-wing parties, my family served and fought for Hitler, principally because we saw the Nazis as being an interim regime which would precede a return to the monarchy. We considered that the Party must be acceptable. The

Crown Prince and two other sons of the Kaiser were in the SA. Also, it would have been unthinkable for any member of our family not to fight for Germany. Hitler, we considered was an aberration. Germany would live after he had gone.

'At the outbreak of war, I gained employment in the War Office as a short-hand typist and the speeds I had achieved brought me to the notice of those in authority. My father was a serving officer and I was considered "politically reliable". That recommendation brought me to a post in a corps forming part of Army Group South in Russia. My first tour of duty in the Soviet Union was at the end of 1942, and the detachment with which I was serving as a lieutenant, was stationed in Kharkov. That was as far east as we women soldiers were allowed to be posted.

'At that time the great Stalingrad battle was at its height and at Corps we could follow the tragedy when our offensive halted and that of the Red Army began. I was also involved in the later retreat of the German Army out of Kharkov. I had had no idea of what a retreat actually involved – what it looks like and feels like. The panic that there was among those who thought they were trapped. The despair of being encircled; the fear as our motorized columns passed through a narrow escape corridor which was lined with Russian guns and tanks. I also saw the Party bigwigs, the so called 'golden pheasants', from the amount of bullion lace which decorated their brown uniforms. These Party 'Bonzen' demanded that the Army escort them to safety. At a time when every one of our panzers should have been in the line, these politicals were demanding to be escorted to safety by panzer regiments.

'When the war ended I was in Schoerner's Army Group in the Protectorate (Bohemia and Moravia). We were attacked by Czech partisans on the day the war ended and during the scrimmage I was struck on the head. That blow knocked me unconscious and also split my scalp so badly that my face was covered in blood. That blow and the amount of blood probably saved me from being raped for it must have seemed that I had been killed. In the following days the effect of the blow puffed my face so much that it was completely deformed for nearly a week.

'Like many of the Blitzmaderln (the Signals Corps girls) I changed into a man's uniform seeking to disguise myself as a man and thus to avoid rape. This deception may have stopped the

sexual attacks but not the beatings which were hard and frequent. In addition, we women disguised as men had to do a man's share of work and. we also received, of course, a man's share of beating. When some of the girls collapsed at work and their identity was discovered the Red Army major in charge of our unit told them that their future was to serve as whores for the Red Army. By not being acknowledged by the Reichs government as soldiers we were, therefore, legally outside the protection of the Hague Convention. Our own army, he told them had described them as "matresses for officers". The Blitzmaderln would fulfill that function for the Russians. Not for officers, but for the ordinary rank and file. The girls were, after all, common whores and not good enough for the officer heroes of the Red Army. What happened to the girls I do not know and all inquiries in post-war years have been fruitless.

'One day I eavesdropped on what some Red Army guards were discussing. I had graduated in Russian and had used it when on duty in the German Army, but as soon as I became a prisoner of war, I did not dare let it be known that I spoke the language. I was afraid that if I did, firstly it would betray that I was a woman and, secondly, it would mark me out as "special", when the object of a prisoner of war is not to be conspicuous. The guards on whom I was eavesdropping were discussing the instructions they had been given. Our open air camp was being broken up. We were being moved to a hutted camp. I did not recognize the name of the place and asked an officer from Staff Intelligence who had also disguised himself as a common soldier. He knew that it was a camp set up in western Siberia and that it was near a mine – he thought a mineral mine.

'We set out and within a few days our column had passed northwards into Brandenburg. One night I managed to escape from an overnight halting place, a transit camp site, by hiding in a latrine trench. I cleaned myself up in a stream and it took a long time without soap. I used mud to scrub, literally scrub, my skin and hair. Even after repeated rinsing in the stream I still felt that I smelled. Later, dressed in army trousers and a civilian jacket, I managed to get home, only to find our family home destroyed and the estate occupied by Poles, who were now the new owners. Early in 1947, still disguised as a man, I managed to escape from eastern Germany via Czechosovakia and into Austria.'

# CONCENTRATION CAMPS

Let us, at this point, consider the phenomenon which was first revealed to the world in July 1944, when the Red Army overran the extermination camp at Maidenek in Poland. From the earliest days of the Third Reich it was generally known that concentration camps existed. They had, in fact, been mentioned very frequently in the German Press and foreign correspondents had been allowed to visit them – albeit in organized parties – to see for themselves the way in which they were run. It was widely believed in Germany at that time that the camps held enemies of the State, such as criminal elements, murderers, sexual perverts or political enemies; trades union officials, Communists or monarchists. The camps, in those early days, had no Jewish inmates imprisoned because they were Jews. Racial laws were passed in 1935, but in the mid 1930s, it was not an offence punishable by a term in a concentration camp to be a Jew. Those Jews who were in camps were imprisoned for some other reason, not because they were Jews.

Those Germans who had been in one of the camps and who had then been released kept quiet about them and the way in which they were run. Not until these former prisoners had left Germany and were in another country did they speak out. They told of the rigorous inspections, the hard work, the lunatic bureaucracy, of the punishments inflicted for the most trivial offences and how those who died in the camps were sent home to their next of kin inside a sealed coffin which was not allowed to be opened. A refinement to this policy was introduced even before the war. The bodies of those who had died in the camps were cremated and the ashes handed over in a small urn. Stories of priests in Dachau being crucified at Eastertime, began to circulate around Europe, but reports of such horrors were generally disbelieved both by the German peoples and those living outside the Reich. Neither the natives nor the foreigners could bring themselves to accept that a nation as civilized as the Germans could behave in so depraved a fashion. Camps for the correction of errors; camps to bring back the erring inmates to the Volksgemeinschaft; these were acceptable. It was also accepted that in handling vicious criminals it might be necessary to use a high degree of

firmness – hardness even. After all, those who had to be beaten or punished must have been guilty of breaking some camp law. But that guards and especially SS men, the élite of the Volksgemeinschaft, would be brutal without cause was unthinkable. Goebbels in one of his cynical pronouncements had once said to his colleagues, that if the German people had known what the Nazi Party intended to do once it had gained power, they would never have voted for it. In that he never spoke a truer word.

But concentration camps had not only become an expression of German penitentiary techniques. They were also to become a source of special labour. In them prisoners could be worked without pay, without concern for their safety and until they died, for the concept of hard labour for the prisoners had long been accepted. As the Reich spread across pre-war Europe more prisoners came in, Austrian monarchists, men of Dolfuss's conservative Party, Socialists and Communists. To their number were added Czech politicals so that new camps in the Greater German Empire, that is the lands outside the 1937 boundaries of the Reich, needed to be set up and more SS guards had to be recruited. The outbreak of war and its spread brought more and newer categories of prisoner. As early as 1939 the first mass executions of Jews in Polish towns had taken place and by the beginning of the 1940s the first round up had begun of Polish Jews. The transit camps in which those first deportees were held eventually became permanent sites, stages on the road of suffering that was trod by millions – Jews and Gentiles alike. Once again the first executions and the first deportations were announced in the German Press but the outcry that might have been anticipated from the German people did not materialize. There was a war on and to many Germans the fate of some bloody foreigners in Poland was of less importance than the difficulties of their own life in war-time. The round up of the Polish Jews and their imprisonment did not affect too greatly those Jews still living in Germany. In 1940 they still numbered 743,000, of whom 47,000 were in Berlin and 72,000 in Vienna.

Special arrangements had to be made to accommodate the great numbers of Polish Jews

Above: Heydrich – athlete, fighter pilot, fine horseman, musician, the very ideal of Aryan superman. Heydrich was responsible for the organization and expansion of the concentration camps into extermination centres in the conquered lands. Germans regarded his rule of Czechoslovakia as benevolent. Above right: Himmler, ex-chicken farmer, believer in the 'Nordic' cult and one of the first members of the Nazi Party. Responsible for the 'final solution', he realized the economic potential of the concentration-camps.

Right: The Warsaw ghetto. The bridge is for non-Jews, who were forbidden to enter the ghetto area. 'Containment' of the racial enemy was just one step along the road to elimination.

The beginning of the persecution of the Third Reich's racial enemies. Polish Jews are forced to haul a German tank to a maintenance depot as a form of ritual humiliation. On the far right of the picture the man with the white armband is an auxiliary policeman, probably a Volksdeutsch. It was probably he who rounded up the victims.

who had been gathered together. Principal camps were established and soon proved to be too small. Satellite camps to the main lager were then set up and this process continued with the satellites having their own satellite camps. Soon even that accommodation was too small because the Jews from Poland had been joined by those from other countries. By 1942, the plan to remove all Jews from Europe was in full swing and eventually even the satellites to the satellites had sub-camps of their own. The number of prisoners ran into millions.

The intention was that the Jews would be put to work and those who were able-bodied would be worked until they died. When the trains bearing the deportees arrived at the camps a selection was made: on one side the fit, the workers; on the other the unfit. Those too old, too young, too weak or too sick were just mouths that would eat but who would be unproductive in the workshops. Dead they had a certain value. Their hair could be sold, some victims might have gold teeth, false teeth, spectacles, little things of value that were theirs as long as they lived. It was, therefore, ensured that they should not live long but should die before they had had a meal or had learned from the other camp inmates how and where to

hide their few treasures and little trinkets. How the old were selected from the strong, the ways in which those selected to die were deceived into a false security; the so-called bath halls in which they were gassed and the crematoria in which they vanished have all been described. I do not need in this book to add to that catalogue of horror.

Let us remind ourselves that in this chapter we are seeing things not from the viewpoint of the martyred, but from that of the SS who selected the work force, who condemned the infirm, who organized the round up which had brought the prisoners to the camps and who owned the prisoners body and soul. The concentration camp captives were the property of the flourishing SS organization and as property, as things, they may not have had rights, but they did have certain skills. Among the Jews of Europe there were artists, designers and craftsmen. The knowledge and skill of these men and women could be put to special use; a simple, brilliant and profitable scheme had been formulated at senior SS level.

The SS would extract from the labour force the artistic specialists and, using their skilled craftsmanship, would create contemporary works of art for sale. The idea was adopted enthusiastically

and put into practise. These prisoners were the cream of the workforce. At their lowest level, those who were first-class tailors were employed in making uniforms for senior officers of the Party, the Services and others able to pay top prices for such quality work. Others, meanwhile, had designed and produced limited editions of porcelain figures, ceramic works of art, Damascene blades and exquisitive leather work. As soon as a supply of these treasures had become available other prisoners produced a glossy catalogue printed in six colours, illustrating the gifts that were on sale to the Party bosses. It was a little gold-mine for the SS.

On a less artistic level other unusual skills were explored, among which was the attempt to undermine confidence in the British economy by using skilled forgers to counterfeit British Bank of England £5 notes. Several millions of these notes were produced and the Germans used some of these to bribe foreign agents or to pay for their services. The British Ambassador to Turkey had a valet who worked for German Intelligence. This agent, 'Cicero', opened the Embassy safe and photographed the documents inside it. 'Cicero', was paid by the SS in forged fivers and it is an illustration of the general lack of European con-

fidence in Hitler's Germany that agents asked to be paid in Sterling, not Reichsmarks.

Below the level of the skilled designers and craftsmen, below the counterfeiters and the tailors was the great mass of other prisoners whose skills could not be exploited for gain. They could be worked to death in quarries or on land reclamation projects, hard and unrelenting toil in all weathers. Under such a regime it is not surprising that many concentration camp inmates chose to throw themselves from the quarry heights on to the boulders below. One SS report enclosed the request form from a quarry owner – a civilian employer – asking the guards to prevent prisoner suicides as the blood, brains and flesh on the boulders were upsetting other workers.

By the middle of the war, in late 1943, the SS Production and Sales organization was in full swing. The personal effects of those who had entered the camp and who had been very quickly killed, were being converted to cash. Those who worked in the camp on non-SS projects for civilian employers, were, indeed, paid for their labour, but the money did not reach the prisoners but passed straight into the SS bank account. Then there was the money earned from the luxury goods scheme. Each of the systems showed a hundred per cent profit. Not only was the SS organization as a whole, making money, but it was also possible for individuals to profit on their own account. Those who were more than usually vicious to the inmates, who could drive them harder or get more work out of their captives were candidates for promotion. They might even be selected to run a camp of their own and this promotion brought with it definite financial reward. A certain proportion of the personal items of prisoners could be creamed off leaving the bulk to go to the SS main office. And for as long as there were Jews in Europe the treasure would flow in.

There were other money-raising ventures. In the early months of 1943, the German Foreign Office and an SS committee met at Belsen and considered the case of Jews who were in possession of foreign passports. Technically, these people could not be considered as Germans, but they were none the less in Belsen. A plan was formulated to separate these alien Jews and to hold them as exchange objects for Germans held in allied internment. Of the four to five thousand Jews involved, only 357 reached freedom. Then there was a fund-raising scheme to sell nearly two thousand Hungarian Jews at a thousand dollars a head. Nothing came of that or any of the other SS fund-raising ventures involving the sale of human beings.

By the end of 1944 secret meetings were being held in neutral countries between medium rank SS officers and Western Jewish leaders on how to save as many as possible from the death camps. These meetings were not a latter-day reversion to humanity on the part of the SS. It was now clear to them that Germany might lose the war and that if she did retribution would follow. The negotiations dragged on and on without result. Meanwhile one concentration camp after another was being overrun in eastern Europe. At senior Party level the decision was taken to evacuate from the camps those prisoners who could still be physically exploited in the workshops and to leave behind the weak and the sick. These latter were not to be found alive by the Red Army. In a final purge they would be shot and the whole site blown up so expertly that no trace would remain to show that once an extermination camp had been sited there.

The SS guards at Auschwitz in Poland did not carry out the orders they had been given and the eight thousand prisoners who were too weak to march were found by the Russians amid the intact gas chambers and crematoria as well as half-destroyed factories and work halls. The spearheads of the Soviet advance were not able, however, to overtake the prisoner columns of those evacuated from Auschwitz. Nor was that the only camp from which marching groups had set out. As the Allies advanced from the east and from the west the orders from SS HQ were insistent, 'Destroy the installations, kill those too ill, form the fit into groups and march them to those provinces which have not yet been overrun by the Allies.' Thousands of prisoners were marched and counter-marched through a shrinking Reich and when they reached journey's end, found that this was usually one of the camps in Germany which had been set up in the first years of the Reich.

In those early days the fearsome bureaucracy and the exaggerated attention to hygiene had ensured that accurate records had been kept, regular meals provided and serious outbreaks of infection kept to a minimum. Into the orderly, well-run hells of Dachau, Mauthhausen, Sachsenhausen, Belsen and their satellites, there then entered in the first months of 1945, hordes of exhausted, starving prisoners who had been foot-marched for long distances. Records which had set out with the prisoners seldom reached the destination camp for these lists, indexes, rosters and other paper work were often lost en route. The unnumbered thousands of lousy, bronchitic prisoners were herded into accommodation that had been intended for a fraction of their number. There were too few taps for drinking water. The washing of clothes, even the washing of one's person, was almost impossible and, inevitably, typhus broke out. This ravaged the weakened prisoners and deaths began to mount. There could be no accurate account kept of those who died and soon there were too many to dispose of. The crematoria could not burn the bodies quickly enough and open air cremations did not consume totally the bodies of the dead. Nor were the inmates strong enough to dig large pits to hold the bodies. A half-hearted attempt was made at piling up the enmaciated dead, but this and other attempts at keeping the camp area clear were unsuccessful.

More and more marching columns came in and a vicious circle soon established itself. Into the overcrowded camps, rife with the most virulent diseases, with inmates starving because food supplies were no longer reaching the camps, there poured in more and more columns of prisoners until the whole administration of the camps collapsed. The SS authorities could do nothing even had they wanted to. In some cases German SS units were withdrawn and were replaced by Hungarian or other foreign SS men upon whom fell the vengeance of both the prisoners and the Allied soldiers when the camps were finally liberated. A final signal from Himmler regarding concentration camps was issued shortly before the liberation of Belsen. This repetition of the order to destroy all evidence of the camps resulted in a bloodbath in which chiefly the German politicals and those of the Resistance were murdered. In several camps the SS commandants stayed on to hand over the festering sites to the liberating forces and obviously expected that the Allies would praise them for their devotion to duty. Those men were horrified to find themselves arrested, tried and convicted as war criminals.

The SS had run the camps and their inmates as a commercial enterprise and it had paid them handsome profits. There can be no doubt that the money obtained from slave labour and from the

Right: The German view of the camps. This sign outside a concentration camp warns that any person crossing the neutral zone will be fired upon. The inmates were little thought of. It stood to reason: if they ended up in prison, they must have deserved their fate.

personal effects of the slaughtered paid not merely for the escape to South American countries of a great number of officers, but also set them up in business once the political climate in Germany changed and those men could return home with new names and fat bank balances. Some remained and gave their services to the Russians. The notorious SS commander, Mohnke, Gauleiter Koch and Muller, Head of the Gestapo, were only three of the many men who removed their swastikas and replaced them with Red stars.

It may be possible to accept that the massive influxes into the permanent concentration camps so overwhelmed the administration that this collapsed and produced the horror which the British found when they liberated Belsen, which the Americans discovered in Dachau and which the Red Army uncovered on its march through eastern Europe. Nothing can forgive the systematic and deliberate torture and killing of the Christians and Jews alike who suffered and perished. Nor should we forget that the same horrors are being employed today, more than four decades after the liberation of Auschwitz, in the slave camps of the Soviet Union.

The terrible story of the concentration camps begs the questions, to what degree did the German people know of the things that were being done by their government, and what could they have done to stop them? In the opening paragraphs of this section of the book it was explained how it was common knowledge that concentration camps existed to hold anti-social elements and opponents of the regime. In pre-war days it was accepted by the general public that people might be punished while imprisoned and that sometimes capital punishment might need to be inflicted. Such things, while being unpleasant, might become necessary when dealing with criminals. The war turned against Germany at about the time that the first stages of the destruction of European Jewry were begun. The 'Final Solution' was a state secret and unauthorized knowledge of that secret or disclosure of details of it was an infringement of the law punishable by death. The threat of arrest, of trial and imprisonment – or even execution by beheading – served to preserve the state secret. Then, too, the air raids upon German cities, the everlasting worries about the men at the front, the problems of rationing and the sheer strain of living in war-time gave the ordinary German scant time to reflect upon any sufferings which the enemies of the state might be experiencing.

Had they known about the horrors in the camps the German people might well have been distressed, but what could they have done to either alleviate or stop it? The honest answer must be – nothing. In a dictatorship protests by the population achieve no result. The Russian people must have known of the murderous tyranny of Stalin and the Communist Party, a tyranny which continues to this day. The Soviet people today know of the Gulags in which dissidents are imprisoned. Do they protest or are they also afraid that any protest from them could lead to their own trial and imprisonment? Dictatorships do not allow their policies to be influenced by the great mass of the people and in that respect the Nazi government would not have allowed itself to be deflected from its policy of murdering European Jews.

In the second part of his Political Testament, dated 29 April 1945, Hitler laid upon his successors and their followers, the obligation to maintain the racial laws and to offer bitter resistance to 'the poisoners of the peoples of the world' – international Jewry. Goebbels wrote in 1940, 'that we were enemies of the Jews was generally known even before 1933. We have, therefore, reaped the disadvantages of anti-Semitism in world propaganda. Now we can enjoy the advantages and remove the Jews from the theatre, the cinema, from public life and from administration.' The genocide, which followed those first expulsions, the destruction and the horror were all considered by him and his Führer to be positive achievements in 'ridding Europe of a race of aliens which had exploited it for centuries'. It was a bitter legacy to leave behind, even for revolutionaries as dedicated to nihilism as were Hitler and his comrades.

Right: How the persecution ended. A few of the millions who suffered and died. These photographs were taken at the end of the war by the liberating armies and show the results of the breakdown in the camp system. The victims were probably prisoners who had been forced to march many miles, without food or drink, to new camps as the perimeter of the Reich shrank. (Imperial War Museum)

# THE PARTY'S VIEW OF GERMANY'S ENEMIES

As the result of her policies and her aggression the Third Reich was eventually at war with three powerful enemies. The resources of a world-wide British Empire, the mighty colossus of the Soviet Union and the industrial might of the United States were all ranged against Germany. She, herself, was a nation of finite resources, lacking many of the basic raw materials vital to maintain a major war. To avoid confrontation by three powerful enemies should have been a major pre-occupation of the Nazi government, yet the Reich had chosen to go to war with Russia and to declare war against America. The leaders of the Reich had planned fast and decisive operations that would knock first Russia and then Britain out of the war before America was fully ready to aid her allies. Yet even when it was clear that Operation 'Barbarossa' could not be concluded successfully in 1941, there was still optimism at Reichsleitung level as to the eventual outcome of the war.

The optimism of the Reichs leaders was based upon their misreading the political situation. They deluded themselves into thinking that their view must be a political imperative. They convinced themselves that the forces of Capitalism must clash with those of Communism. The most significant word in that sentence is 'must'. It was not a hope, not a belief that the capitalist West would fight the Soviet East. No! Such a clash was seen by the leaders of the Nazi government as politically inevitable and as the tide of war turned against Germany more and more, efforts were made by the leaders to ensure that it occurred before the Fatherland was overrun. And when the clash did come about the Reich could capitalize upon it by making peace with either the West or the East and then, as an ally of one or the other of the warring factions, would enter the war in a new partnership. To the pragmatic revolutionaries, Hitler and Goebbels, it mattered little whether the new ally was the Communist East or the Capitalist West. The Party's propaganda machine would influence the masses towards whichever nation showed itself willing to work with Germany, although at Reichsleitung level an alliance with the West was favoured over one with the East. The first hints of that future co-operation were reinforced in

Europe by the spreading of an alleged prophecy by the Swedish clairvoyant, Gruneberg, that the West, allied with Germany, would win the war. Germany must play for time. The war must continue until either the war-weariness of the Allied nations or historic inevitability of a Capitalist/Communist clash would begin to work for Germany.

The Nazi leaders saw it as inconceivable that a die-hard Tory like Churchill could have a rapport with the Bolshevik, proletarian thug, Stalin, or that the latter could reach any sort of understanding with the Yankee patrician, Roosevelt. An alliance between such conflicting personalities must produce strains sufficient to smash the alliance. The Nazi explanation for their own Treaty of Friendship with the Soviets in the autumn of 1939, had been that both the Reds and they were working class and revolutionary ideologies. Churchill, an aristocrat, and Roosevelt, from a distinguished New York family, were neither working class nor revolutionary. They could, therefore, have nothing in common with the Communists and this wartime alliance must inevitably break up when the financial and/or ideological differences between East and West became more important than the military alliance against Germany. In their pursuit of signs of strain and dissolution every complaint, every grumble by one Ally about another was seized upon by Hitler and Goebbels in particular, who inspected and analyzed those complaints seeking to find in them the signs of an irreparable rupture.

The wrong conclusions which the National Socialist leaders drew from their perspective shows how much they were prepared to delude themselves. The Casablanca Conference of January 1943, was seen by them as evidence of Allied discord because Stalin was not present. The Generalissimo's invitation was, in fact, not taken up because he was involved with problems connected with the closing stages of the Stalingrad campaign, but his absence, as the Reich leaders saw it, was an affront to the West. That action was as much a deliberate insult as was the failure of Soviet newspapers to report in detail Anglo-American military operations. Such affronts, so it

Above: Winston Churchill with (left) Charles de Gaulle, head of the Free France organization, and General Sir John Dill (right), Chief of the Imperial General Staff, in late 1940/41. In the background to the right is General Wladyslaw Sikorsky, head of the Polish Government in exile. Germans saw Churchill as the arch-enemy, an evil warmonger who had conspired against Germany between the wars. (Imperial War Museum)

was believed at Reichsleitung level, must be resented in the West.

Russian complaints during 1942 and 1943, that the Anglo-Americans had not opened a Second Front were also seen as proof of a rift, and in an effort to divide the Allies it was proposed at the highest level of Reichs government that feelers be put out to the dissatisfied Stalin, offering an arrangement with Germany. Hitler's view had always been that the Soviets were the one partner in the Alliance that could be the most easily detached. The Anglo-Americans had electorates to consider; the Communist dictatorship had not. Another proposal to take Russia out of the war was that advanced during April 1944. The Soviet Union was offered a free hand in a whole area of eastern Europe extending from Norway to Greece. It was all a far cry from Operation 'Barbarossa', when the Reich had gone to war with Russia in order to gain a line running from Archangelsk to the Black Sea.

The San Francisco Conference, early in 1945, was another straw at which the Nazi leadership clutched. They hoped that the Soviet demand for an increase in the number of votes allotted to her in the infant United Nations assembly, would create friction which must lead to open hostility between the Allies. When that rift did not develop the Nazi leaders placed their expectations upon the Yalta Conference. Britain had gone to war for the independence of Poland and yet the outcome of Yalta was that the Poles were still not free, but had exchanged, as the Nazis saw it, the benevolent German overlordship for a Russian tyranny worse than that which they had suffered under the Tsars.

When it became clear that despite the disagreements at Yalta no positive break had occurred, the Reichs leaders rationalized their chagrin by declaring that Britain was now militarily impotent to act against the Soviet Union and that America had no interest in Europe generally, or in Poland, specifically. The West had abandoned Europe; therefore, it was in Germany's best interest to seek an accommodation with the more powerful Russians who did have an intense interest in the Continent. Were such an alliance to be concluded Germany could turn westwards once again and together with the Soviet Union deal with Britain, the mischief-maker of Europe.

There would have to be some absolutely compelling reason to force Russia to come to the negotiating table and as the Nazi leaders saw it the German Army on the Eastern Front would need to win several swift victories; battles which would cause the Reds such losses that they would be prepared to negotiate. The time for such devastating blows had come, so they believed. They based their calculations upon reports from the front which showed that large numbers of Red Army troops were still deserting to the Germans. The interrogation of these deserters as well as that of ordinary Russian prisoners showed evidence of a great war-weariness. The Nazi leaders believed that the signs were favourable for a series of quick strikes to produce the victories, after which negotiations between Germany and the Soviets could begin. The question must surely have been asked at some time during the planning, from where, at that stage of the war, would the forces and equipment come to undertake and to achieve these necessary victories? The Supreme Command was clearly so out of touch with reality that it did not consider the procurement of men and materials to be a difficult problem.

In their perspective of the West the Nazi leaders saw two plutocratic nations, Britain and America, whose struggle for supremacy had resulted in the destruction of Britain as a world power. As Goebbels saw it the political blunderings of Churchill had led directly to Russia's becoming the dominant land power and America the dominant sea power. Britain had lost her paramount position and had no influence on Allied policies which were now, and would be in the future, decided by the two major powers, Soviet Russia and the United States of America.

The Nazis viewed Great Britain with a mixture of envy and hatred. Frequent and repeated propaganda campaigns stessed the theme that Britain was the aggressor against Europe. Britain had sought allies; nations whose soldiers she would send to fight her battles. She had found them and

then lost them as the German Army won victory after victory during 1940 and 1941. During that period Britain reached a stage when she had no Allies she could dominate. Instead her new ally, America, was more powerful than she and Great Britain had been forced to accept the inferior position *vis-à-vis* the USA. For their part, the Americans were determined to usurp her place. The unequal exchange of British bases in the Caribbean for a handful of old destroyers was evidence of how the Americans were determined to exploit their superior position. In pursuit of their ambition to reduce her it was, therefore, irrelevant to the US leaders whether Britain won or lost the war. Either way she was declining in power and the Reich leaders were determined to hasten that decline by supporting any enemy of Britain and any revolt made against British imperialism.

So they came to pay court to Hitler. Subhas Chandra Bose, the Indian traitor who preferred the genocide policies of the Reich to the British Raj. Raschid Ali, who fomented a revolt in Iraq during May 1941, the Mufti of Jerusalem, who supported the Nazi solution to the Jewish question and, finally, the German-dominated government of Vichy France which began an uprising in Syria. All these attempts to undermine the influence of Britain were supported and the Arab and Indian leaders were received as honoured guests of the Reich. To support these traitors and to foment more trouble, Goebbels set up a number of transmitters broadcasting German propaganda but purporting to be independent 'pirate' stations located in Britain. One of these, set up as early as October 1939, put out IRA propaganda.

The National Socialist perspective of America was no less distorted than that which they had of Britain. America was a plutocracy, decadent and disorganized, run by Jews whose only concern was to make money out of wars fought by Christians. Several entries in the Goebbels diaries refer to Allied military victories as having a depressing effect upon Wall Street, as 'Jewish financiers realized that the war would soon be at an end and with it the huge profits they had made.'

In pre-war years it had been a source of great annoyance to the Nazi leaders that German youth should spend its time viewing American films, that they should prefer American, Negro jazz to German music and that German girls should want to paint their faces, lips and nails in the fashion of Yankee harlots.

Even before Germany declared war on America in December 1941, the Reichsleitung had been well aware of US power and ability, that America was capable of expanding her arms production and that she had an enormous economic growth potential. Nazi experts accepted that American industrial output must eventually exceed that of the Reich, but projected that the Americans would need many years to achieve that position. Before the USA could realize her potential the war against the Soviet Union would have been won and England, too, would have been subdued. By that time, too, Europe, the workshop of the world and now extending from the Channel to the Volga, would be working for Germany. The Greater German Empire would be more than a match for the Americans. Not that the Reich had any aggressive intentions towards the United States. Indeed, from the earliest days Nazi representatives had sought to assure America that the Fatherland had no hostility towards her and no intention of interfering in her sphere of influence in the New World. As a quid pro quo, the Reichsleitung expected America not to interfere in European affairs or politics and was bitter at the partisan attitude of President Roosevelt.

What Hitler had hoped to gain by the lunatic declaration of war upon America is hard to see, but reports from SD sources following that declaration, spoke of the pessimism and despair evident in many ordinary Germans who were aware, even if their leaders were not, that with the entry of America the war was as good as lost.

The Nazi view of Russia was principally a racial one; the superior Teuton versus the primitive Slav although there were certain influences which modified that view. Throughout the history of Germany and Russia there had been interchanges of ideas and customs and this love/hate relationship had continued even when Naziism confronted Bolshevism. The Soviets had brought about the first modern revolution to succeed and the Nazi leaders, who considered themselves to be revolutionaries, had been and continued to be influenced by the Russian experience. Also there were still in German society, in factories, offices and in the services, five million people who had voted for the Communists in the 1933 elections. There were also students who were known to be infected with the disease of Bolshevism and it was a worry that German coal-miners and workers in heavy industry considered those Russians who had been brought into German mines and factories, not as racial or ideological enemies but as comrades.

Of what glorious things in the Soviet Union could the Russian workers tell their German counterparts? There could be nothing; an exhibition, 'The Workers' Paradise', showed to German civilians the primitive conditions and way of life

Right: Russian and German officers meet in Poland, 1939, while a Pole interprets. Good relations with the Soviet Union were seen as important and beneficial by the German people; from Russia came supplies of oil and grain to counter the effects of the British naval blockade. The reversal of German policy towards Russia in 1941 was sudden and unexpected.

suffered by the common people under Communism. Those things that the German soldiers had met when they entered Russia. A depressed population living in verminous hovels lit by oil-lamps, with no gas, electricity, running water or proper lavatories. The food they ate was of so inferior a quality as to be a subsistence diet and their lice-infested, tatty clothing was held together with safety-pins. That was the Workers' Paradise in reality. The fraternal feelings between German and Russian workers brought with them a reminder that the spread of Communism in the Imperial Fleet had led to revolution in Germany and to the overthrow of the Kaiser. The spectre of 1918 haunted the Nazi leaders.

Europe must be united and brought into the war against Russia. To bring that about it would be necessary for Germany to produce an argument, a unifying motif. The Nazi government soon produced it. They had attacked Russia in a pre-emptive strike. Proof existed to show that the Soviets were about to sweep westwards in another attempt to overrun the whole of Europe. If that happened Europe, with its ancient culture, its priceless heritage, its centuries of Christian traditions, would be endangered. If the Red plan succeeded Western values would be perverted by Bolshevik distortions. The heritage of law would vanish and be replaced by the torture chambers of the OGPU. Bolshevik hatred of culture would take

Europe back to the Dark Ages. The Germans had struck the first blows in a war for freedom, but it was a European duty to unite with the Reich and join the crusade against the common enemy – Russian Bolshevism.

The campaign had a certain appeal, not only to native fascist parties and capitalists, but to a great number of ordinary people of the countries of western Europe who did see civilization and themselves as under threat and, therefore, enlisted in the war against the Godless Bolshevik state. Very soon there were battalions, then regiments and finally, divisions of Nordic men, the first to be enlisted, in units of the army or SS ready to fight on the Eastern Front. The appeal was then widened to take in the non-Nordic peoples who clamoured to join and the German Army's Order of Battle then included Frenchmen, Belgians, Italians, Spaniards and Hungarians. As the German Army advanced deeper into Soviet territory the minorities of Russia came forward to fight alongside their European liberators. Cossacks, Ukrainians, Uzbekis and Tartars volunteered and even if they were not at first allowed to serve in the fighting line, they proved their worth on anti-partisan operations and were willing supporters of the German Army. From the German point of view the politically aware peoples of the whole of Europe were marching with the Reich in a cause common to all; a crusade for Western civilization.

Left: The day war broke out – in Germany. Civilians listen to the announcement that Britain and France have declared war on Germany, September 1939. The news was greeted with sober 'realism'; war had been forced upon Germany, and she would fight.

# THE PARTY'S PERSPECTIVE OF EUROPE

Nazi policy *vis-à-vis* the races of western Europe moved from mildness into furious repression as the war developed. Towards those nations that had been beaten in battle there was, to begin with, the natural pride of a conquerer, but the Germans soon passed out of that stage and into one of paternalism. Towards the middle years of the war when there was a need for workers in German factories, active recruiting campaigns were mounted as a result of which thousands of Europeans went voluntarily to work for the occupation authorities. Whether the attraction was a job, the higher wages which German employers paid, better rations or the increased social benefits given by the Reich, is immaterial. These non-German people volunteered to help Hitler by working in his factories. Then there were those who had come forward as a result of military recruiting campaigns to serve in the German Army or in the SS. None of these volunteers to industry or to the services saw themselves as traitors to their countries. Many considered that they were participants in a new, united Europe.

In the belief that German policies *vis-à-vis* beaten nations should be as mild as possible, Josef Goebbels, suggested that acts against the German forces of occupation ought to be met by counter-measures of like nature. Thus if, for example, the people of a city boycotted for one day the local tram service as a gesture of protest, the German authorities should withdraw the tram service for a few weeks. He also suggested that instead of shooting hostages, which was a standard reprisal tactic, all civilian bicycles should be confiscated and turned over to the German Army. If the execution of hostages was unavoidable, it was wrong, as a matter of common sense, to execute their families as well. Instead the Party comrades of the hostages should be shot. They were all criminals together.

It was, of course, in the interests of the Nazi government that Occupied Europe should work harmoniously for the Reich. That Germany had liberated Europe from British hegemony was one of the most frequently stated expressions of the Nazi media. With Britain driven from Europe, that continent could settle down and enter an era of collaboration and co-operation. The more strident expressions of Party dogma were toned down and skilfully blended in with the general hopes of most Europeans for peace. Goebbels was particularly mocking of British attempts to gain French support in highlighting the differences between Bonaparte and Hitler. The armies of Napoleon, the British government had proclaimed, had carried with them the spirit of Freedom and Equality as expressed in the French Revolution. Exactly, scoffed Goebbels, and that is why you British fought him, just as you are fighting contemporary, National Socialist ideas of freedom in Europe.

Of all the nations of western Europe France was the most important. The size of her fleet, the accessibility of her North African possessions for food supplies, her sophisticated and extensive industries might all have been brought into the German sphere, had the Nazis so wished it. For some reason Hitler rejected the attempts of the Vichy government to gain close collaboration with Germany and permitted only such cosmetic exercises as the return to France of the body of Napoleon's son. The 'Eaglet' was taken from the Habsburg burial vault in the Capuchin church in Vienna and re-interred in France, the cortège and the reburial being accorded the highest military honours. Little more than that was allowed by the Führer. The consequence was that France, a possible supporter of the New European order, was allowed to drift into the Allied camp.

The Nazi attitude towards the Germanic/Nordic nations was fraternal – that of a big brother advising the smaller ones – and it was a source of bitter disappointment to the German authorities when the peoples of those nations, their own Nordic brothers, rose in open revolt. German reprisals were carried out more in sorrow than in anger, but there were reprisals and harsh ones, too.

The Czechs were a special case. The skill of the Czech workers and the importance of the Skoda armaments industry to the Reich, required that the nation be governed with a very light hand. The Protectorate was also so far removed in distance from RAF bases in Britain that it was beyond the range of even the Lancaster bomber. Thus, neither Prague, Pilsen nor any other of the principal cities of Czechoslovakia was bombed. That immunity through distance from the air raids which had destroyed the towns of the Reich, a ration scale for the Czechs as good as that which the Germans themselves had, and a light touch of government gave the Czechs little to complain about. Indeed, Heydrich, who was *de facto* the Vice-Regent of the Protectorate, enjoyed such good relations with the native population that he drove unescorted and in an open car through Prague. That popularity was to kill him. A team of heroic individuals, recruited and trained in Great Britain, was flown to Prague where they attempted to kill him. Heydrich died of his wounds and despite public protests by some Czechs against his death, German retribution was neither delayed nor moderate. The Nazis took the Allied bait and reacted mercilessly, destroying the village of Lidice and its inhabitants. Despite this terrible act the scale of Czech partisan operations remained low until the Red Army drew near. Then it flared. But between the death of Heydrich in June 1942 and April 1945, Czechoslovakia was one country which seemed to be untouched by war. It was, in fact, one of the last to be liberated and Prague, itself was not entered by the Red Army until the last days of the war.

This special treatment for the Czechs was unique in the history of the German Occupation and was a model of how a moderate approach paid dividends. There was no such mildness in the case of Yugoslavia or Greece, where armed resistance by partisan units was put down with murderous ferocity. In the case of the occupied areas of Russia no attempt was made at Reichsleitung level to win the support of the masses, and yet the Minister responsible for the administration of the Eastern Areas must have known that the peoples of the Baltic States, of Belorussia and of the Ukraine were hostile to the Soviet government in Moscow.

It was a firmly held conviction of many senior men in the Reichs government that German occupation policy in western Europe was benevolent and that foreign workers going home on leave or upon expiry of contract would be the best propagandists for the German way of life. They would tell their compatriots of living conditions in the Reich, of its social habits and manners, which could only have a good effect upon the political strategy of forming Europe into a single political and economic bloc. The strength of such a united Europe, the genius of Europe which had enriched the world, the moral leadership which Europe had always given; all these things united would form a power bloc that could never be overcome. German-arranged sports meetings, football matches, a pan-European Youth congress and travelling exhibitions illustrating the dynamics of Western civilization, all served to reinforce the message that the West had a common heritage, a precious gift not shared by the barbarians in the east nor by the English who were aggressors against Europe, nor by the Americans who were plutocrats living off the blood of Europe.

How far the propaganda viewpoint of a Europe endangered by Bolshevism was accepted is shown by the number of volunteers who served in German industry and in the military forces. That the Germans manipulated the feelings of the people of occupied Europe to produce hostility towards the Anglo-Americans is illustrated by the experience of Jeff Brady of the Queen's Brigade which served with 7th Armoured Division in Normandy. His is not an uncommon theme but is one remarked upon by many who served in North-West Europe.

'One place where we were dug in was a fairly big farm. In peace time it must have been a gold-mine. There were cows, chickens, geese, apples, wheat – it must have been self-sufficient. The family living there made its own bread, had hams hanging in a smoke house, made cider and a spirit called Calvados from the apples. There was certainly no sign here of the starvation which we had been told to expect in Europe, after so many years of occupation. The people in Normandy were living better than were our own families in the UK. That farmer had been lucky. Only a few of his cows had been killed, but it was enough for him and his family to go on and on about it all the time. "Why had we come there? Why hadn't we landed up the coast a bit, somewhere else?, Who wanted to be liberated if it meant dead livestock? The Germans? They had been fair, honest and generous and had paid cash for everything they took." There were a lot of people like that, and not only in Normandy in June but even in Belgium in September and October. They really didn't want us. Not all of them anyway.'

Of course, for those in the big cities of occupied Europe life was hard and unpleasant. There were the shortages of food that occur in urban areas and any attempts to supplement the poor rations by going out into the country to barter with the farmers were often frustrated by checks carried out by local police and occupation troops. Then, too, in many big cities there were factories working for the Germans and these were targets for Allied bombers. Losses among the local population as a result of air raids were seized upon by the German authorities in an attempt to alienate public opinion against the Anglo-American terror bombers. The natural feelings of the bereaved were exploited by Goebbels' propaganda machine which worked on the emotions and to the instincts – never to the intellect. There could be fewer more effective emotional arguments against the Western allies than a German soldier bandaging up those wounded by Allied bombers and caring for those families who had been bombed out of their houses by the Anglo-American air armadas.

It was not, however, all German salvation and soup-kitchens. There came a time when the infiltration of Allied agents into occupied Europe became a serious problem for the Germans. In 1940 and 1941, the days of Britain's weakness, the few agents who entered Europe were in danger of betrayal by the Communists who were at that time the allies of Germany; from those workers who collaborated with the Germans, or from the local civil population as from the Germans themselves. When, during the long years, from 1943 to the end of the war, the number of infiltrated Allied agents increased dramatically, the scale of attacks against the Germans grew and losses to their troops mounted. Their reprisals became harsh, ruthless and vicious. Thousands of hostages were taken and murdered, whole villages were burned down and entire communities slaughtered. It was a long way removed from the confiscation of bicycles.

It was during those years, as the number of attacks brought about a rise in the frequency and scale of reprisals, that the numbers fell of those volunteering to work in Germany. There was not only the reluctance to work for a nation that was executing citizens of one's own country. Rather more important was the fact that the resistance movements in the individuals' countries had

Right: German soldiers on occupation duties in France. In the background is a French factory, now working for Germany. Far from seeing themselves as an occupying power, Germans believed that they were fulfilling the Fatherland's role in uniting Europe.

warned the volunteers workers that revenge would be taken if they continued to work for Germany, for this was treason. The numbers of volunteer workers to German factories declined but the need was still there. To the Germans the situation was serious but not insoluble. If no volunteers would come forward they would be compelled if necessary and taken as slave labour to the Reich. This was the time of round ups, of deportations and of young men escaping industrial conscription by slipping away to join the partisan forces. As a consequence the underground units became strong enough to undertake more raids which resulted in more reprisals. These, in turn, engendered more attacks upon the German forces. Yes, it really was a long way from the confiscation of bicycles.

As the Allied blockade began to affect food supplies in Europe there were discussions at senior level in the Nazi Party, on how the captive populations were to be fed. The problem was chiefly one of transport. There were enough of the basic foodstuffs to meet the standard ration, but it was difficult to distribute fairly the richnesses of Normandy, of eastern Holland or of Denmark. The fertility of the soil and the more intensive farming

methods in western Europe might have made it possible to supplement the poor official ration scale, but there were other regions in south-eastern Europe and the Balkans where this was impossible. In those places hunger became the norm and starvation an unpleasant but accepted way of life. Goering had once threatened that whoever starved in Europe it would not be the Germans and that boast was soon borne out and nowhere more tragically than in Greece and Yugoslavia. In the German view it was hardly their fault if people went hungry in Europe. It was the fault of the British and their blockade.

Despite the hunger that had descended upon much of Europe as a result of occupation policies, or as the Germans claimed, the Allied blockade, it was still held to be true by those in authority that German rule was more beneficial to the people of Europe than that which the Anglo-Americans or the Russians had inflicted. It was a strongly held view, that the people of Roumania and Bulgaria, into whose lands the Red Army had advanced during 1944, were pining for a return of the Germans and remembering with sad nostalgia the days when they were protected by the power of the Third Reich.

In western Europe, too, now occupied by the Anglo-Americans, the food shortages in France and Belgium, the public demonstrations against the low ration scales should have convinced the populations of those countries just how benign and well-organized had been German rule. It was clear that Roosevelt would do little to feed Europe if this meant cutting down the lavish American ration scales. Indeed, Roosevelt had so reduced food supplies to the United Kingdom that it was common knowledge that famine and strikes were features of daily life there. Oh, if only the British had known at first hand the blessings of German rule and efficiency, might they not, too, have wanted to exchange the despotism of Churchill for the benefits of occupation by the Reich?

Left: A recruiting poster for a Walloon SS armoured division. Recruits – members of a common European civilization – would join Germany's crusade to unite the continent.

# PARTY CONTROL IN THE LAST YEAR OF THE WAR

The task of the Party in the last year of the war was to unite the masses and so inspire them with the will to resist that the invading Allied armies would be confronted by eighty million Germans who, as Goebbels hoped, would sooner go down to ruin than submit to their country being ruled by the enemy.

There is no doubt that the crassness of American politicians helped the German propaganda machine in its task of stiffening the resolve of the German people. Roosevelt's blurting out that unconditional surrender was the Allied demand gave Goebbels a trump card. It was, as he repeated to the German nation time and again, a matter of victory of death for them. In an unconditional surrender the loser had no say. Whatever the victors did: forced emigration, slave labour, sterilization . . . anything, any horror which served the plutocratic, Jewish, Bolshevik interest could be inflicted upon the Germans who would have no choice but to accept their fate. Then there was the lunatic suggestion of Morgenthau, the American Secretary of the Treasury, that Germany should be stripped of all her industries, her cities should be destroyed and that millions of her people should be deported leaving in Central Europe a nation organized into rural, peasant communities. That new German nation, now of manageable size, would have no army; would need no army, because the occupation of this rural Germany by Allied Forces would be indefinite. Those and other US pronouncements prolonged the war. The Russians, by contrast, disclosed very little of their post-war plans for Germany and the British were, by this time, only an echo of the voice of the Americans whose wilder excesses they sought to control success.

In view of these threats Goebbels realized he would have to inspire the German people to rise up and fight. The former claim 'The German Army is the German people under arms', he intended to change to 'The German people under arms has become the German Army', for now he intended that the whole nation would engage in the conflict. He was aware that it would not be an easy task to produce the blinding rage that would inspire women and children to go into unequal battle against Allied tank armadas. Goebbels knew that this was a difficult task and gave the reasons why in an article for *Das Reich*, a Party magazine. On 6 September 1942, he wrote of the Germans that 'This was a people that had not yet learned to hate . . . We are not well suited to chauvinism and if anyone wants to bring our national soul to the boil he has to set about it carefully . . . In moments of crisis when our life as a nation is imperilled we should not make objective judgements. A mania for justice as well as German sentimentality could prevent the Germans from fulfilling their mission in the world.'

The horror of the two years of war that passed between that article in September 1942 and the situation in the last six months of the war had still not been drastic enough to rouse the German nation to the boil. In fact, it seemed that the suffering had had an adverse effect, certainly in western Germany. The Anglo-American bombing offensive had destroyed six million of the 1939 total of twenty-three million dwellings. By the end of December 1944, 353,000 civilians had been killed in air raids and nearly half a million injured. Despite their ordeal, the people of the western regions of Germany had not fought and were not fighting the advancing enemy armies as the Party had hoped they would. In the areas into which the Anglo-Americans had advanced the reception from the local population had fluctuated between coldness towards the foreign invaders of the Fatherland and an enthusiastic welcome to the Allies as liberators. Nowhere had the masses risen, as the Party had hoped they would, with weapons in their hands to confront the imperialistic invaders. The peoples of the western Gaus, through which the American armies were driving, had learned very quickly that resistance to the US forces equalled destruction by the US forces. The military philosophy of the American troops was a simple one. Any house not flying a white flag was deemed to be inhabited by hostile elements and was fired upon. Any resistance near a village – even a single rifle shot or a bazooka being fired – brought down upon that village savage and immediate retribution by US artillery which continued until the place was destroyed completely.

Left: As the situation deteriorated, one way of maintaining civilian morale was through 'Wunschkonzerten', a sort of family favourites programme. This photograph shows the singer Zarah Leander at a concert in Berlin; her most famous song at the time was 'Es wird ein Wunder geschehen' – 'A Miracle will Happen'.

Any town whose inhabitants sought to obstruct the US advance was destroyed by aerial bombing and shell fire. Faced with such deterrents it is no wonder that the whole of Central Germany was one huge mass of white flags.

Against such expressions of defeatism the Party could do little. The town of Aschaffenburg was recaptured from the Americans and punishment was meted out by the Party upon those traitors who by displaying the emblems of surrender had betrayed the Führer and the Volksgemeinschaft. Acts of retribution in recaptured towns, and isolated cases of revenge by the Wehrwolf were all that the Party could do.

In the east it should have been a different matter. There the Red Army had initiated an orgy of rape, looting and destruction. Reports of that wave of horror galvanized the eastern Gaus and inspired their populations to desperate resistance. Where German Army counter-attacks recaptured towns and villages soldiers saw for themselves what bestialities had been committed by the Soviets upon German civilians. Age was no protection against rape. Females from the age of 11 upwards were violated and then mutilated. In one village all the women had been impaled and the men castrated. Reports of such terrible things spread quickly and were seized upon and reported in the German news media. There was little need for a propaganda campaign; the deeds spoke for themselves.

But if the Party expected the masses as a whole to resist, its officials had to set an example to be followed and there had been no sacrifices by the Party élite to match those which the people had had to endure. At a time when under-age youths were being conscripted for the army and when young children were being expected to stand and defend the Fatherland with bazookas, the Party organizations were still fully manned, absorbing as much man power in the straitened conditions of 1944/45 as they had at the high noon of German power, Hitler's year of destiny, 1942. That many of the offices, particularly those concerned with the administration of the conquered regions of the east, were redundant was not seen as a reason for releasing the men in them for active service. The Party officers at Reichsleitung or Gauleitung level did not wish to see their carefully constructed bureaucratic empires dismantled. The Foreign Office, for example, had a propaganda department which, in terms of manpower, was actually larger than that of the official ministry run by Goebbels. Each of the Party bosses had his own Intelligence-gathering service, his own private group of art experts to advise him of what to loot and where to find it. Most of the senior officers at Reichsleitung level had their own private armies. Himmler had his SS military formations while Goering had his Luftwaffe and paratroop divisions. The officers of those private armies had the right of direct approach to the Reichsführer or to Reichs-marschall Goering over the heads of the army leaders to whom they were nominally subordinate. It was a ludicrous situation.

In the last months of the war, although the Luftwaffe had shrunk to being little more than a small fighter force, the need for bombers and long-range reconnaissance aircraft having long since passed, its strength, in March 1945, was still more than a million and a half men of whom only a fraction were employed operationally. Even when the keenly anticipated Me 262 began to enter service there were an overwhelming number of under-employed men in the German Air Force who could have been released to flesh out the under-strength infantry divisions of the army. Goering would not release them. The Kriegs-marine, too, needed a thorough comb out and a posting of redundant men to the army. It was a

time of national crisis but the services seemed unaware of it. But then, in Goebbels' opinion, the military leaders had constantly betrayed Hitler so badly and had so often acted against the orders he had given that he could place no reliance upon them.

Even quite late in the war there might still have been time to arouse the masses. All that Germany needed was a breathing-space during which her industry could produce the weapons to arm the masses; for there were no more wonderful secret weapons to rely on. Now it was the German people who would have to gain the breathing-space that was needed and while they were holding the advancing Allied armies, Speer would repair the railways so that weapons parts already manufactured could be taken to central workshops for assembly. The production schedule of the new jet, the Me 262, was for more than a thousand machines per month. Within a few months there would be a strong force in front-line service as well as in reserve. Then the 262s would be launched against the Anglo-American air forces and could claw these from the skies in such numbers that the scale and weight of the terror raids would be broken. With the respite that such a victory would produce more arms could be turned out, new tanks constructed, infra-red sights fitted to those tanks; night sights, which the conservative-minded army leaders had rejected as unnecessary. These new weapons would halt the flood of Allied armies across Germany. A series of bitter battles fought with revolutionary élan would cause the Western Allies to recoil in horror at the losses that they had sustained while the defeats which would be inflicted upon the Soviet Army would bring the Russians to the negotiating table. All this the Party would do. To further demonstrate the close links between the Party and the masses, the army divisions which would be raised using men of the next age group to be conscripted would be formed into new 'Volksgrenadier' Divisions (VG) some of which would bear the name of a past, illustrious German hero: Clausewitz, Schlageter, Schill. With those names to inspire them the Volksgrenadier Divisions must triumph in battle. The combat prowess of the Party's VG Divisions would stiffen the old, traditional, conservative divisions and inspire them to emulate the National Socialist units.

A new spirit would infuse the German soldier – a revolutionary one. Behind that wall of inflamed

Nazi warriors would stand a second line of Party-raised troops, the Volkssturm and those in that organization who were veterans of former wars would be infected by the revolutionary spirit of their youthful comrades, boys who had not yet reached military age. Together youth and maturity would form a second National Socialist bulwark against which the enemy hordes would fling themselves in vain. Then, too, in those areas of the Fatherland into which the depraved Bolsheviks or the forces of the plutocratic Anglo-Americans had already penetrated, a new, secret, Party organization, a partisan force, the Wehrwolf, would rise. It would strike terror into the hearts of the enemy as well as into the hearts of those German traitors who were collaborating with the foe. The most ruthless measures would be employed against those who betrayed the Volksgemeinschaft.

To strengthen the moral fibre of the people, each Gau was to provide a team of first-class speakers who would undertake a fast lecture tour. They would also talk to front-line formations, reinforcing the political lines set out by the National Socialist Leadership officers in military units. It is perhaps a comment of how close were the tactics of the dictatorships of Russia and Germany that the Nazis introduced into the German Army, leadership officers who were a combination of political agitator and commissar.

How different from the dream perspective was the reality of the situation in Germany in those last months of the Second World War. All the ruthless application of more than 800,000 men could not make the railways run. Allied bombing smashed the systems faster than they could be repaired. Aircraft parts which could not be moved, piled up in factories which had been decentralized to maintain production. The aircraft could not be assembled and the Luftwaffe did not receive the machines which it needed to attack the Allied bomber fleets. Then came a hammer blow to Hitler's hopes. Speer, his Armaments Minister, advised the Führer on 14 March that Germany's economic decline was so advanced that within a few weeks the war must end. Speer's was the voice of doom for he alone, of all the hierarchy, knew the true picture. Desperate not to believe him and confident still that the Fatherland could win at least a compromise peace if it held out long enough, the most fanatical orders were issued from the Party Chancery.

Populations were ordered to be evacuated into those areas of central Germany which had not yet been overrun by the Allies. A large number of civilians had already left the threatened areas of their own accord, because of air raids, making long treks to reach safety. Others had been ecnouraged to leave the principal cities of the Reich. More than 17,000,000 people had already left their homes. Now that number was to be added to by the forced evacuation ordered by the Party. This move was necessary, the Party claimed, first to deny the manpower resources to the enemy and, secondly, because the Party intended to destroy everything in those areas through which the Allies must advance. The enemy armies would face a depopulated desert, a scorched earth from which everything that might have been of use had been either destroyed or removed.

One of the intentions behind the evacuation of the fit prisoners from the concentration camps of the east, may well have been to deny that work force to the Russians. The Red Army was notorious for its ruthless conscription of all manpower on its line of advance. Anybody could be taken to act as a porter, lugging boxes of ammunition or carrying a couple of artillery shells. In more extreme cases of conscription, every available man, woman and child would be formed up to advance across German minefields. It was Slav reasoning that a tank costs money – human lives are cheap. If some civilians were to be killed when the mines exploded, their sacrifice saved a tank from being knocked out. In the most extreme cases civilians would be used as infantry to thicken an assault wave. Goebbels feared that when the Russians reached Berlin they would conscript the 100,000 foreign workers in the city into Red Army infantry battalions.

Thus, any person capable of working, or of being turned against Germany, was to be brought into the central provinces from where the last stand would be made and from where a revolutionary Germany would arise phoenix-like from the ashes of its ruined cities to sweep away and destroy her enemies. The long columns of Allied prisoners of war, concentration camp inmates and German refugees being herded along the roads and byways of Germany knew nothing of this glorious dream. Most lived on a day to day basis; the concentration camp people on a minute to minute basis, for which of them knew whether the

**Above:** One means of attempting to halt the Allied advance was to construct barricades in the streets of German cities. In this picture, taken in the Rhineland, soldiers and party members work side by side.

Above: The end of the dream. A German woman watches in bewilderment as American troops advance through the bomb-damaged streets of her home town.

next halting place might not be the site at which they would all be slaughtered.

The evacuation into the central provinces of Germany from other regions was not a success. However much the Nazi authorities may have preached the benefits of the Volksgemeinschaft, it did not work well in adversity. Millions of refugees and bombed-out people moved into Saxony and Thuringia and swamped the local administration. There were shortages of accommodation, food and medical services, and relations between the locals and the refugees deteriorated from acceptance of a necessary evil to a downright hated of each other.

In considering the advance of the Allies into the Fatherland, Goebbels displayed the nihilistic side of his revolutionary character and began to revel in destruction. 'The fewer cities there are left in Germany', he declared in the last months of the war, 'the more free we are to fight.' It was an attitude unlikely to have been shared by those who still lived in those cities or who, having been evacuated, hoped one day to return home to them. The Party Chancery demanded the most severe punishments for those who failed to meet the revolutionary challenge. The principle that the family of an officer condemned for treason should also be imprisoned and/or executed was activated, and the officers who failed to blow up the Remagen bridge paid for their failure. To halt the surrender of German troops it was proposed at Reichsleitung level that Germany should withdraw from the Geneva Convention and begin killing the Allied prisoners of war. This would bring reprisals of the same nature from the Allies, but it would deter other German troops from surrendering if they knew that what awaited them was not a prison camp but summary execution.

That proposal was not taken up, but a more direct method was introduced. To ensure that troops did not abandon their positions, 'flying courts-martial', were set up by Hitler on 9 March 1945. Under the control of Lieutenant-General Rudolf Huebner, these mock courts were empowered to try any member of the services or the Waffen SS, without consideration of rank and to carry out any sentence of execution which the court might pass upon the accused. It was under this law that the officers of the Remagen bridgehead were tried, condemned and executed. Similar terror faced civilians, regardless of sex, who in the opinion of the Party-established court 'was guilty of endangering German will to resist or German determination to fight on'. Although it is impossible to obtain full and accurate figures of those service personnel murdered by such courts, approximately 500 convictions and executions each month is generally accepted as being correct and compares with the 180 cases monthly of those condemned and executed during the First World War.

Despite the judicial terror and the ruthlessness of the sentences, the authority of the Party began to collapse. By the end of March 1945, the Reich had shrunk to a narrow strip of land running from the Baltic down to Bosnia-Herzegovina in Yugoslavia. Letters received by Party offices at that time – for the post office was still working efficiently – demanded to know why no peace was being sought, now that Germany had all but ceased to exist. Accusations were made against Goering for the impotence of the Luftwaffe, against Gauleiters and Kreisleiters for their failure to look after the people for whom they were responsible and even against the Führer who had not visited the cities which had been destroyed in air raids.

To a great degree the criticisms of the ordinary people were justified. Goering had failed; Hitler had not visited one ruined city and in a great number of cases the leaders of the Party at Gau level had proved cowardly. The Rhineland city of Cologne had fallen without much fighting. No proper defence plan for the city had been prepared and the Gauleiter had simply abandoned his people. It was chiefly in the western regions that this dereliction of duty was most evident. Chiefly, but not completely for there were in the east certain Gauleiters who had no intention of dying with the masses. Those men evacuated themselves, using the authority that was theirs to commandeer trains to carry personal belongings to ports from which specially chartered ships carried them to safety in the west. The two most notorious of these men were Forster of Danzig, who had helped to foment the Second World War, and Koch, whom we have met formerly as Reichs Kommissar for the Ukraine.

By contrast there were Gauleiters who held true to the Party and who defended their city or their Gau with the demanded revolutionary fervour. One such was Hanke of Breslau, whose 72-day-long defence of that city helped to confound the march of the Red Army towards Berlin. Goebbels noted in his diary that no such defence as that of Breslau had been made by any German city in the west and ascribed that failure to treason. Another Gauleiter determined to make a stand for Volk, Führer and Fatherland, was Ueberreither of Styria in Austria. His erection of barricades around the Gau offices on the castle hill in Graz was seen by the people of Graz as their Gauleiter's eccentricity. Since the local army commanders rejected completely the Gauleiter's defence stance and since he himself had no troops to back his authority as Reichs Defence Commissar, his dream of holding the Red hordes on the slopes of the Schlossberg, remained unfulfilled.

Gauleiter Hofer of Tyrol was another whose attempts at a heroic defence were ignored by the military who were more concerned with the safety of their own units than taking part in the Gauleiter's pantomime heroics. Those Gauleiters who wanted to continue the struggle saw themselves as heroes defending the Fatherland. We can only see them as pathetic little men trying to hold off what was in March/April 1945, the inevitable – defeat of Germany.

But while Hofer and Ueberreither are girding their loins for combat, while Hanke is conducting a staunch defence prior to being flown out in the last aircraft to leave Breslau and before Koch and Forster have deserted their peoples, let us look at the Party's military organizations named in the opening paragraphs of this section of the book – the Volkssturm and the Wehrwolf – and see how they and the other Party militias conducted themselves.

# THE POLITICAL MILITARY FORCES

Seen from the perspective of the Party leadership the army had failed the Führer. A clique of generals had conspired to confound the plans of the 'greatest military genius of all time' and had compounded their conspiracy of disobedience by an assassination attempt. It was clear that all the old-fashioned elements of the nation were in conspiratorial league and only the Party was holding true to the revolutionary doctrines of National Socialism. During the autumn of 1944, certain Party revolutionaries were promoted to senior positions of command and were expected to halt the Allied advances towards and into Germany. To aid the dilettante commanders in their task it was vital that new military forces be found. These would need to be inspired with revolutionary *élan* if they were to succeed in the task of defending the Reich, where the traditional army had failed. A memorandum written by General Heusinger in 1943, had proposed a Home Defence Force, an idea which had been rejected as unnecessary at that time by Hitler. The proposal

was raised again in July 1944, in the light of experience gained by those Gauleiters who had raised civilian labour forces to dig defences along the Reich frontiers. Out of that successful application of Reich Defence Commissar powers, which Hitler had given to the Gauleiters, evolved the concept of a military force raised by the Party, and, therefore, free from negative, reactionary influences. The leadership of the organization would be that of the Party at every level – national, regional and unit. The only part that the Regular Army would play would be in arming and equipping the new force. Even at that level the influence of the Party would be strong, because Himmler, in his new role as Commander of Replacement Armies, was responsible for the supply of weapons.

At that period of the war there was no uncommitted manpower source from which a new, full time, military force might be obtained. The wave of soldiers who might have been used had already been called to the colours and posted to their

units. The next call-up was months away and time could not wait until the next class of conscripted men came of age. The need for a great mass of men was now urgent. Those who would make up the new force would need to be in reasonably good health, not too old and based locally. The only body which met these requirements and which was not already in the armed forces or registered for military service, was the work force in the factories. It was obvious that among the thirteen million men in industry there would be many who met the criteria demanded.

The standard procedure to call up men to the colours was slow and cumbersome. A newer method needed to be found. The solution lay in the Party's own organization. The Gauleiters could establish from Party records which men in the factories were available for local defence service and under their authority as Reichs Commissars could conscript the factory workers as temporary soldiers to defend the factories and their own homes. That was the original intention; for the Volkssturm to be a local unit defending its own area for a limited period of time.

The tactical unit would be a battalion and this would be activated by the Gauleiter under his Reichs Defence Commissar powers. The men of the battalion, now armed and equipped as soldiers, would occupy the trenches which another directed body of workers would have already dug. The Volkssturm men would hold those field fortifications until the well-armed and better trained Regular Army arrived to relieve them. The Volkssturmbattalion would then be stood down and its men would go back to work in the factories until some new crisis caused them to be reactivated.

In German history there had been many instances of local men being called up to guard or, if necessary, to fight in defence of their own areas. From the earliest days of the Prussian Army the Landsturm, as such a body was named, had formed a part of the military establishment. What was unique was that the new force would be totally outside the control of the army until the time came for the battalions to go into action. Hitler, acting through the Party Chancery, would advise the Gauleiter to activate the battalions within his Gau. His units would take post and only then would they come under military control.

The proposal made in 1943 by General Heusinger was warmly received in Berlin in 1944, and on 6 September Hitler directed Martin Bormann, to undertake the raising of a National Socialist military militia to which he gave the name 'Volkssturm'. Within three weeks the basic organization had been completed. Hitler's Decree of 25 September, which formally raised the new body, is interesting reading. It opens with a blazing condemnation of Germany's allies for having failed her but claims that the situation in September 1944 was similar to that which had faced Germany in 1939, when she had stood alone against her enemies. At that time, by a first ruthless application of the Reich's potential, difficult military problems had been solved and Germany's future, as indeed of the whole of Europe, had been assured. These enemies of the Reich who were now approaching the Reich's frontiers would be met by a second massive effort of the German people. This would not only fling back the enemy but would hold him at bay until the future of Germany and all Europe could be guaranteed. Against the nihilistic plan of Jewish international interests Germany would set the assault of the whole German people.

The Führer's Decree ordered that all men between the ages of 16 and 60, who were capable of bearing arms, were to be enlisted into the Volkssturm. Each Gauleiter was made responsible for raising and commanding the Volkssturm battalions within his Gau and he was to use every Party organization to enable him to carry out the task. The Chief of Staff of the SA, Schepmann, was named as the Volkssturm's Inspector-General, responsible for training, and Kraus, leader of the NSKK (National Sozialistisch Kraftfahr Korps, the Nazi Motorized Corps) was given the post of Inspector-General of Transport and was to ensure the mobility of the Volkssturm.

Left: German men called up for the Volkssturm marching through Berlin on their first parade. Most are armed with Panzerfaust anti-tank rocket launchers. Generally these were men from reserved occupations – such as skilled engineers, steelworkers, miners and shipbuilders. Service in the Volkssturm was seen as but a temporary measure, to meet the needs of the immediate crisis.

The future warriors were assured that during the period of their service they would be soldiers as that term was understood in military law. Himmler, in his capacity as Commander of the Replacement Army, was not only responsible for the arming and equipping of the entire organization, but was also the channel through which Hitler's orders concerning Volkssturm operations were to be passed.

To conclude his proclamation Hitler declared that the National Socialist Party was fulfilling its duty by using its own organization to bear the main burden of the battle. The Volkssturm Decree was made public on 18 October and promulgated in the official Gazette two days later. A special postage stamp was also issued bearing the motto, 'A people arises', and a new film *Kolberg*, showing the heroism of the citizens of a beleaguered city, was released.

The Party's plan was for four waves of the Volkssturm to be raised. The men of the first wave could be called up as long as their conscription did not prejudice the national war effort, and only battalions from that wave might, with authority, be used outside their local territorial areas. The second wave would not be activated until the imminent approach of the enemy whereupon they would be mustered and go into action. The men of the second wave were, generally, younger than those in the first wave, and were without military training. The average age of the men of the first wave was 52 and many would have seen service during the First World War. The third and fourth waves were made up of practically every other reasonably fit male person. Fit was a relative term to some dedicated Gauleiters who did not scruple to enrol cripples or amputees and then not only for simple guard duties, but also for active service.

The problem of arming the six million men who, theoretically, might be liable for Volkssturm service was not easily resolved. The first wave alone, comprising 30 per cent of the whole, would provide 1.2 million men who would be formed into 1,850 battalions. These first-wave men had to be armed, but there was a crisis in the production of the German Army's standard infantry rifle. Not only had production declined to 200,000 pieces per month, but the army had to replace the 3,500,000 rifles which had been lost between April and August 1944. The Army Ordnance Depot designed several types of robust, cheap and easily made Volkssturm weapons, relying upon pressed metal and not precision machined parts. The weapon finally selected was the VGI-5 of which 10,000 were to be produced each month. It was planned that production would be carried out in decentralized workshops and that final assembly would be made in centralized factories. Raids by the RAF halted the flow of weapons parts and local gunsmiths had to be employed on the task of arming the Party's Army. To cover deficiencies in machine-guns the Luftwaffe was directed to supply such weapons from its stocks. Two consignments, one of 150,000 and one of 180,000 pieces, were issued for Volkssturm use. The Regular Army intended to stand aloof from the task of arming the Volkssturm, particularly since their own firearms and supplies position was critical. An Army Order dated 12 December, made the point on rations very clear. 'The equipping . . . of the Volkssturm is a Party matter . . . only on active service will their units be fed from Army resources'.

Tactically, each battalion of the Volkssturm would have four companies, each of which was divided into four platoons each of four sections. Since the units were locally based there was no need for a staff system or for rear echelon detachments. Such liaison officers as would be needed would be Party members who had had military experience. The Gauleiter chose the battalion commanders who then appointed company commanders. They in turn selected the platoon commanders who nominated the section leaders. This was in some respects an excellent system since the men of the smaller detachments – section and platoon – would have usually served together in a Party 'block'. To overcome the problem of a Party official expecting to hold rank in the Volkssturm because of his political position, it was ordered that no major Party formation could join the Volkssturm *en bloc*.

The clothing of the Volkssturm was as simple as its organization. Under the terms of the Geneva Convention it is not necessary for a combatant to wear full uniform. So long as he can be recognized as a soldier is sufficient and in that context an armband provides identification. Certainly, Germany in the desperate situation of 1944, could never have supplied uniforms to the new Volkssturm army. The only items on general issue were identity documents, identity tags and the necessary armbands. These carried the words 'Deutscher Volkssturm – Wehrmacht' sometimes, but not always, followed by numbers indicating the Gau, battalion and company. Party members wore their usual uniforms from which the collar patches and shoulder strap insignia had been removed. The Volkssturm rank insignia consisted of silver stars worn on two black rectangular collar patches; four stars in the case of a battalion commander, three, two and one for ranks from company commander down to section leader respectively. In an effort to clothe men with warm garments a final collection was made by the Party's charity organizations and was very successful. Some Gauleiters were able to provide from such sources the stout boots, warm clothing and overcoats that each Sturmmann was recommended to wear. Each man supplied his own equipment: a rucksack, blanket, water-bottle, mug and eating utensils.

The weapons establishment for a first-wave battalion was 649 rifles, 31 light and six heavy machine-guns. For a second wave unit 576 rifles, thirty light and three heavy machine-guns, while no establishment was laid down for the third and fourth waves for whom, it was anticipated, that shotguns or hunting rifles would be sufficient. Mortars were on establishment but were seldom used as they were often commandeered by Regular Army units to increase their own establishment of such weapons. The familiar picture of a Volkssturm man is of an elderly gentleman armed with one or other of the newly introduced types of rocket-launcher, either the Panzerfaust or the Panzerschreck. Six of each of these were on issue to each battalion. It must be appreciated that these numbers of men and women were the laid down establishments. They were seldom met and it was not unusual for the battalion to be issued with fewer weapons than expected or for those weapons to be practically useless. Great numbers of captured enemy guns were issued for which there was little ammunition. The equality of sacrifice demanded by the National Socialist Party was unusually rigid in the matter of the issue of firearms to the Volkssturm. It might have been expected that in those Gaus where there was little immediate danger, few weapons would have been distributed to the battalions and that more lavish supply would have been made to the units in the provinces facing the most immediate danger. This did not happen. The Volkssturm battalions in the eastern provinces which were activated to face the Red Army received only the same number of weapons as those battalions in unthreatened areas of central Germany. Thus, in East Prussia, some battalions went into action with its men armed with foreign rifles and thirty rounds of ammunition and with no prospect of further supplies.

Although the Volkssturm was conceived as an infantry force there were certain anomalies. One Prussian battalion obtained a battery of 75mm field guns from a museum and soon had them in firing condition, using the artillery pieces to support the attacks launched by their own infantry companies. Some units with NSKK leaders converted soft skin vehicles to armoured cars for reconnaissance missions. Gauleiter Koch, always an innovator, formed a night-fighter squadron made up of civilian light aircraft piloted by Volkssturm men who had been trained by the Luftwaffe. Koch's flying circus never saw action. Lack of petrol grounded the machines.

Although the Volkssturm was conceived as a stopgap force, whose men would only be called from their factories when the enemy drew near, inevitably there were occasions when the battalions were put into action as front-line troops. One of the Party criticisms concerning Volkssturm was that the battalions in the west, which had had a longer time to train and to prepare for battle, did not perform so well as the units in the east. It says a lot for the morale of the Volkssturm men of the east that they stood firm. Consider how they must have felt as they, armed with a miscellany of firearms and equipped only for a short infantry action, marched towards the front passing on their march heavily armed panzer units which were withdrawing in front of the Red Army. The panzers were pulling back, yet they, the Volkssturm, undertrained and poorly armed were expected to hold back the Red hordes. The feelings of the Volkssturmmänner can also be well imagined when the 'No retreat!' orders were issued. The author of one report stated how he rang an army unit to ask for permission to withdraw from a village which he and a handful of men was still holding. The army officer at the other end of the telephone line was adamant. 'There will be no withdrawal. Any man leaving his post will be shot.' To that tirade the writer of the report asked who would form the firing-squad for the army had abandoned the place days earlier. The Army officer hung up.

Inevitably, there were some units which showed incredible bravery and others which broke up leaving the men to return home. Among those units which demonstrated the devotion to duty for which the Party had hoped were the East Prussian battalions in beleaguered Königsberg. The Volkssturm there, organized into eleven battalions, fought alongside army units and one Sturmmann won the Knight's Cross of the Iron Cross for his bravery in destroying enemy tanks at close quarters. In Pomerania the Volkssturm destroyed nearly four hundred Russian armoured fighting vehicles using Panzerfaust rocket-launchers. The tank-busting detachments rode around the province on bicycles and one group, having knocked out fifteen tanks during one morning, received an alarm call during the afternoon and promptly smashed a further six enemy machines. At Kolberg, on the Baltic coast, the scene of action of Goebbels' propaganda film, the Volkssturm garrison held out for three weeks to cover the evacuation of 80,000 refugees and wounded. The Berlin Volkssturm was called out during November and was employed in constructing field defences and minelaying along the Oder river line. Some battalions were then put straight into battle during January and March against the attacks launched by 1st Belorussian Front which had broken through the German defences. In the Reichs capital about thirty battalions of Volkssturm saw service and their arms included fifteen different types of rifle and ten types of machine-gun. Most men were issued with only ten rounds and one battalion was disbanded in the Berlin Olympic stadium when the unit ran out of rifle ammunition.

The Volkssturm battalions in Breslau had, perhaps, the most impressive record. The garrison of 35,000 army troops, and an SS regiment, together with some miscellaneous units of the army and the Luftwaffe, was backed by 15,000 Volkssturmmänner. This determined garrison held the Silesian city from 14 February until 6 May, obstructing the advance of three Soviet Army Corps and tying down the Red divisions until the war's end.

An example of the deployment of a Volkssturm battalion outside its own Gau area is that of one from upper Austria which was activated during January 1945. Three days training was given; conducted entirely in the open air and then the unit, 560 men strong, was entrained and sent to the Oder front. During the first week the battalion not only held its sector in the face of Red Army tank assaults but also launched counter-attacks fighting its way forward through massed artillery barrages. Such courage was costly and within that first week half the battalion had been killed in action. For six weeks the Austrians held the line and their short period out of action was brought to an end when they were put back in to face the Soviet assault on 16 April. The Austrian battalion held and flung back the assaults of the 362nd Red Army Infantry Division, but such an unequal contest could have only one result. The Soviets broke through at last and the remnants of the battalion conducted a fighting retreat towards Berlin. In their withdrawal they destroyed a further seventeen Russian tanks. The Austrians were submerged in the fighting to the south-east of Berlin, some of the survivors managing to reach the west and to pass into American prisoner-of-war camps. The others were taken by the Russians but were not shot as partisans, which had been the fate of those who had surrendered in Königsberg, in Breslau and in many other places.

In retrospect the idea of a locally based militia defending home and hearth and the factories in which its men worked was a good one. In practice, however, the concept was seldom met. The fighting capabilities of the battalions depended to a very marked degree upon the Gauleiter. If he was an anxious man and called them out too early, factory production suffered and the aggressive edge of the men was lost in the waiting time. Other Gauleiters waited so long to activate their battalions that when they were formed they were untrained and ill-equipped. It is a fact that the greatest number of men who were eligible for Volkssturm service were not called up or saw little or no active service.

As we have seen the battalions differed in quality. Some fought well, others very bravely indeed. There were battalions that dissolved under fire and not a few that broke up before they ever reached the combat area. In any case, the battalions had only local significance. At a national level the Volkssturm achieved little and the concept of a people's militia rising spontaneously and battling with National Socialist ferocity, proved to be just another of the Nazi Party's unrealized ambitions.

In each of the lands which it had conquered and occupied the German Army had to deal with the problem of fighting a secret army – the partisans. At Command level the actions to counter these guerrilla forces meant that soldiers had to be taken from combat duties, thus weakening the battle line. At a personal level the German troops' need to be vigilant at all times coupled with the knowledge that they were nowhere safe from partisan attack, had a serious effect upon their morale. Neither the importance of partisan movements nor the success of their operations was lost upon the Germans and as the Allied armies closed in on the Reich, plans were laid to create a German guerrilla movement – Wehrwolf. This would operate behind Allied lines and inflict upon their troops the fear and the uncertainty that the Germans had had to suffer.

As in the case of the Volkssturm the raising and direction of Wehrwolf was not entrusted to the army. In the opinion of the Reichsleitung, the Generals, with their bourgeois concepts of warfare, would have no idea of how to use this new, revolutionary force. Nor could the military be trusted after the July bomb plot. Wehrwolf would, therefore, be raised and administered by the Party. The Reichsleitung would select the targets to be attacked and the Wehrwolf activists would carry out the missions. The OKW would be the *de jure* Head of organization in order to give to the underground force the authority of being a military body.

Discussions at the highest level emphasized that the prime consideration for a volunteer to be selected as a Wehrwolf agent was the fervency of his or her belief in National Socialist principles and a staunch adherence to the Führer. Military experience was not, at first, considered essential. Candidates would be trained by SS officers each of whom was expert in anti-partisan operations. In the final weeks of the war when it was no longer possible to give proper training to the Wehrwolves, military experience was the next consideration – after loyalty to Hitler and to the Party.

As the Reichsleitung first envisaged it, Wehrwolf would be a small group of agents whose drive would create a momentum strong enough to inspire the great mass of the people. It was accepted that most civilians would be unsuited to serve on active field operations, but they could feed, hide, supply and support the activists. In addition to operations directed against Allied troops and installations in Germany, the Wehrwolf would also paint slogans and flypost placards to intimidate those Germans who collaborated with the occupying powers, or else to keep the other civilians true to National Socialist principles.

Gruppenführer Prutzmann, who had been given the task of raising and training Wehrwolf, was a skilled and ruthless administrator. Armed with absolute power to comandeer and to direct, he set up in certain eastern and western provinces of Germany, isolated training centres. In these the recruits would undergo instruction, which would be given by the most skilled instructors in anti-partisan operations whom Prutzmann withdrew from army and SS units. Together with those experts he drew up a training programme and tested its efficiency. Next he laid out numerous well-hidden ammunition and supply dumps on whose stocks the Wehrwolf agents would draw. The first candidates arrived; mostly volunteers, but including some who had been approached and asked to join. The courses were rigorous and exhausting for they had been designed to test the candidates to the limit of their physical and emotional limits. Those who could not meet the exacting demands of Prutzmann and his staff were dismissed with the solemn warning that Wehrwolf was a state secret; to betray it was high treason.

The candidates passed from a regime designed to break them physically and emotionally, through intense political indoctrination and on to practical training. This included the manufacture and use of explosives, close-quarter combat, camouflage and communications. Intensive training in survival techniques ensured that the activists would remain at liberty and also operational in enemy-occupied territory. At the end of the course the candidates who had now become agents were sent home to await developments. When their own region was overrun and occupied by the enemy they were to slip quietly away and go underground.

To keep the Wehrwolf politically indoctrinated as well as to relay instructions to the scattered agents, Goebbels, allotted stations on the Deutschlandsender radio network exclusively for Wehrwolf use. Those stations broadcast slogans from the Kampfzeit years; slogans which increased the fervour of the activists to a fanaticism and inspired them to go out to fight, to suffer and to die for the Führer.

Mention was made in earlier pages that the attitudes of the civil population in the western Gaus was a disappointment to the Party leadership. In that connection Prutzmann reported that the mass of the civil population in the west wanted nothing to do with the Wehrwolf or the Party. So far as the civilians were concerned the arrival of Allied troops would bring an end to the bombing and the fighting. The Nazi Party had brought disaster upon Germany and the civilians had no intention of compounding that disaster by supporting the snotty Hitler Youth brats of the Wehrwolf in their efforts to restore Party discipline. So far as the masses were concerned the war had gone on too long. Too much had been sacrificed. Too many had been lost. It was time for the Nazis to accept defeat and to face up to reality.

The Party, of course, would not tolerate such cowardly attitudes and its activists swore revenge upon those traitors to the Volksgemeinschaft. Prominent German men who had been appointed by the American or British occupation authorities to positions of civil authority were warned by Deutschlandsender that their treachery would be punished. Some were murdered, the most important being the Lord Mayor of Aachen. The news of his assassination was broadcast over the Wehrwolf network and its success boosted Wehrwolf morale. By painting slogans and posting placards Wehrwolf warned the German people that they must remain loyal to Hitler. In some towns and villages the slogans were scrubbed out by civilians before the Allies entered, while in other places opponents of the dying Nazi regime painted their own slogans. The most famous of these was a question. 'Did Hitler need four years to achieve this?' This question was a bitterly sarcastic comment upon Hitler's demand in his first years of power. At that time he had stated, 'Give me four years and you will not recognize Germany.' The bitter question painted on the walls of bomb-damaged houses illustrated the feelings of many people in western Germany.

Prutzmann may have been dissatisfied with the response of the German civilians in the west, but he could have had no complaints to make about the civilians in the eastern regions. To begin with Wehrwolf activity was better supported in those areas threatened by the Red Army, and the radio broadcast numerous accounts of the courage of the German partisans. There are no post-operation reports on the missions Wehrwolf undertook and thus it is not possible to determine their scope, success rate and effect. What did happen was that such operations inevitably reduced as the grip of the Red Army tightened on the areas of Germany and Austria that it had occupied. The boasts and threats of the Wehrwolf stations of Deutschlandsender served only to heighten the Red Army's awareness of the underground army and the Russians took fast and dramatic action following any real or suspected Wehrwolf operation. The NKVD was also able to 'turn' those operators whom it caught and through them discover the Wehrwolf cells and destroy them.

There was a variant of Prutzmann's Wehrwolf underground army of highly trained, specialists. This new Wehrwolf was announced in a broadcast made by Goebbels. He called upon the whole German nation to become Wehrwolves, rise and to take up arms against the invaders. In response to the Reichminister's call there were reports received from American troops that they had been fired upon by civilians. Such attacks were few, isolated and swiftly dealt with. Destruction was visited upon those localities from which opposition came. The razing of a village or a town by US ground and air forces served to warn other localities along the lines of the US advance that any opposition would be beaten down without mercy. Along the Red Army's thrust line there was almost no response to Goebbels' Wehrwolf cry. The countryside was devoid of people. In many cases they had fled out of fear of the avenging Soviet soldiers. In other cases the civilians, having been despoiled and looted by the Soviet soldiers, were then rounded up to work either as carriers or porters for the Red Army, or else were grouped into road repair gangs.

For a number of reasons neither of the two Wehrwolf organizations had a chance of succeeding. The Goebbels one was naïve in concept. There cannot have been many civilians who would attempt, by themselves and only lightly armed, to stop an Allied tank armada. More particularly was it naïve to expect such heroism from civilians who were well aware that the Allies would exact a fearful retribution for a single act of bravado. The instinct for self-preservation kept the German masses docile as the Allied armies advanced and overran them. Those civilians must have been few in number who, having endured and survived nearly six years of war, would hazard their life in so pointless an operation.

Although excellent in concept, Prutzmann's Wehrwolf organization was doomed to fail. To be successful any partisan organization must have a home base from which weapons and supplies are received, in which plans can be drawn up and from which instructions are issued. The partisan groups in western Europe had had the United Kingdom as their base; their source of hope and inspiration. To the Russian partisans operating behind German lines, that home base had been the great, unconquered mass of the Soviet Union. From both those bases went out the support which the guerrillas needed to sustain them in the field. For the Wehrwolf no such base existed in a rapidly shrinking Fatherland nor could one operate once the Allies had overrun all of Germany. Neither did Wehrwolf have popular support. It lacked those who would be prepared to take risks to help the agents, to feed them and to encourage them. Lacking those things the movement could not succeed. The Party notion that National Socialist fervour and political slogans from the Kampfzeit would be the foundations of military victory was shown to be absurd. Slogans are no substitute for food; nor have they the power to command the support of the war-weary masses.

The Volkssturm, the Party's attempt to produce a workers' factory militia similar to that in the Soviet Union, had failed. Attempts to slow down or even to halt the Allied advances through Germany by Wehrwolf, another Party organization, had come to naught. A third Party-inspired effort, produced in the final weeks of the war, was for a Freikorps.

This was an emotive name. Freikorps had been formed from volunteer detachments which had held Germany's eastern border in the years immediately following the Great War. Once again, a host of volunteers, loyal, true and politically inspired, would be formed and would march to the sound of the guns – towards Berlin where the Führer, Party Comrade Hitler, was besieged. As with most Party-inspired projects the raising of the Freikorps involved a great attention to petty detail, first in who would be eligible to serve in its ranks and, secondly, in how the groups from each Kreis were to meet and amalgamate before the whole host set off to smash the Russian ring around Berlin.

The most important requirement for any Freikorps man was his political reliability and staunchness to the ideals of National Socialism. Gauleiters were requested to forward the names of men of their staff who most fitted the requirements. If the nominees were fit they would join the Freikorps, would assemble, clad in suitable clothing and with packed lunches, ready to ride their bicycles towards Berlin. No written records remain, if indeed any ever existed, to describe the military service rendered by the 1945 version of Freikorps. If any detachments actually reached the Reichs capital they would, I feel, have been swallowed up in the anonymity of that great battle.

Once the bicycling Freikorps set off, pedalling its way to Berlin, there was no other male source from which soldiers could be gained and which the Party could send into battle for National Socialism. There may have been no more men upon whom the Party could call, but there were women. Great numbers of them had written to Hitler and to Goebbels demanding the right to fight. The inspiration was there; the will to fight was there and the weapons were there. Only the decision by the Party leaders was missing.

The Reichsleitung did not feel itself able, even at that stage of the war, to jeopardize the future mothers of Germany by putting them into battle. The soul-searching went on and on. Then at last, in March 1945, came the decision that, because of the grave crisis facing the state; in these hours of Germany's danger, women might be permitted to bear arms and become soldiers. A women's force, 'Adolf Hitler', was born – but it was stillborn. The pettifogging, bureaucratic details, that were considered so essential by the Party, took so long to resolve that the war ended before the units could be formed and activated.

With that last abortive effort the Third Reich died and with it passed also the Party that had created it. The Party organizations whose fervour and fanaticism it had been hoped would produce victory out of defeat, had failed in their endeavour.

# II. ECONOMIC PERSPECTIVE

EARLIER in this book it was stated that for a nation to undertake and to prosecute a war to a victorious outcome requires, among other things, the efficient use of its economic potential. In that respect National Socialist Germany can be considered as having been ill-prepared for war. This section of the book deals with economic Germany and the preparations which the Nazi leaders made for that conflict. A national battle plan which sets out the strategy to be followed determines not only the weapons which will be used, but also the raw materials which industry will require to produce those weapons. Let us see, to begin with, the Nazi view of how the war would be fought and then go on to the matters of production.

In their appreciations of the economic demands that war would entail the Nazi party leaders demonstrated as great a lack of forward planning as they had in the planning of military grand strategy. They foresaw, wrongly as it turned out, the war being fought as a series of fast and mobile campaigns, each of which would be won within weeks or months. The fundamental flaw in this military appreciation was the belief that Germany would only have to fight land campaigns. Economic planning was based on the same false premise. As a result not only was industry organized for short-run campaigns but only weapons of limited capabilities were designed, produced and taken into service.

The scenario for war, as envisaged by the German leaders, was that ahead of the fast and hardhitting panzer columns the Luftwaffe would fly, destroying the enemy's air forces on their aerodromes or in the air. With air superiority gained the Luftwaffe would go on to act as long-range artillery, bombing the enemy and making him 'sturmreif', that is to say, 'softened up' ready for the final assault. Employing the tactics of overwhelming fire power and rapid movement a campaign could be begun and concluded quickly. Each such success would be another step along the road to final victory.

This plan placed the greatest emphasis on the army and its combatant arms of service; infantry, artillery and panzer. The roles foreseen for the navy and the Luftwaffe were supportive to the ground operations. In such a role the Kriegsmarine would not need a vast fleet of surface warships. A certain number would indeed be required, but its greatest strength would be in the U-boat arm whose task would be to blockade enemy countries dependent on imports from overseas to feed their peoples and to fuel their war effort.

The flaws in this grand strategy were apparent as early as the spring of 1940 and the campaign against Norway. The Kriegsmarine was powerless to counter the Royal Navy and despite the heroism of the German crews, lost ships out of all proportion to the numbers which it put into that operation. Thereafter, for all the subsequent years of the war, with the exception of isolated and abortive attempts to use its pocket-battleships, the Kriegsmarine surface fleet was dead. When the Allies invaded North-West Europe in the summer of 1944, German surface ships could not intervene effectively and the Navy was restricted to such *ad hoc* devices as explosive motor-boats, one-man submarines and human torpedoes.

The construction of surface units is admittedly, a long and expensive business, and it is accepted that the number of pocket-battleships could never be large. Nevertheless, a programme to construct smaller units should have been undertaken. It was not and as a result of that failure to replace the losses incurred, the total number of destroyers in commission with the Kriegsmarine during the summer of 1940 was just four.

Hitler had not anticipated the complexity of a global war and in his allocation of even basic materials such as steel, gave to the Kriegsmarine a lower priority for all its ship construction than that given to the army for its needs. There was little flexibility in the allocation of priorities in the first years of war. Each service foughts its battles in competition with and not in co-operation with the sister services. Appeals to Hitler were not helpful. His decisions were reached by snap judgements, by emotion, by the propaganda effect to be gained and seldom by logical thought or reasoned argument. This was not economic planning but economic pragmatism and so far as this concerned the Kriegsmarine, the Führer lacked an understanding of surface ship capability.

The most severe tests to which the Kriegsmarine put the Allied navies were the several offensives known as the battles of the Atlantic. These were fought by the U-boat, the only German naval weapon to cause the Allies long periods of deep crisis. Throughout the war the number of U-boats at sea remained high enough to demand the strongest effort on the part of the Allies to defeat them. German U-boat successes ensured that that arm of service received the highest priority in materials and shipyard space so that large numbers and more modern vessels were built. The bulk of the steel made available to the Kriegsmarine was devoted solely to submarine construction. As we shall see in the chapter on Operation 'Sealion', the projected invasion of the United Kingdom, Germany had neither the shipyard capacity nor materials enough to enable work to be undertaken on more than one naval construction programme at any one particular time.

The other supporting Service, the Luftwaffe, was the most National Socialist in outlook and was commanded by Goering, one of the senior men in the Party. He was also in charge of the Four Year Plan for the restructuring of German economics. With such influence he should have been able to produce an incomparable fighting force. He did not. The apparently invincible, shining weapon of National Socialist Germany was fatally flawed. As the result of a shortage of basic materials and the false premise of Germany's grand strategy, an air force was created which did not have strategic capability but only tactical potential. There was not, in its whole arsenal of aircraft types, a single heavy bomber type. To define that statement more precisely, the German Air Force lacked a bomber capable of flying long distances while carrying a havy bomb load. The Royal Air Force had among the aircraft on its establishment, the Lancaster, a machine which could carry a 10-ton bomb to middle distance targets or a less heavy bomb load from the United Kingdom to the most easterly of German cities. The Americans had the Boeings which carried a lighter bomb load than the Lancaster, but which were so strongly armoured that they deserved their name, 'Flying Fortress'. The Luftwaffe had no equivalent aircraft, but had to be content with improving the performances of the Heinkel and Junkers bombers with which it had entered the war. That the Junkers and Heinkels of 1944/45 were superior in performance to the original marks produced during 1938/39 does not alter the fact that the Luftwaffe lacked a specially designed bomber comparable to the long-range, heavy machines in service with the RAF and the USAAF.

During the First World War the German Imperial government had designed, built and employed airships and aircraft on long-range,

Hermann Goering, ex-fighter ace, commander of the Luftwaffe, loyal Party member and economic supremo. He was also a very popular man in Germany, seeming to epitomise the martial virtues of the nation by dint of his heroic First World War service, while also demonstrating an exemplary enjoyment of life. In both his principal roles, as chief of the Air Force and in charge of industry, he failed miserably, however. Indolent and incompetent, he appeared to the industrialists as a self-important nuisance with no knowledge of the problems afflicting German manufacturing.

overseas bombing missions, but the lessons of those operations seem to have been ignored by those who directed the affairs of the Third Reich in the years immediately preceding the Second World War. There were, of course, many senior German air force officers, among them General Wever, who proposed the setting up of a long-range bomber striking force. With his death in an air crash in 1936, the chance of directing Luftwaffe thinking along lines already laid out by such writers on aerial strategy as Douhet, Billy Mitchell and Arthur Harris, were lost. Two factors were chiefly responsible for this; that of personality and that of economics. Reorganization of the German air arm following Wever's death brought into senior command positions, men of the same type as Goering, the Commander-in-Chief of the Luftwaffe. These were former fighter pilot aces of the Great War. Their viewpoints accorded with the general policy of the Supreme Command, that tactical fighters and bombers were vitally important. The second factor, the economic one, arose out of Adolf Hitler's political demands. He exploited the fear of aerial bombardment felt by the civilians of Europe. The effect of bombing from the air had been demonstrated in Abyssinia, in Spain and in China. The terrifying prophecy of the experts was that the bomber would always get through and when it did the destruction it created was fearful. In the mid 1930s Hitler was determined to impose his will upon the nations of Europe and threatened their populations with the weapon which they feared most – the bomber. Fleets of these flew in practice flights across German skies and soon pictures of those sinister squadrons were reproduced world-wide in newspapers and newsreels. It was a crude but effective form of political blackmail.

Goering, in his dual capacity of administrator of the Reich's Four Year plan and Commander-in-Chief of the Luftwaffe, had been ordered to produce the aircraft which Hitler demanded for his increasingly aggressive political stance. The Reichsmarschall was later to complain that to the Führer the performance of the machines was immaterial. What he insisted upon were numbers. Goering produced bombers in the numbers which Hitler demanded, but to achieve that goal resorted to a simple but fateful compromise. Aluminium, an important component in the construction of aircraft, was in desperately short supply in Germany. The equivalent amount of aluminium

required to build three heavy bombers would build five, short-range machines. Goering decided to produce a greater number of short-range bombers, a solution which not only met Hitler's demands but also fitted in with the grand strategy concept of continental land battles. Thus the Luftwaffe entered into what it thought would be a tactical war and was armed with weapons built for a war of that nature. The German airmen soon found that they were fighting British and American forces, both of which were equipped with modern weapons which also had strategic capabilities.

The situation of German air force inferiority did not improve during the war despite new aircraft types which were brought into service. It was no longer a shortage of aluminium which was responsible. That was now available in abundance; the fruit of conquest and exploitation. There were instead, other factors. The most important of these were the political interference of Adolf Hitler in Luftwaffe tactics and the fuel shortage. The German Air Force had a fast new jet fighter, the Me 262. This machine, had it been produced in the numbers which had been planned – 1,000 per month – could have been used to combat the Allied bombers. The high speed of the 262 made it faster than any fighter aircraft in service with the Allied air forces. Used in the role for which it had been designed, the 262 might have inflicted upon the RAF and the USAAF such losses that the strategic bombing offensive would have had to be curtailed or even shut down completely for a very long period. By the time that the Me 262 came into squadron service Germany was everywhere on the defensive. The great days of conquest were past and the Reich was suffering under a bomber offensive in the air and reverses in the land war. The overwhelming need was for a defensive posture, but that was rejected by Hitler who demanded the offensive in every situation. Fighter aircraft he considered defensive; but bombers were offensive weapons. His orders were that the Me 262 fighter was to be converted to a bomber. The Führer rejected the warning of the Luftwaffe experts that the fitting of external bomb racks would alter the aircraft's configuration and reduce, thereby, the performance of the 262 to that of a conventional, propeller-driven fighter. The advantages which the jet fighter enjoyed would be lost; its potential for destroying the USAAF bomber formations would be untried. In

Above: The lack of long-range bombers forced recourse to makeshift measures. This combination aircraft, Mistel, was to be used in the last months of the war for a raid on the bridges over the River Oder. (The photograph shows a captured example bearing RAF roundels.)

the Führer's opinion its future role as a high-speed bombing machine justified the conversion which he had ordered.

It was at this time that fuel shortages played their part in diminishing the Luftwaffe. Fuel supplies, which had never ever been copious, were drying up as oil fields in eastern Europe were overrun by the Red Army. Fuel was now the key to survival. Luftwaffe official figures showed that only 30,000 tons of petrol would be available up to the end of March 1945. There would be no further supplies until the autumn. There was, therefore, insufficient fuel for the petrol-engined aircraft. There was now no shortage of aircraft and enough pilots were being trained. But the fuel which would improve their skills was not available for the purposes of training. Fuel had to be conserved for combat operations. As a result these men were sent in only half-trained, against the more numerous, better trained and battle tested crews of the Allied air forces. Small wonder then that 60 per cent of German pilots were lost in action during the last weeks of February 1945.

The lack of a forward planning perspective is encapsulated in one of the very few raids on a strategic target planned by the Luftwaffe. This was Operation 'Eisenhammer', a bombing mission to

be launched against three main generating stations, at Moscow and Gorki, whose output supplied electricity to the whole of western Russia. Destruction of the plant would paralyze Soviet war industry. In 1943, when the idea was first discussed, Operation 'Eisenhammer' would have had significance and a disastrous effect upon Soviet production. In March 1945, when the operation was finally authorized, it had neither any chance of success nor practical purpose.

To begin with the nearest point to the target from which the raid could be flown was more than 1,000 miles away. Adjustments to the flight course would need to be carried out on the flight to the target area, in order to delude the Russian air-controllers. The round trip was, therefore, in excess of 2,300 miles. There were no aircraft in service capable both of flying such a vast distance and carrying a bomb load sufficient to destroy the targets. The crack, special operations squadron, KG 200, whose men had been selected to fly this mission, were therefore trained on the 'Mistel' combination. This was a version of the pre-war, British invention of a pick-a-back, mother and daughter aircraft, linked together. The German variant used a fighter aircraft as the 'mother'. A Heinkel bomber, loaded with explosives and fuel was the 'daughter' and was fitted below the mother machine. For the duration of the flight to the target the pilot in the mother aircraft would draw upon the fuel supplies carried in the bomber. Close to the target he would launch the daughter machine and this would glide in a shallow dive on to the target. The fighter pilot would then head for his base relying on auxiliary tanks. Even with those extra supplies whether the pilots reached German territory would depend totally and absolutely upon favourable tail-winds. Lacking these the pilots would certainly come down in Russia. Even with tail-winds to help them the chance of landing in enemy territory was high. In the event the mission was never flown. An air raid by the American Air Force destroyed most of the Mistel combinations which had been gathered together and which were waiting for a combination of favourable tail-winds on both the outward and inward flights.

It can be seen from the outline of Operation 'Eisenhammer', that first and foremost, the failure to build a strategic air force had reduced the scope of Luftwaffe operations and forced the service to depend upon improvizations to overcome the basic defect in its structure. Secondly, there was a lack of a strategic planning group at senior level to select targets whose destruction would bring the best strategic results. Thirdly, there was no efficient economic planning group which would have ensured the thorough testing of the specially designed explosive produced for Operation 'Eisenhammer'. One of the Mistels which was destroyed in the American air raid was carrying a bomb filled with the super-explosive compound. It should have detonated with frightening force but it failed to explode and the filling burnt gently for days. The Luftwaffe showed its lack of forward-looking officers at every stage of its operations and at every Command level.

The Army was the principal arm of service yet even the equipment and weapons on issue to the military were, by and large, inferior to those in service with the armies of Germany's enemies. In the matter of artillery the most successful weapon, the 88mm FlaK/PaK gun, was only a variant of a piece of ordnance which had entered the service towards the end of the Great War. The German gunners had nothing to compare with the British 25pdr, the Red Army's 7.62cm anti-tank gun, the best in the world at that time, nor the US Long Tom. The German leaders concentrated instead upon super-heavy artillery, with all the defects of such weapons. Even in the matter of armoured fighting vehicles, those on the establishment of panzer divisions at the end of the war were little more than upgunned and uparmoured versions of those vehicles with which they had begun the first campaigns in 1939 and 1940. The Panzer VI, the Tiger, the Panther and the Panzer V were the exceptions. It was the handling of armour in the mass that gave the Germans the edge in panzer operations, just as it was in training and familiarity with their weapons that brought its soldiers the victories they had achieved. It was the skill of the operators that was significant, rather more than the inherently good characteristics or the numbers of weapons. That German scientists and ordnance experts did make great efforts to produce new weapons cannot be denied. But these remained tactical ones designed and manufactured to counter new Allied weapons and were not innovations. Once again, Hitler interfered, this time in the production of weapons for the army and we shall consider, later in this chapter, some of the expensive military projects with which he amused himself.

In the view of the leaders of Nazi Germany, the Reich had been at war from the first days of their government. They were well aware that their racial policies had antagonized the Western world. The Nazi party's political victory over the parties of the Left had made it the deadly foe of those outside the Reich who supported the Soviet system. German military victories in Spain had helped to bring Franco to power – another cause for condemnation from the Left. So far as the Nazi hierarchy was concerned on every front Germany was embattled. Soon the political and economic wars would be replaced by the military one.

For a nation at war there can be only the options of victory or defeat. There are no half-measures, no compromises. To achieve victory all the resources of the state must be ruthlessly exploited. During the Second World War such total conscription was applied in Britain and in America. In the Soviet Union the pressures of conscription upon citizen and industry already existed and needed only to be tightened in order to fight the German invasion. That same degree of conscription was not applied in Nazi Germany and, to quote Speer, 'It was one of the most surprising developments of the war that Hitler wished to spare the German people those trials and burdens which Churchill and Roosevelt had laid without hesitation upon their peoples.' In Britain the government exercised strict control over industry, laying down the objectives to be gained and limiting the profits which could be made. All the resources and energies of capitalist America were employed in war production. Russia had been subjected to pressures to industrialize since 1917. The same degree of official control was not exercised in Germany. Instead, it is true to say that in economic Germany the Nazi leaders had been guilty not merely of a dissipation of effort, nor of overestimating available war materials but, more seriously, of wasting the nation's limited manpower resources.

# THE PARTY'S STRUGGLE WITH THE INDUSTRIALISTS

In 1933 the National Socialist government confronted the capitalist industrialists. The Party had come to power on a manifesto which included, among its more extreme measures, state ownership of industry. But big business, whose leaders were opposed to political interference in their industry, had financed the Party in its time of struggle. Hitler still needed their help and could not yet act against them. The delay in carrying out this part of the Party manifesto, this hesitation *vis-à-vis* the capitalists, was condemned by the Party's left wing, represented principally by the SA. In the opinion of Roehm and his brown-shirt legions it was not financial backing but their fists and their aggression which had defeated the Red menace and had brought the Party to victory. Now that victory had been won they expected nothing less than the full socialist programme to be implemented. The capitalists had, however, a strong ally in the military, who also feared the SA, and a coming together of the weapon-makers and the weapon-bearers was a combination of power that Hitler was neither willing nor able to oppose in that first period of government. A direct confrontation had to be avoided with those powerful, conservative elements. If it was to be a choice of treating with the Reaction or the Brown Shirts, it was the SA who would be sacrificed in the Party's immediate interests. In the long term there would be revenge exacted against that coalition of capitalism and militarism that had dared to challenge the Führer's leadership. When the time was ripe he would divide his opponents, would meet them and crush them separately.

The choice of Schacht, an arch-capitalist, to head the Reichsbank seemed to the radical elements in the Party, to have strengthened the forces of reaction and to have betrayed the socialist principles for which they had fought. Hitler knew what he was doing in the case of Schacht. The task of the new man was to unite the

disparate elements of economic power and to produce a strong fiscal economy. In these tasks Schacht was brilliantly successful and under his control German industry prospered and profits in the steel-making industry, the sector of the economy with which we shall soon deal, rose from 32 to 65 million Reichsmarks between 1933 and 1935. There had been a general upturn in the world economy and Germany had benefited from that universal improvement. Not only capital profited; the people, too, prospered.

Hitler, to whom war was an instrument of policy, showed, by the reintroduction of military conscription together with the naval construction programme made possible by the Anglo-German Naval Treaty, the road he was set to follow. The Führer was aware that Germany was in no position to meet the financial burden of an arms programme and, at the same time, pay for the extensive programme of social reform which had been promised in the Party manifesto. He deter-

mined to take advantage of the growing prosperity in German society. There was rebuilding, construction and almost full employment. The citizens had money to spend on a vast range of consumer goods which were being produced. In that happy climate of prosperity Hitler calculated that the Volksgenossen would be prepared to be more than usually generous in the matter of donations to the Party's several welfare projects. To exploit the charitable feelings of the masses the Party increased the scope of its welfare appeals. Senior Nazi leaders were seen more often in the streets of their cities holding collecting boxes in their hands and inviting the Volksgenossen to give generously for the old, for the sick and for the poor at wintertime. The citizens responded and indeed so generously that their charity relieved the Party of much of its responsibility towards those in need. Indirectly and unknowingly the people of Germany helped to finance Hitler's programme of armament for war.

Left: The German industrialists who supported Hitler and who were outmanouevred by Goering in his role as head of the Four Year Plan. Below: Industry followed the armies. This factory sign bears the name Krupp; the location is Russia.

FRIED.KRUPP A.G.
NEUE MASCHINENFABRIK
KRAMATORSK.
TREUHANDBETRIEB
DER
B.H.O.M.B.H.BERLIN.

The intention to rearm produced from the Army commanders a demand for greater control by the state over industry and weapons production. The other arms of service, the Luftwaffe and the Kriegsmarine, made their own demands. Opposing the standpoint of the forces for central control and the limited profits which would result, stood Schacht and the industrialists hoping to maintain the capitalist viewpoint of major profit yield. The introduction of the Party's Four Year Plan in 1936, confounded the aspirations of all the interested parties. German economy was to be neither capitalist nor military but was to be brought under Party control. Leadership of the Plan was invested in Hermann Goering. As a Party comrade he would obediently and completely fulfill his Führer's orders and bring German economy into line with Party policy.

The first task for Goering was to obtain the acceptance of the reactionary elements to Party control of industry. His was to be a long and hard task despite the fact that he was, without doubt, the best choice for the job. Goering had charisma. As a fighter ace of the Great War he had been awarded the Pour le Mérite, Prussia's highest decoration. He had also formed the Gestapo, had organized the provincial police forces during his period of office as Prime Minister of Prussia, and had acted vigorously and effectively against Communist militants. He was, therefore, a brave and ruthless man but one with charm. He was a cultivated son of the minor aristocracy. On his magnificent estate he lived like a Renaissance prince and his visitors were entertained accordingly. They were flattered by being guests of a man so close to the centre of political power and Goering fed that flattery. But when ruthlessness was needed he showed how hard he could be. Eventually, through a combination of guile, ruthlessness and charm, he had isolated the opponents to the Party's economic plans and by 1938, the German iron and steel corporations were faced with the stark alternatives of submitting to state control under his direction or of withering away without the lucrative contracts that he alone could issue.

As leader of the Four Year Plan Goering was faced with the need to increase the production of German iron ore. He ordered the industry to prospect and to find new sources of the mineral. It was, as he saw it, vitally important to exploit fully all possible native sources. His orders met with opposition from the industrialists. Iron ore production, which in 1913 had produced 66 per cent of the nation's requirements, had fallen to 26 per cent by 1936. The industrialists' defence was a standard one of profit margins. Foreign ore was of a higher grade than German and it was cheaper in price.

Goering was not the man to tolerate arguments against his orders and he threatened with the compulsory purchase of their mineral rights those companies which would not prospect. Continuing this threatening stance Goering stressed, during a conference in March 1937, that if German private enterprise proved incapable of meeting the national demands for iron ore the state would take over and show them how this could be achieved. It was not, he explained, sound economics for Germany to run down her balance in foreign currencies by purchasing iron ore from abroad when this could be mined in the Reich. He stressed the danger of the Fatherland becoming too dependent upon foreign suppliers whose government by changing its policies, might adopt a hostile attitude towards the Reich and cut off supplies.

The setting up, in 1937, of a state steel concern, the Reichswerke Hermann Goering, was a direct threat to the capitalist sector. The industrialists argued that if they aceded to government demand and used expensive native iron ore their profits would be reduced and as a result there would be less money for prospecting or for the replacement of worn-out plant. The Party's position on the matter of state management produced from Schacht the bitter comment that German economy had now passed into the hands of amateurs. He feared, indeed, that the incompetence and extravagance of the Party men would bring about an inflation, out of which would come despair, food shortages, civil unrest and finally, Communism. The fears he expressed were very much those felt by other bourgeois elements.

Goering's demand for the industrialists to obey the Party's economic policies produced the response which such orders and such situations evoke. Senior industrialists and ministry officials, unwilling to change the system which had served them well, colluded in ways to circumvent the new regulations. Schacht, privy to the conspiracy, played his part by suggesting that the Reichsbank refuse to release funds to set up the State's Reichswerke Hermann Goering. The Party's response to such expressions of opposition was to counter-attack and to split the opposition. The firm of Krupps, the biggest of the steel combines, was secretly advised of the special and unique benefits which would be theirs if they collaborated with the state. The other major industrialists were made no such offer. Instead, each received a telegram stressing the dangers of intrigues which 'more and more take on the form of sabotage'. The final move to destroy the capitalist opposition was a telegram to Schwerin von Krosigk, the Finance Minister, warning him not to block the movement of money from the Reichsbank.

In view of such threats the revolt of the iron and steel masters collapsed. It was now a matter of firms acting individually and exploiting their position to gain lucrative contracts. Following the collapse of the opposition Goering set out to deal with major as well as minor companies and even individual people. Schacht, for example, was forced to resign and the Economics Ministry was then absorbed into the larger Four Year Plan organization.

The fears which the Ruhr steel barons had advanced that there would be insufficient capital to replace old plant were realized when a great proportion of their company profits were appropriated and used to develop other sectors of the industry – notably the Reichswerke. Goering's appetite for economic power was insatiable and the Reichswerke increased its capital holdings so that it could buy up other smaller companies. One of these was the gun-producing firm, Rheinmetall Borsig, a takeover which brought Goering out of general steel production and into the more specialized field of arms production.

Confiscation and expropriations in the iron and steel trades of Austria and Czechoslovakia, following the annexation of the one in 1938 and the occupation of the other during 1939, resulted in an expansion of state control of those industries. In the race to seize the spoils of those aggressions the private sector gained only the smaller and less profitable companies. Major concerns like Styrian Erzberg near Trofaich and the Skoda Works at Pilsen both passed to Goering. With the successful conclusion to the Polish campaign in 1939, the great factory complexes of western Poland also became part of the Reichswerke holdings as did the iron mills in Belgium when they too were put to work for Germany after the campaign in the west during 1940.

The final phrase of the preceding sentence is, perhaps, not strictly true. Although all these mines did produce for Germany their greatest asset was that they gave Goering personal power. This he exploited in the struggles for prestige which were carried on between the Party comrades. Hitler made no effort to intervene in this strife. His philosophy had always been that by dividing the opposition he could rule it and he tolerated conspiracies between his comrades so long as the conspiracy was not directed at him.

The policy of *divide et impera* served Hitler well, and below his isolated place as Führer the others of his immediate circle strove to obtain or to maintain their privileged positions. Thus Goering, as director of the Four Year plan, had created his own empire. Himmler had created another. Each senior Party comrade worked against the other comrades so as to become if not the *de jure* then certainly the *de facto* second man in the Reich. Bormann, who had no opportunity to create an industrial empire such as Goering's, and had no nations of slaves under his control as had Himmler, nevertheless, accrued a great deal of power for he made himself the sole channel through which all the other Party comrades had to go if they wished to see Hitler.

Himmler's SS fought for control of Germany's Intelligence services against the established Abwehr organization. The SS sought to become the paramount influence within the Nazi state and thus had its own private industrial and economic structure which worked less for the broad interests of the Reich and rather more for the narrow interests of the SS corporation and its leader, the Reichsführer Himmler. It was a shrewd policy. The more power that the Reichsführer gained, that much more influence was gained by his organizations and, therefore, by his subordinates. Goering's industrial organizations worked to gain him influence and this policy of personal prestige worked against the economic interests of the Fatherland. There was no control at the centre of power to wrest the privileges and the opportunities for exploitation from the hands of the individual Party leaders and place them at the disposition of the nation, except by Hitler, and he would not act.

Not in the matter of economic power alone, but in the lengths to which the senior Party officers went to preserve, or better still to increase, their individual empires in other spheres of influence, can be seen, in the creation of their own, personal Intelligence services outside of and often in conflict with the State body. Each 'Bonze' had his own economics department whose experts advised him on the best paintings and sculpture to loot. At a lower, more personal level, the Party leaders insisted upon all the privileges of rank and office being extended to them. Thus, the private railway trains which each had acquired, had had specially built or had looted from the railway systems of Europe, traversed Germany bearing the Nazi minister, his swollen entourage and, usually, a guard detachment of soldiers. It will be understood that these private facilities and the demands by the Party leaders for special priority treatment threw the whole railway timetable system into confusion and interrupted services to the general public as well as obstructing the flow of war supplies across Germany. Consideration for the Volksgenossen or the transport of weapons and materials were of less importance than the travelling comfort of the Party leaders.

Hitler received warnings from senior officers of the Transport Ministry, that such privileged transport as private trains damaged the railway system and with it the Reichs economy, but he would not act to forbid their use and Goering had ceased to exercise his authority in the economic sector. He spent more and more time in his Karinhall estate playing with the model railway network installed there and critics soon sneered that the only railway timetable in all the Reich that could be relied upon was the Reichsmarschall's toy one. Even when Hitler was advised during May 1942, that a shortage of rolling-stock and locomotives made it impossible to guarantee railway services in the Reich, the Führer still refused to act against his Party comrades in the matter of private trains.

If it is accepted that absolute power corrupts absolutely, it can be no surprise to learn how infamously corrupt certain Party officials became. A Party which carried the word 'Socialist' in its name should be seen to practise some socialist principles and those in authority must be the ones

to set the example. Many in the Nazi hierarchy did not lead the modest lives with which the ordinary working class citizens could identify, but surrouded themselves with every privilege. They ceased to be revolutionaries and had become voluptuaries. One example of this greed was in the matter of private trains another was the personal air raid shelter. Many Party officers down to Gauleiter level had these bunkers constructed for themselves and their families. Nor was it just air raid shelters that were built. Other types of luxury building continued to drain manpower and material resources. In Burg Veldenstein, one of Goering's castles, an underground complex of rooms was constructed each of which was appointed with specially designed furniture. The Reichsmarschall was the most flamboyant of the Party leaders and his excesses were the most notorious, but his demands were by no means unique. Even Hitler had builders working on his chalet in Berchtesgaden up to the end of the war.

Had such building requisitions and demands for such luxury been made in a peacetime economy they would still have been considered wasteful. For them to be insisted upon in wartime and at a stage in that war when the Fatherland was in crisis, shows an attitude that can only be described as a criminal offence against the German people into whose lives a drabness had come. Living standards began to fall in 1938 and continued thereafter. The Eintopfgericht, pilot rationing schemes which, all too soon, became a reality and the increasing use of substitutes for food and clothing were the daily burden of the Volksgenossen.

Goebbels was one Minister who refused to abuse his position and was indeed, fervent in his denunciations of luxury especially when this was indulged in by high Party comrades. At one stage of the war he organized an SA squad to smash the windows of a top Berlin restaurant which was one of Goering's favourite eating places. Demands by the owner for police protection against the SA thugs was turned down by Goebbels, the Gauleiter

Goebbels was one who realized that industry was not being run as ruthlessly as the situation demanded. Above right: At a Party function, Goebbels talks to some of industry's eminent men, including Heinkel (left) and Messerschmitt (centre). Right: As Minister of Propaganda, he also toured factories, making speeches to boost morale, committment to the war effort and production, as here in a Berlin tank factory.

of Berlin, on the grounds that such luxury was unseemly. The owner was advised to close his restaurant. Goering solved the problem. The restaurant was closed as a public eating place and re-opened immediately as a Luftwaffe officers' mess, using the same staff of chefs and waiters.

Not for the Volksgenossen the luxury of restaurants or private air raid shelters, but strict rationing and the cellars of private houses where they endured nights of bombardment. Not for them special teams to construct new buildings. Indeed, the vast amount of damage to workers' houses, the result of allied air raids, could not all be made good. The labourers who might have been used to carry out the urgent repairs were busy erecting new buildings for the Party or for its Ministers.

There was no central allocation of labour into industry and, as we have seen, no compulsion of women to take up war work. There was so great a labour shortage in Germany that some factories worked only one shift and that at a time when the workshops of Germany's enemies were working round the clock. At that time of national shortages the attitude of certain Gauleiters towards the work forces in the Gau was nothing less than feudal and many of these senior officers refused to allow THEIR factory workers to seek employment outside the Gau. This selfish attitude persisted even where they could offer no work but where employment was available in factories in neighbouring Gaue.

Nor were these German factories employed solely upon war production. At the beginning of 1942, the range and output of consumer goods for the home market was running only 3 per cent below that of peacetime and very little effort was being made to reduce this wasteful drain upon the nation's limited resources. Indeed, Eva Braun, prevailed upon Hitler to allow the cosmetics industry to continue production. As a concession to the needs of wartime Hitler did decree that there was to be no future production of new rollers for hairdressing salons and that rollers broken or damaged would have to be repaired and not replaced. It must have been a consolation to Grenadiers freezing on the steppes of Russia or thirsting in the deserts of Africa to know that there was electricity and staff for salons where German women could still have their hair permananently waved. It must have been comforting to learn that those women could then go on to sit

for hours over coffee and cakes in the cafehauser of the Fatherland rather than sweat over a lathe or a drilling machine producing weapons for the front. Nor did many of these women need to do their own housework. Sauckel, who had the task of finding workers for factories, ordered that the administrators in eastern territories supply, 'Four to five hundred thousand specially selected, healthy and capable girls to work in the Reich.' These would be used principally as house servants. It was a bizarre situation. The factories lacked personnel, but there were still more than a million housemaids in Germany. And those servants did the housework for their perfumed, coiffeured and cake-eating mistresses.

The greatest lack in the Party's organization of wartime industry was that there was no co-ordinator with ministerial powers. Lacking that authority which would have needed to be backed by the Führer, any Gauleiter could ignore orders that might be issued. Quite early in the war Goering ceased to be anything other than a cipher; idle, unable to make a decision, influenced by anyone who pandered to his desires or practises. Under Goering German industry declined dramatically. In 1940 and 1941, despite improvements in techniques and more efficient machinery, output had not reached those levels attained during the First World War. Comparing output during the first year of the war with Russia and that of autumn 1918, produces the statistic that only a quarter the number of guns and ammunition made in 1918 were produced in 1941/2. Even in 1944, production of ammunition was still below that of the Great War. The belief, even up to the autumn of 1941, was that the war would be won by short campaigns of limited duration, and Goering arranged his work-load upon that mistaken assessment. The decline in Germany's fortunes during 1942 suddenly brought to Hitler's attention the desperately poor state of Germany's economy. The Führer looked for a man who could replace Goering and found Albert Speer. He placed the authority for planning and control in the hands of his young and able architect.

Alber Speer, the architect who became Hitler's industrial mainspring.

# INDUSTRY UNDER SPEER

When Speer took over direction of the Reich's war effort, the situation he found was catastrophic. Goering had done nothing to overcome problems and on those few occasions when he had sought to intervene the result was chaos. He worked, in Speer's words, 'on the basis of impulsive inspiration' and did not think a problem through. He refused to accept the official US figures for aircraft production, probably convincing himself that the totals were a Yankee propaganda myth.

Speer found that steel production was stagnant and the percentage of that material reaching war factories had declined from 46.5 to 37.5 per cent (1942 figures). The demand for steel by non-essential, consumer industries was being met at the expense of the battle fronts. Direction of labour was the key to overcoming low production. The Minister reduced the number of workers in

the non-essential industries and gained, as a result, half a million people whom he could direct into arms production. The over-manning which had been a feature of German Home Front factories allowed that half million to be taken away without seriously impairing output. Speer had little further success in reducing either the numbers employed in or the waste of materials used on producing consumer goods. The Führer's fear that shortages would bring about Communism made him choose to divert men and materials into non-essential goods rather than risk revolution.

Hitler could not understand that there would be a manpower shortage of such proportion as to impair war production. Europe, he argued, had a population of more than 250 millions. From that vast number, surely there must be a work-force sufficient to produce all that Germany needed. He seemed not to accept that the use of forced labour, the result of round-ups in the occupied countries, had the inbuilt disadvantage of sabotage. Also, those foreign workers entering German industry were usually unskilled labourers and seldom the specialists that were required. In addition the accommodation given to workers was of a poor standard and there were too few interpreters to help resolve the personal problems which arose. It was also a fact that many young men were escaping to fight with the Resistance rather than work for Germany. The use of concentration-camp labour swelled the numbers which Speer demanded for the war factories, but did not significantly raise production.

Turning his attention to practical production matters, Speer was able to raise output through the use of practices not known in German industry. He introduced the concept of rationalization and of streamlining. He also set up discussion groups at every level from shop floor to management involving the workers in talks about the weapons they were making and inviting them to advance ideas on how production could be increased. Using worker involvement and other practices of consultation and discussion Speer inspired the work-force and output rose to double that which had formerly been achieved. But even

The low level of productive efficiency before Speer took over control of industry is shown in this photograph (above) of Ju 52 construction. By the end of the war, jet aircraft were being built in factories safe underground on a mass-production basis (left), and tanks were rolling along proper production lines (right).

its peak in 1944, did not meet the target figures that had been achieved during the Great War. To what extent the great bureaucratic machinery was responsible cannot be determined, but swollen ministerial staffs do not necessarily speed production. The Ministers, too, still empire building, refused to cut their staffs. The Weapons Department, for example, had ten times more personnel than had been employed during the First World War. Nor were the office workers in industry prepared to make sacrifices in the national effort and they refused categorically Speer's demand that they work the same hours as factory workers. He, himself, reduced the number of officials in his Ministry to just two hundred and eighteen.

Speer found that there were major problems connected with the shortage of strategic war materials: oil, wolfram, chrome, copper, ball-bearings and rubber. When wolfram supplies from Portugal were cut off, the only suitable and immediately available material capable of hardening steel for anti-tank shells was the stockpile of 1,200 tons of uranium. That material had been set aside for use in the building of a German atomic bomb (the anticipated target date was 1947). From 1943 onwards the uranium stock was steadily depleted to meet immediate demands. The synthetics industry had achieved excellent results and had helped to make good some of the shortfall in supplies. The best efforts of that industry could not, however, supply all that was needed when those nations upon whom war production depended halted deliveries. The proud prophecy of the *Das Reich* article in May 1940, was a hollow boast. With the sources of strategic materials cut off and with stockpiles of these materials dwindling it could only be a matter of time before the factories ceased production. The Führer then declared that fuel was the paramount need and to protect such remaining vital areas as the oil fields in Roumania and Hungary showed unusual resolution and a singleness of purpose. He mounted military offensives to regain those which had been lost or else protected those that were

Above: Speer with German workers who have just been presented with the Knight's Cross of the War Service Cross, awarded for outstanding work in industry.

unendangered on the ground but within range of the Allied bombers by encircling them with regiments of Flak artillery. During 1943, ten thousand Flak guns were being used for anti-aircraft and not for anti-tank purposes. One-third of the optical industry was employed in making sights for anti-aircraft guns and more than half of the electrical companies were producing anti-aircraft rangefinders and predictors.

Paradoxically, it was in those last months of the war that German war production reached its peak. The rationalization programme, conveyer belt techniques which turned out numbers of vehicles instead of fewer, almost hand-built machines, had all played their part in raising output. Allied air raids had not affected, significantly, the attendance of the work forces nor the effort they put into turning out weapons and equipment.

The strategic materials famine reached crisis point and during March 1945, Speer was forced to lay before the Führer the terrible ultimatum that supplies were only sufficient for a few more weeks of production. Then the war must end. That grim prediction seems to have fallen on deaf ears, for as late as 20 March, Hitler decided to initiate a programme of arms production. The notice given by Bormann and Goebbels, at the end of April that Red Army soldiers were only hundreds of yards away from the bunker, was the final proof that the end which had long been in sight had arrived.

In the warning that Speer gave to Hitler in March, he made no condemnation of the blatant waste of opportunities, of manpower, of materials, of intellect, of which Hitler stood guilty. Speer might have mentioned that Hitler's dilettante approach to problems had led him into a succession of extravagant developments such as over-weight tanks, super-heavy artillery of limited range and the rocket programme. The rocket programme was, in Speer's words, 'not only our largest but also our most wasteful failure'. Of the fields of mistaken endeavour let us consider briefly those areas of weapons development in which Hitler interfered; tanks, guns and rockets.

# THE FÜHRER'S MILITARY TOY PROJECTS

The perfect armoured fighting vehicle is one that combines speed, heavy armour and a powerful gun. The factors which govern the design and production of a tank are a careful balance of compromises. Any increase in the weight of defensive armour will demand a stronger engine. The new engine may be larger in size than the original and require more fuel. To meet these requirements might encroach upon the limited area inside a tank which can often only be met by reducing the crew space or the ammunition stowage area. The mounting of a bigger gun also raises the vehicle's weight and brings with it the need to produce a larger turret, which in turn will lead to another weight increase. Then, too, the design of the metal gun box, which is in essence all that a tank is, must be so simple that mass production is possible of parts that are easily machined and, finally, an assembly that is uncomplicated. It must be possible to replace damaged parts swiftly and under battlefield conditions.

Very few tanks of the Second World War met all these criteria. The Red Army's T-34 was one which did. Not one of the German armoured fighting vehicles did until the later marks of the Panther tank came into service. The fearful reputation of the German panzers was, as I have already said, due more to an ability to handle armour in the mass and not to an inherently good vehicle design or the numbers produced.

Hitler, who had been an infantry soldier during the Great War, did not allow that fact to inhibit him in discussions regarding the weight/power/gun ratio in panzer design. On 7 July 1941, he ordered AFVs to be uparmoured by fitting spaced metal plates to counter the effect of hollow-charge shells, even though the increase in weight brought about by these plates lowered the speed and restricted the manoeuvrability of the vehicles. Later that month he decided that the number of Panzer divisions was to be increased to thirty-six. The 1941 figures of total production of all types of armoured fighting vehicles was only 3,256. To have equipped the extra Panzer Divisions which the Führer required would have necessitated a threefold output. Hitler was not able to accept the simple economic fact that German industry was incapable of meeting the extravagant demands he made upon it.

German tank production had always been inhibited by the lack of a native-designed vehicle. Not until 1935 and the Panzer III did the German tank-building industry produce a design which was not dependent upon foreign inspiration. The Panzer III was selected as one of Germany's two projected types of battle tank. The Panzer IV was the other. One surprising fact was that no thought seemed to have been given to whether the contracted companies had experience of mass production. The only conclusion that can be drawn from this is that in the opinion of those in authority conveyer-belt techniques would not be required. It was obviously expected that standard production would be able to make good those losses in vehicles suffered in the projected series of short wars and that, therefore, there would be no need to go into mass production. Indeed, the Ford and Opel Car Companies, both with great knowledge and ability, were excluded from the panzer construction programme. As a consequence, until Speer's reorganization of production methods late in the war, panzers were almost hand-built by craftsmen.

Concurrent with Hitler's order for Speer to take over war production was the change in direction of the Führer's thinking. He decided, during 1943, that the overriding priority was for tanks and demanded them in large numbers. The demand could not be met for a variety of reasons; principally because industry had not been allowed to concentrate upon a small number of really good designs. During the short years from the advent of Hitler to the end of the war, no fewer than 230 different types of armoured fighting vehicle, including prototypes, were in service. Of those 94 were fighting tanks, ten were various sorts of tank hunters, 42 were armoured personnel carriers, 19 armoured reconnaissance vehicles, twelve were anti-aircraft tanks, ten were SP carriages, nine armoured gun and infantry carriages. The tragedy for the panzer force was that there were too many types, each of too short a run, and brought too late into service. The problem of providing spare parts for this wide variety of vehicles was enormous. Another factor which affected adversely German tank design was the decision taken before the war,

to halt the development of medium-weight vehicles in favour of light machines whose battlefield role would be reconnaissance. That High Command decision, pushed through at the insistence of the cavalry arm, was to have the most serious effect upon the application of armour in military operations.

On the matter of armament a discussion at the Berghof during May 1941, produced from Hitler the order to fit a 5cm gun into the Panzer IV. Only a month later this weapon was to be found to be ineffective against most Russian armoured vehicles. The experience gained by panzer units on the Eastern Front during the first months of battle, seem to have had a sobering effect upon the Führer's thoughts concerning panzer construction. On 14 November 1941, Keitel's memorandum to the Army High Command read, in part: 'The Führer sees it necessary, having regard to our over-stretched and limited production capacity, to restrict the tank programme regarding the various models and to determine future types . . . to ease the pressure upon the industrial and military drawing officers and to release engineers for other production, those current developments whose production would, in any case, soon have been terminated will now be discarded. The Führer demands a simplification and a limiting of the programme so that mass production can be more easily introduced . . .'

This just did not happen. Prestige struggles between Party bosses, together with the conflicting views of senior military commanders on the development of the panzer arm were sufficient to ensure that Hitler's clearly expressed wishes were totally ignored. The obsolete Panzer II was still being produced in 1944 and the 38(t) until 1942. Production of chassis of the latter vehicle, to be used as the carriages of SP guns, was actually increased after that year. A lecture given by Guderian on 9 March 1943, showed that the Panzer IV, which had been in service since 1936, was still Germany's principal battle tank and that it was planned for production to be continued at maximum rate throughout 1944/45. There were also conflicts within the political leadership in an effort to phase out the Panzer IV in favour of SP guns. Such divergences of opinion did not make for a progressive production programme.

The Panzer V (Panther), was one vehicle which showed the effect of Hitler's direct interference. Drawings and prototypes of tanks heavier than the

Panzer IV had been produced by several companies, but the Supreme Command had shown no interest, declaring that there was no need for them. The T-34 soon proved the OKW's declaration to be untrue. There was a need for a heavier German tank and that need was urgent. Production of the Panzer began during November 1942, and the first vehicles to be produced showed weaknesses resulting from rushed development. Guderian warned, during the lecture already referred to, that the fundamental faults in the Panzer V were of so serious a nature that the vehicle could not enter troop service until July 1943. Hitler was impatient to bring the new machine into service and actually postponed Operation 'Citadel', the German offensive against Kursk, in order to use the Panther as the principal weapon in that operation. The routes of advance to the Kursk battlefield were marked with broken-down Panthers whose transmissions had not been able to cope with the great weight they had to bear, and other tanks which had caught fire because of faults in the cooling system. The poor performance of the Panthers was acknowledged in a High Command memorandum which went on to highlight the fault of German production methods: '. . . The demand for replacement parts (for the Pv V) could not be met . . . without interfering with production of the vehicles . . .'

The Panzer VI (Tiger) went into production during August 1942 and ran until August 1944. Then, as a result of Germany's supply shortages, production was concentrated on the Panzer V; in the same number of man-hours two Panthers could be built but only one Tiger. A further reason was that the Tiger was not adaptable for the mass production which was essential. Hitler interfered with the tactical employment of the first Tigers to be built. He ordered the whole batch, eighty-three vehicles, to be put into action on the Leningrad Front. The Führer, some 500 miles removed from the battle and without knowledge of ground conditions, laid out the tactics for the whole operation. Every one of the Tigers was lost.

The introduction into services of the Mark II Tiger, or König Tiger, reflected the German tendency towards huge and heavily armed monster tanks, of which the Maus, was the outcome. During 1943, the Army Weapons Department initiated a new series of AFVs. The construction of these machines would be met by drawing upon the potential of companies which

had not hitherto been employed on tank production. Included in this, so called E series development, were plans for the Adler Company to produce a tank of more than 140 tons in weight.

The way in which the vehicle was contracted is indicative of Hitler's spontaneous actions in pursuit of a single, not necessarily desirable objective. The oral contract was given by Hitler to Professor Porsche on 8 June 1942. A model of the vehicle was shown to Hitler during January 1943, but there was little further development until August, when the first prototype was produced. In June 1944, the turret and gun were delivered for the prototype. Although work continued on the Maus it was never completed and did not enter service.

Even had the 188-ton monster gone into action the operations in which it could have taken part would have been limited. To have moved the Maus across country would have placed a strain upon the 1200hp engine. Vast quantities of petrol would have been used at a time when fuel supplies were fast diminishing. To have transported the Maus by rail would have required special wagons to be designed and constructed.

Hitler, in commissioning the Maus, had ordered the construction of a vehicle that was little more than a slow-moving pillbox. It could not move on made-up roads, nor cross bridges because of its great weight, and it had to be waterproofed so that it would not flood when crossing rivers, for one of the contractual conditions was that it had to be capable of submerging to a depth of eight metres. To construct one 25-ton Panzer IV batle tank, required among other things, 39,000kg of steel, 195kg of copper, 238kg of aluminium, 63kg of lead, 66kg of zink and 116kg of rubber. The amounts of material which were wasted in constructing the Maus were shockingly high and the use of so scarce a material as rubber can only be described as an abuse.

That the Führer could waste not just the material alone but the energies of a vast number of skilled technicians and a great amount of shop floor capacity is indicative of how the Reich's resources were dissipated. The Maus, with its 12.8cm gun was one area which Hitler had explored in his manic search for weapons of great size. Another was in the production of super-heavy guns of which the 60cm mortar, Karl or Thor, described below, is representative.

The rationale behind the construction of this monstrous piece of ordnance was the need to destroy armoured fortifications. Obviously, the Maginot Line was meant. The use of heavy-calibre artillery pieces to bombard such fixed targets was not new. Before the Great War the Austrian High Command had constructed 42cm weapons to destroy the Italian alpine fortresses. In those early days the aeroplane was an untried weapon. By 1935, however, flying-machines could cover vast distances to drop armour-piercing bombs on such static targets as fortresses. The day of the super-heavy gun being used to smash forts was over, and yet, upon Hitler's orders, the construction of such artillery pieces was pushed ahead.

The Karl mortar, named after General Karl Becker, the officer most closely associated with its development, bore the official description, Gerät 040. The first plans for its construction were laid at the end of 1935 and following certain technical discussions the Army Weapons Testing Department laid down guide-lines during the following year. The gun was to fire a 2,000kg shell over a distance of 3,000m. A fleet of nine heavy trucks would be required to transport the loads into which the 55-ton piece would be broken down. To assemble the gun ready for firing required six hours from the time of its arrival at the firing site.

As the time taken to set up the Karl was found to exceed the projected six hours, it was then proposed to make the gun self-propelled.

Further developments increased the range to 4,000m and the weight of the gun to 64,500kg. In March 1938, production of the final plans was ordered. Within six months an electrically driven, working model on a 1 to 10 scale had been produced. The proposed weight of the gun had now risen to 94,770kg and the range to 10,000m. First firing trials were carried out in the middle weeks of June 1939. By that time plans had been perfected for the gun to be transported as one piece on a specially constructed railway wagon. Consider: to bring a super-heavy piece of ordnance into action required, to begin with, a railway whose gauge was compatible. Those in Russia were not. Once in the target area, a curved spur line had to be constructed to take up the gun's recoil, ammunition had to be brought forward and a camp for the crews established. Thousands of men were employed to prepare the route and to serve the gun as well as to man the anti-aircraft batteries and the defence units.

And the end result of all that endeavour? One lucky shot during the fighting in the Crimea

Right: Wasted effort. The V1 and V2 rockets were the secret weapons with which, Goebbels promised the German people, the war would yet be won. Fake illustrations showing London ablaze from end to end were produced to show their effectiveness.

destroyed a strong Russian fortress. The other shells fired in that artillery bombardment created deep and symmetric holes in the earth. During the destruction of Warsaw, following the collapse of the Polish Home Army, the Karl destroyed blocks of houses and flats. Hitler had ordered the production of super-heavy artillery and the pieces had been created. For the excavation of a number of holes, one fort destroyed and some city buildings demolished, millions of man-hours had been misused, thousands of tons of steel wasted and confusion brought to the railway system as the ponderous artillery train crawled across Europe.

The last of the Führer's toys was the one which Speer had described as Germany's most costly and greatest mistake. The V weapons programme was based on the false premise that indiscriminate destruction would smash British morale. Experts, in pre-war years, had predicted that air raids would cause widespread destruction and produce panic among the civil population. Their predictions were incorrect. Both in Britain and then in Germany it was demonstrated that aerial bombing did not break morale but that suffering, paradoxically, stiffened it. Few reports came back to Hitler to show what damage was being caused by his V weapons and he based his hopes not upon facts but upon what he believed to be facts. Lacking accurate Intelligence he continued the random destruction and his actions can be seen not as the application of a thought-out strategy but as the wild blows of a blindfolded man in a dark room.

Into the production of rocket weapons the Führer poured money, men and materials. Upon these revolutionary projectiles he placed his hopes of finding the war-winning weapon. The rockets failed him just as the super-heavy guns had failed him. The Maus did not even have the chance to show that it too would have failed.

Had all Germany's wasted resources been controlled, used productively on proper weapons and employed correctly, the outcome of certain battles and campaigns might well have been different. Thanks to Goering's indolence, the Führer's interference and the fact that Speer was not given the power he needed until it was too late, industrial Germany was not the thundering forge of Vulcan which she had been thought to be. Instead she was an almost undirected economy, working along bourgeois lines, at a low, almost peacetime level of production and riddled with rivalries, inefficiency and corruption.

# III. MILITARY PERSPECTIVES

IN a game of chess, a logical, intellectual game, there comes a point where one player will cry 'checkmate'. That player has manoeuvred his opponent into a situation from which there is no escape. The opponent had been defeated. The game ends.

In warfare, too, a point is reached where logic dictates that the armies of one nation, having been defeated, must surrender. The war has ended. What happens, however, if the losing side refuses to accept that it has been beaten; where the loser, defying logic, continues to resist? In the game of chess it cannot happen. In warfare it should not, but frequently does occur.

The German General Staff which fought the Second World War was the most professional military network of any army. Through its trained, collective consciousness ran what was to them the inescapable logic of the military equation, that defeat results in a surrender which, in turn, equals the war's end. Those logical German minds were confounded when challenged in a 'checkmate' situation by opponents who acted illogically and did not capitulate.

The history of the Second World War affords a number of examples of the German perspective in a military context; I have selected two major and three minor examples. The two principal topics are Operation 'Sea Lion', the proposed invasion of Great Britain, and Operation 'Barbarossa', the attack upon the Soviet Union. The minor ones are the Balkan campaign of 1941 which links the two principal themes. The other choices are the Battle of Bastogne in December 1944 and the politico/ military delusion in 1945 that the British and Americans would ally themselves with Germany against Russia.

The rationale for my selection of the two principal themes is that the failure to appreciate the determination of Britain to resist led to a situation where an invasion operation could not be undertaken. That failure to invade led to the attack upon Russia, whose resources had been underestimated and whose determination to fight back had not been appreciated. In both cases logic had determined what the outcome must be. In both cases the logic was not followed and the outcome was different from that projected.

Between the two operations lies the Balkan campaign of 1941. The German High Command saw the Balkans as a flank open to British assault, and entered upon a war which had little purpose, given Britain's military weakness both at home and overseas. It is a widely held belief that the Balkan campaign so reduced the German military build-up that the time-table for 'Barbarossa' was irreparably compromised. This is not altogether true but it is accepted that the spring campaign during which Yugoslavia, Greece and Crete were subdued, must have had some effect upon German plans. With hindsight and seeing the situation from the German point of view, it would have been a better solution to have merely contained, until a more suitable time, the unrest in the Balkans and the British expedition which was sent to aid Greece. That containment would not have been of long duration for, from the German General Staff viewpoint, the war against the Soviet Union would be concluded within five months.

The German perspective of Russia was of a bloody dictatorship hated by its unfortunate citizens. The Red Army was the usual Russian human steam-roller, unwieldy, inflexible, badly armed and poorly led. Logically, there was no reason why the triumphant and invincible Wehrmacht should not achieve victory in twenty weeks over the dispirited and unthinking moujiks of the Red Army.

Above: Warlord and bodyguard. Hitler inspects Leibstandarte SS Adolf Hitler during the winter of 1939. This regiment, his personal bodyguard, had its origins in the street battles of the 1920s when the first SA detachments were organized in the early days of the Party to protect him while speaking in public.

A similar lack of understanding led to the German demand for the surrender of Bastogne during December 1944. The town was surrounded; its US garrison outnumbered and denied supplies. Logic dictated an honourable surrender as the only decision which General McAuliffe could make. His reply must have baffled the German High Command both for its semantic brevity as much as for its refusal to see the obvious logic of defeat.

The final choice I have made describes a belief held by a great many Germans, at senior command level as well as at the level of the common soldier. That belief was that we – the Western Allies – were fighting on the wrong side. That we and the Germans should be allied against the evils of Communist Russia. Dispassionate logic argued that Capitalism must inevitably fight Communism. The Wehrmacht had experience of war against the Soviets. What better ally could the well-equipped, capitalist West have than skilled, battle-hardened German veterans. Logically, we in the West must want our political system to triumph. Therefore, we must ally ourselves in the same crusade against Bolshevism that Europe had been fighting for four long years. The Germans – commanders and men – were not just astonished when the Western Allies refused to change sides, they were distressed at our illogicality, at our refusal to see the most obvious threat.

These then, are the examples of the German military perspective which I have chosen. Both at high and low, at official and at personal level, there are hundreds of others which might have been included. There was the logical demand of the negotiators of the armistice in Italy that no announcement of their act of betrayal be made until Berlin had fallen. When the Reichs capital surrendered this would betoken that the Führer was dead and therefore, that their oath of allegiance to him was no longer binding. History would not then judge them harshly as traitors to their Führer. Equally as logical to the Germans, but baffling to the Allies, was the rejection by Rear-Admiral Frisisus, the commander of Dunkirk, that he surrender the town. He refused to be included in the local act of surrender which embraced the German forces in North-West Europe and held out until the general surrender came into effect only a few days later. He could, thereby, claim that his forces had not been defeated.

Let us then enter the military arena of the Second World War and see that vast conflict through German eyes. The first campaign against Poland in September 1939, had produced the war for which the Führer had so ardently striven. The short successful enterprise had not only defeated the Poles but had brought Germans and Russians face to face across a common frontier which divided between the two aggressor nations the former sovereign territory of Poland.

In the early spring of 1940, German troops had crossed into Denmark and had occupied that country, while other formations had invaded Norway. While fighting was continuing to secure the Norwegian iron ore, other German armies had opened a massive assault in the West. Within weeks the Allied forces in North-West Europe had been shattered and their remnants, chiefly British and French units, were being evacuated by the Royal Navy from the flat and sandy beaches outside the port of Dunkirk.

Right: Oil tanks burn as Dunkirk is evacuated by the defeated British and French. (Imperial War Museum)

# THE PLAN TO INVADE GREAT BRITAIN

In his book, *The Longest Day*, Cornelius Ryan records the impression of a German artillery officer who saw, appearing out of the pre-dawn darkness and seemingly heading straight towards him, an armada of ships carrying the Allied invasion armies to the coast of Normandy.

Other Germans who faced the assaults of that momentous day have described how Allied ships had covered the sea; how their aircraft had filled the skies and how, from the bellies of giant landing craft masses of armoured fighting vehicles had rumbled ashore. The Allied invasion of Normandy had begun. The lodgement areas which the Anglo/US armies had gained on that first day were small; unlinked, separate, narrow and shallow beaches which, by last light on 6 June, extended inland no more than six miles. And yet those landings in Normandy were the result of years of planning, organization, construction and production by two industrial powers, America and Britain. The preparations had lasted four years and even after that length of time there were still some shortages of material, and some commanders who feared that the landings might not be successful, and that the fighting in France might degenerate into trench warfare. In the event the landings were successful and in time the Allied troops fought their way inland. The Americans had entered western Europe but the British had re-entered it. For them the wheel had turned full circle.

Four years earlier, on 4 June 1940, the Royal Navy had wound up Operation 'Dynamo', the

lifting off of the British Expeditionary Force from the beaches around Dunkirk. Now, in June 1944, the Western Allies had returned in a successful sea-borne invasion; an operation which the German armed forces at the height of their power had not dared to undertake against Britain.

The German armed forces at the height of their power, in the summer of 1940, were the mightiest in Europe. On 10 May, they had opened the campaign in the West, Operation 'Gelb' and although fewer in number than their adversaries and less lavishly equipped, had demonstrated a singleness of purpose and a flexibility in action that had brought them victory in fewer than six weeks. Within days of the opening of Operation 'Gelb' the Belgian and Dutch Armies had been so savaged that they posed no threat to the right flank of the German panzer formations as these thrust across northern France. The armies of France and Great Britain, which had been tied to conventional military methods, were outgeneral-led by the new tactics of blitzkrieg and were forced back towards the Channel port of Dunkirk. At 0900 hrs on 4 June, General Beaufrere formally surrendered the shattered perimeter around the town. Some thirty to forty thousand, mainly French troops, the last survivors of the allied units which had manned the defence line, marched into captivity. Their staunch defences had allowed the Royal Navy, backed by a mass of little ships, to carry out an enterprise which over the course of a few weeks, had taken off more than 365,000 French and British soldiers.

Those Germans who stood victorious on the beaches of Dunkirk must have been astounded at the scale of destruction which they saw around them. Out to sea, were the wrecks of large ships that had been bombed and sunk during the evacuation. Heavy lorries had been driven into the shallow sea and lined up side by side to form temporary moles from which the lines of patient men had embarked. Field guns stood empty and

useless with their breechblocks removed. Light anti-aircraft guns, which had defended the perimeter until ammunition ran out, still pointed their barrels to the sky but they no longer posed a threat. Their muzzles had been shattered to deny the guns to the enemy. Allied prisoners, dejected and exhausted by the fury of the fighting, sat in groups waiting for their captors to march them away. And everywhere were the dead. Some lay in the fields or on the sand, corrupting in the heat of the June day; others bobbed up and down, mingling with the flotsam in the gentle swell of the waves. Strewn across the beaches like discarded toys were rifles and machine-guns in vast numbers. And all that nightmare scene lay darkened, overshadowed by smoke which rose in black rolling clouds from the burning oil tanks.

German soldiers who had fought their way across Flanders and then through the Dunkirk perimeter to the beaches would have seen, during those weeks of battle, the vast material losses which the Allies had suffered. Those soldiers, remembering the devastation they had witnessed and seeing the shambles of the beaches, knew that their army had gained a great victory. It was unfortunate that the British Expeditionary Force had managed to escape to England, but it had left behind all its heavy equipment and lacking such weapons was almost defenceless.

A great victory had been gained in Flanders, but Walter von Reichenau, commander of Sixth Army, which had captured Dunkirk, warned his troops that the final battle had yet to be fought. In the event, that final battle, an offensive undertaken to destroy the Allied armies south of the Somme, was brief but decisive. An armistice, requested by Marshal Pétain, came into effect at 01.35 hrs on 25 June. The pride of the German Armed Forces at what they had achieved is evident in the Order of the Day issued by Fedor von Bock, commanding Army Group B. This announced that '. . . in 44 days the armies of this

Far left: The scene that met the German troops who arrived at the beaches of Dunkirk. Left: Those who did not get away. Allied prisoners await transportation to POW camps. The spectacular success of the campaign in the west enhanced Hitler's reputation in the eyes of the German people, who were convinced that this was the end of the war. (Imperial War Museum)

Army Group have stormed and captured the Dutch and Belgian fortifications; have forced the armies of both those States to capitulate and in a bloody battle have beaten decisively the Anglo-French armies . . .'

Any German viewing the destruction of the Allied forces and learning of the surrender of the nations of western Europe could not doubt that the war must be almost over. Only those islands lying off the European mainland – the British Isles – remained to be taken and their reduction could only be a matter of time. That the British must soon capitulate was a matter of inescapable logic. From northern Norway to the Pyrenees the whole of western Europe was now under German domination. Britain must see the hopelessness of her isolated position and must soon come to offer her own surrender. The British were defenceless. Their guns had been abandoned in Flanders. Their tank forces were no more than hulks rusting around Arras and St Valéry. The Royal Navy did not dare to leave the anchorage at Scapa Flow for fear of the Stukas and the aircraft of the Royal Air Force would soon fall like game birds to the fighter aces of the Luftwaffe. Soon the war would be over. A sharp lesson had been taught to every one of those nations that had sought to subjugate Germany, except one. That single exception was Britain and she could save herself the frightfulness of modern war by taking the Führer's proffered olive-branch.

In Berlin, so great was the confidence in an imminent, final victory that plans were drawn up to demobilize thirty-five army divisions. Now that it seemed Germany's military objectives had been achieved, it would be possible to release a large number of veteran soldiers. The war, however, was not over yet, not quite, and to hasten its end it had to be prosecuted with vigour in every sphere, military, civil, economic and, particularly, on the political front; one on which battles of a different nature are fought, but whose influence is as decisive as any military operation. One aspect of the political front is that which covers relations with other nations. These may be allies who will give unquestioning support and loyalty, or enemy nations whose downfall is the principal war aim. In the middle ground stand the neutral nations –

Left: 'This was not the way the Allies thought it would be.' The famous German propaganda picture showing discarded British and French helmets, intended to bring home to the Germans the magnitude of the defeat their armies had inflicted on the enemy.

those whom one hopes to enlist as allies or at least seeks to prevent from becoming active enemies.

In the summer of 1940, the nations of western Europe, seen from the German perspective, were either defeated or, in the case of Spain, benevolently neutral. In central and south-eastern Europe German influence was strong enough to keep the neutrals there kindly disposed towards the Reich. There remained only two countries: England, the principal enemy in the west, and in the east a political enemy, Russia. There might have been a case for the Reich authorities to have considered the USSR a benevolent neutral since a non-aggression treaty existed between her and Germany. In view of her ideological position, however, it was considered that Russia's benevolence might be of such short duration that it would be better to view her not as a friendly neutral but as a potential enemy.

During the summer of 1940, Hitler was faced with the threat which England and Russia represented to his new Europe. It was clear, if he was to avoid fighting a war on two fronts, he must first defeat one of these two nations before he could turn about and destroy the other. Logically, the initial strike should be against the weaker of the two. The first victim must, therefore, be England.

In the Führer's opinion, England's political pragmatism would compel her to surrender before she was invaded. There were stories of peace feelers being put out. It was reported, that Lloyd George and the Duke of Windsor had written to the King. According to information received, the British Ambassador in Washington had acknowledged that England had lost the war, and Joseph Kennedy, the US Ambassador to the Court of St James's, had written to President Roosevelt forecasting an imminent British defeat. Hitler hoped that from the reported reshuffle of the British Cabinet such politicians as Lloyd George, Halifax or Chamberlain would come to power, accept that Britain's position was hopeless and sue for peace. In General Halder's opinion the delay in calling together the Reichstag was due to Hitler's expectations born of that reported reshuffle.

The Führer's buoyant conviction that England's hopeless position must soon compel her surrender changed to frustrated annoyance when this did not happen immediately, and produced in him the conviction that he would have to invade and teach the English a lesson. This was not, he confessed, an operation that he wished to undertake, for in his opinion the destruction of the British homeland would lead to a collapse of the British Empire and the loss to the world of its stabilizing influence. Any invasion and battle for England would result in German blood being spilled and those who would benefit from that sacrifice and from the subsequent collapse of the British Empire would be two neutral and non-European nations, Japan and the United States of America.

Hitler's political reasoning accepted it as self-evident that England would work to bring Russia or America – both or either – into the war as her allies against Germany. America's present neutrality was not, in any case, impartial. Jewish interests in America, declared the Führer, made her hostile to the Third Reich and, therefore, benevolently inclined towards Britain. It was equally clear that Russia would not want to see Germany as the dominant power in Europe and that Britain might reach an accommodation with the Soviets by making concessions to Russian colonial expansion in the Middle East; probably in Iran. Another factor was that although the Russian leaders might continue publicly to proclaim their peaceful intentions towards Germany, in their private conversations they spoke with another voice. Kalinin, the Soviet President, for example, had discussed with the Yugoslav Ambassador, the possibility of a war with Germany.

Then there were those in German political circles who reinforced Hitler's suspicion of Russia by arguing that the Reich should undertake an actively hostile policy against the USSR. Russia so they claimed, was making territorial gains in eastern and south-eastern Europe at Germany's expense. The whole political attention of the Reich, so these factions argued, was absorbed in the war with England, but Russia was the more powerful, more dangerous enemy with a common land frontier across which she could attack Germany. Under the influence of these people, Hitler than considered the advantages that might be gained from fighting a lightning campaign in the east. Once that was successfully concluded, there would come the time to deal with England.

The Führer reasoned there would be no danger from the English while the putative war with Russia was being fought, for England was powerless to make a land attack against Germany. As a weapon which would weaken England still more, Admiral Doenitz had forecast, that by the spring of 1941, 120 U-boats would be in service and that these would be able to strangle the enemy by sea blockade as efficiently as the Luftwaffe would be able to bomb and destroy the industries of Britain from the air. With Soviet Russia defeated by the autumn of 1941; with the U-boat blockade tightening its grip on England, and with her centres of production smashed by German air power, a sea-borne assault might not be required.

But the war against Russia could not be launched in the summer of 1940 as Hitler demanded. His senior military commanders told him that as they had had no directive from him for such an undertaking, no detailed plans had been prepared, nor had any military preparations been put in hand. And even supposing, as they pointed out, that planning and preparation were begun immediately and pushed ahead with all speed, the time expended in completing just the basic preparations would leave only a few weeks of campaigning weather before the onset of winter. In that late summer of 1940 Hitler was in a dilemma. He was unwilling to invade Britain and unable to attack Russia. Yet he must do something. Germany must retain in her hands the military and political initiative. The Führer baulked in his intention to make war with Russia, was forced to turn his attentions westwards once again. Overcoming the reluctance he felt, he issued a Directive for an invasion of England to be planned.

A number of documents already existed concerning such an undertaking. There were minutes of meetings and personal briefings on which the staffs could work. Major powers produce, even in times of peace, plans for war against their neighbours and, in that context, it follows that the German High Commands must have had some plans for the invasion of Great Britain, probably prepared in the days of the German Empire and merely updated as necessity demanded. There was too a more recent document of November 1939; a study prepared by the Directorate of Naval Operations on the feasibility of landing troops in England. The first section of that report concluded that the detection of, and attacks upon, the invasion fleet by enemy aircraft would rob the aggressors of the valuable element of surprise. Therefore, such an operation could only succeed and crippling losses in both men and matériel be avoided, if the attacker gained and held both naval and air superiority.

Moving on to an examination of ports at which the invading host could take ship, the writer produced a number of options. When it is remembered that the memorandum was written in 1939, it shows an unusual degree of clairvoyance for him to have included not only Amsterdam and Rotterdam but also the French Channel ports as embarkation areas from which the German Army could undertake an assault against Britain. Any attack, the writer stressed, would have to be made on England's east coast, for the problem of supply as well as the low speeds of the naval convoys, ruled out any longer sea voyage, such as one to the British west coast or even Ireland. It was essential for the landing areas to be as close as possible to the embarkation ports.

In view of the inclusion of Dutch and French ports, it is surprising that the writer did not suggest an invasion to be mounted against the south-eastern coastal area of England – Kent and Sussex. Instead he proposed as landing points, areas between the Tyne and the Thames, despite the disadvantages of small harbours and the lack of protected anchorages against high winds.

To summarize his arguments, the writer concluded that if the situation were to arise where it was possible to siphon off German military strength from the Western Front and make it available for other military operations, an invasion across the North Sea against Britain might be one way of breaking a military stalemate in Flanders and of forcing the enemies of the Reich to sue for peace.

Another document concerned with an invasion of Great Britain was 'Studie Nordwest' also produced during November 1939, and by a Major Stieff of the General Staff. His proposal also foresaw a landing in East Anglia, on the east coast of Britain, followed by a scythe stroke of seventeen divisions aimed at capturing London from the north. Stieff's memorandum was submitted to the navy and to the Luftwaffe High Commands for comment.

The navy's reply was not long in coming. Behind the formally expressed explanations one can detect the raised eyebrows of the Naval Operations Staff at the ignorance of the landlubber who had penned this document. There was no way, declared the naval authors, to guarantee that the minefields which had been swept would remain cleared, for it was obvious that the enemy would immediately relay them. The navy estimate was that 400 vessels was the absolute minimum number required to carry just the first assault wave and that figure did not include the mass of tugs, ferries and other ancillary craft which would have to ply between the troop transports and the shore. To assemble a 400-ship convoy to carry the assault wave would require not less than 36 hours to complete. There were, the authors pointed out acidly, the problems of passing the ships one by one through the lock gates of the Kaiser Wilhelm Canal out of the Baltic and into the North Sea.

The naval authors pointed out that there were no specialized landing barges available and that any programme to build such craft could only be undertaken at the expense of U-boat construction. Furthermore, such a programme would take a year to complete. The Navy also needed to know who would destroy the heavy guns which were mounted on the British east coast; naval armament could not be used against such targets. Nor was the German Navy strong enough to prevent the Royal Navy from launching attacks against the German armada during the operation. It would not be able to take part in deception operations as the army author had proposed, for to undertake these must inevitably reduce not only the number of ships available to carry the assault wave but also, of course, the size of their escort.

The Naval Operations Staff stressed that there could be no guarantee of a successful co-operation between the Kriegsmarine and the Luftwaffe during the sea crossing because of the problems of poor visibility leading to failure to identify correctly own or enemy forces. Finally, almost triumphantly one feels, the naval authors concluded by stressing the problems of seamanship and navigation in winter weather and proposed the postponement of an invasion until the summer of 1940. The negative reaction of the navy was reinforced when the Luftwaffe responded in a single-page, three-paragraph rejection. The author of the document laid down as an essential factor, the gaining of air superiority. Any invasion, in the opinion of the Luftwaffe author, should only be undertaken as the final act in a war which was being successfully prosecuted.

The army's proposals of December 1939, outlined in 'Studie Nordwest', and which had been turned down by both the Kriegsmarine and the Luftwaffe; were among the proposals reappraised in the summer of 1940 in the light of the strategic situation which then obtained. On 25 June, the day on which the armistice with the French came into effect, Major von Falkenstein, an officer on

the Luftwaffe General Staff at Führer Headquarters, minuted his superior, Colonel von Waldau. '. . . Plans for a crossing of the Channel are to be laid before the Führer within the course of the next few days . . .' and Halder's diary entry for 30 June says that England might need another demonstration of German military force before she surrendered. Not yet aware that the Führer had already begun to consider a campaign against Russia, German service commanders came to accept that the last act of the war in the west would have to be played out. Britain would have to be invaded.

Commanders about to undertake a military operation of any size must have a clearly defined objective, must know the routes by which their forces are to reach the target area, must be assured that reinforcement and supplies will flow and must be aware of the enemy's strength. With these factors known, more detailed planning can begin.

The German Army commanders who stood triumphant on the cliffs of Cap Gris Nez, in June 1940, could see shining in the bright sunlight the white cliffs of Dover. Over the sea and, seemingly, not too distant lay their next objective. England was certain to be the next military target. On the assumption that an intelligent anticipation of orders pays dividends, commanders at every level began to make their plans and to undertake the training of their men.

At lowest level, that of the regiment, this training was begun very much out of a need to keep the soldiers employed, for there was little to divert them in the closed and shuttered seaside towns of the French Channel coast. Then, too, there is a limit to the amount of time that fit young men want to spend sitting about on shingle beaches and sightseeing quickly palls. It was still too soon for canteens to have been opened, nor had entertainment for the troops been organized. Drill parades were unsuitable for veteran soldiers, but training to strengthen the body, to sharpen reflexes and to prepare for new battles – that was productive and was accepted by the troops.

The Department of Army High Command which dealt with Western foreign forces issued an Intelligence Appreciation of the British Army. This began by detailing the military units that had been available in the United Kingdom at the outbreak of war and estimated that fourteen divisions had served in France during the 1940 campaign.

These had then been evacuated to England, 'having suffered', in the words of that Paper, 'very heavy casualties and the total loss of all their vehicles, together with most of their artillery and anti-tank weapons'.

These remnants were not fit for active service operations and thus there remained for the defence of the United Kingdom, only eleven infantry divisions of the Territorial Army at full strength, together with a single armoured division. A further eight Territorial divisions were available but these were understrength and not completely equipped. Excepting the local defence units, which were considered to be of doubtful value, the only other fully combatant groups were those detachments of the French, Belgian, Polish and Czech Armies which had been evacuated from the Continent to Great Britain.

German Intelligence officers located the bulk of the available military forces in Great Britain in the south-eastern corner of the country and forecast that in the event of invasion reinforcements could not be brought down to that area by road transport, for this had all been lost in Flanders. The British would have to rely upon the railways to move the divisions, or else the units would have to march to the invasion areas.

The picture thus presented to the German High Command was of an enemy army, the great mass of which was made up of untried Territorial infantry divisions backed by the shattered remnants of the defeated Expeditionary Force. The enemy's largely immobile host had but one single armoured division to strengthen it.

Armed with that report the German Army High Command had its next objective and knew the strength of the enemy forces which would defend it. Now it was necessary to determine upon which areas of the enemy coast the landings would take place, how the assault divisions would be brought to the landing areas and how they would be reinforced and supplied. It was the failure of the German army and navy to resolve these points that caused Operation 'Sealion' to be aborted, and changed, thereby, the direction of German strategy.

Agreement between the navy and the army was absolutely essential if the invasion was to succeed. Without full mutual support and absolute co-operation between those two services, 'Sealion' had no chance at all. The navy and the army both had major tasks to undertake. The former to

ensure the crossings and the supply structure and the latter to destroy the enemy in the field. Of the three fighting services the Luftwaffe had a minor role – or so it seemed at the outset. The task of the fighter squadrons was to smash the Royal Air Force in a fast and destructive operation. This ought not to take long for the Luftwaffe had achieved air superiority very quickly in both the Polish and the Western campaigns. To destroy an RAF which was numerically inferior and poorly trained – so the Intelligence officers thought – should be a short, simple and straightforward undertaking. Once the Luftwaffe had gained command of the air, the army, under the escort of the navy, would cross the Channel and land in England. On British airfields the Luftwaffe squadrons would take up the task of being the long-range, fast and flexible artillery component of the ground troops.

In the opinion of the Supreme Command the Luftwaffe could undertake its destructive task without delay. It was to be expected that during the time it took to drive the RAF from the skies and to win the battle for Britain, the divergent views of the army and the navy concerning 'Sealion' should have been, if not completely resolved, then at least narrowed. What were these divergent views, the failure to reconcile which caused the invasion to be postponed and then abandoned? To the army the operation was a variant of a standard river crossing; nothing more, and in the opinion of its planners it ought to be a simple matter for the navy to collect the troop transports ready to convey the soldiers on their short sea journey. The familiar stages of a river-crossing operation would then be followed. The troops would move to their embarkation areas, embark, cross the water, debark, establish a beachhead, receive reinforcement and, once firmly established, would move out and defeat the enemy.

In order to split the British forces OKH proposed an invasion front extending from Ramsgate to Lyme Bay. Originally nine, later reduced to seven, infantry divisions would make the initial landings along this expanse of south-eastern England running from Kent to Dorset. Those areas in which the assault units made the greatest progress would be quickly and massively reinforced, and against these moves the British High Command would, so it was believed at OKH, react very slowly. Then, once the major panzer units

THE PLAN TO INVADE GREAT BRITAIN

had landed and were in action the British would be totally defeated in a blitzkrieg operation. The army plan was a simple one, leaving so OKH believed, only a few tactical problems to be solved. Little did the army leaders know the morass which would soon engulf them in myriad small, but important, details inseparable from the tasks of assembling and preparing a seaborne landing of the scale which they proposed.

The Kriegsmarine, was opposed to 'Sealion'. The chief objection was the extent of the landing area; it was far too wide. According to the Directorate of Naval Operations the service did not have ships enough to protect the invasion armada or the subsequent reinforcement and also supply convoys across an area as vast as that which OKH proposed. A drastic reduction in the size of the bridgehead was necessary before the navy would even consider detailed planning of its part of the operation. Kriegsmarine proposed a narrow beachhead between Folkestone and Beachy Head, on which three divisions would be debarked. Such a width of front was, in the navy's view, a realizable target well within its competence. The second point was that there were no specialized landing craft, nor could any be constructed without loss to German war production in other sectors. Then there were points of a tactical nature such as the hour on which the assault would go in. The whole operation was risky and the navy was adamant. Unless the German forces had aerial superiority 'Sealion' stood absolutely no chance of success.

The naval planners were told that the divisions of the first wave would be accompanied by thousands of horses, for the German Army was still very dependent upon cattle to tow its carts and guns. Then, there were the motor vehicles on the establishment of each assault division and in addition to those, the first wave infantry would be taking in with them, 26,000 bicycles and 2,600 mortars, as well as various types of light artillery. Rations, ammunition, fuel and other supplies had also to be lifted. The navy pointed out, seemingly in vain, that every piece of superfluous equipment reduced the number of men who could be shipped in the first wave.

Among those officers who was anticipating intelligently the course of future operations, was Generalmajor Alfred Jodl, Chief of the Wehrmacht Führungs Stab. As early as 30 June, he had written in an *aide-mémoire* that an attack upon

Great Britain had to be the next logical step. To Jodl final victory for Germany was only a matter of time, for Britain could undertake no offensive operations against the Reich, and being weak, could not counter any course of action which Germany might choose. If political pressure did not compel her to sue for peace, Britain's will to resist would have to be broken by force, but in his opinion, a military landing should only be carried out as a sort of *coup de grâce* to a country which had been garrotted by the Kriegsmarine and whose industries had been destroyed by the Luftwaffe's aerial bombardment.

In his *aide-mémoire* Jodl thought that the earliest date on which the death thrust could go in was the end of August or the beginning of September. The confidence expressed in such an estimate is staggering. It was the opinion of this senior commander that within eight to nine weeks from the date of committing his proposals to paper, the Luftwaffe would have gained ascendancy in the air. The navy would have blockaded British industry into ruin and brought together the fleet of transport vessels sufficient to convey the invading armies; foot, guns, horse and armour. That the army would have worked out the necessary logistics, completed its plans and undertaken its training. All that in a maximum of nine weeks – 63 days.

Opposition from the British would come, Jodl thought, from about twenty divisions. It would require, therefore, a minimum of thirty divisions to overcome them. The General would not say how long military operations on the British mainland might last, but it was evident he did not think that these would be of long duration. The enthusiasm which Jodl felt at the end of June was replaced by a more sober note on 12 July. The opening sentence of his formal Paper, 'First thoughts on a landing in England', sets the tone of the document. 'The landing will be difficult.' Since Britain had naval superiority the crossing from France to England would have to be made across the narrowest point of the Channel, where German air superiority – not yet gained but taken for granted by Jodl – would redress the balance.

There was no more talk of a death thrust to a weakened England. Rather there was recognition that the British ground forces would be ready and waiting for the Germans to land for it could be no secret to them that an invasion fleet was being prepared. Any analysis of aerial reconnaissance

# EXTRACTS FROM SIXTEENTH ARMY OPERATIONAL ORDERS

**SECRET**

Sixteenth Army

Provisional directives for the carrying out of Operation 'Sealion'

(1)  The Supreme Commander of the Armed Forces has ordered preparations to be undertaken with the aim of making an armed landing in England. These preparations will be completed in time for the operation to be carried out after 20 September.

(2)  The enemy's situation. . . .

(3)  The Army's task, in conjunction with the Navy and the Luftwaffe, is to land strong forces in southern England, to smash the English Army, to capture London and other areas of England as the situation develops.

(4)  Army Group A will carry out the Army's part of the operation.

(5)  The operation has the code-name 'Sealion'. The following are provisional dates.
   (a) Earliest date for the sailing of the transport fleets: 20.9 S-Day (the day of the landings) 21.9
   (b) The order to begin the operation will be issued on S-Day minus 10, that is by 11.9 at the earliest.
   (c) The firm date of S-Day and of S-Hour (that is the time of the first landings) will be given by S minus 3 at the latest.

(6)  The task of 16th Army is to depart the area Rotterdam – Calais (both places inclusive) and to land on the English coast in the area Folkestone – St Leonards (inclusive).
   The Army will throw back the enemy coastal defence forces, and will defeat his reserves hurrying to the battle. Using the Divisions of the 1st Wave, a bridgehead will be established along a general line Canterbury – the course of the Great Stour – Ashford – Tenterden – Etchingham. These Divisions will then dig in along that general line and go over to the defence. With the arrival of other forces, in 8 to 10 days, the Army will then continue the attack so as to reach the heights to the south of London.
   The Main of 9th Army will land between St Leonards (exclusively) and Eastbourne, with elements on either side of Brighton and will establish a bridgehead along a general line Heathfield – Uckfield – Burgess Hill – and to the north of Worthing. 9th Army will go over to the assault with its right wing in the direction of East Grinstead.

(7)  Boundary lines. . . .

(8)  The first wave will consist of:
XIII Corps with 17th and 35th Divisions and Corps troops.
VII Corps with 7th and 1st Mountain Divisions and Corps troops.

(9)  XIII Corps first wave troops will depart from Ostend and Dunkirk and force a landing between Folkestone and Greatstone-on-Sea (Landing area B). . . .
   Corps task is to establish a bridgehead along the general line, Canterbury – course of the Great Stour – Ashford – Biddenden – to the south of Sissinghurst. Simultaneously Corps will move from its beachhead to the west of Folkestone and using mobile force will take the towns and harbours of Folkestone and Dover from the west and the north. It will then win the coastal area Ramsgate – Deal and will occupy it. Moving out from the coastal area Ramsgate – Deal, touch will be gained with the bridgehead positions near Canterbury – Chilham. A regiment of paratroops will be dropped to the northwest of Dover to support the assault upon Dover.

(10)  VII Corps first wave will depart Calais and force a landing on the coastal section between Greatstone-on-Sea and St Leonards (Inclusive) (Landing area C). . . .
   Corps has the task of establishing a bridgehead along a general line, south of Sissinghurst – Cranbrook – Flimwell – west of Burwash. Touch will be gained and kept with the most advanced elements of 9th Army (XXXVIII Corps' 34th Division).

(11)  The general defence line after the first landings. . . .
   The Corps must be prepared to hold their positions for a minimum of 8 days without further reinforcement or supplies of food, ammunition, or fuel. They will defend their positions against the counter-attacks of the enemy's strategic reserve – which will include tanks . . . Mines will be laid and minefield traces prepared so that the mines which have been laid can be lifted quickly. . . .

(12)  The first wave of XIII Corps will have under command:
Panzer Detachment (submersible) B – Ostend
Panzer Detachment (submersible) D (minus one Company) – Dunkirk.
With VII Corps: Panzer Detachment (submersible) A – Calais

The submersible panzer detachments are to be deployed among the advanced units so that they reach the coast simultaneously. . . .

(13)  It is proposed to equip the advance units with a number of flame-throwing panzer from 100th (Flame-throwing) Panzer Battalion, in order to give the assault detachments greater support when landing. . . .

(14)  The second wave will consist of:
V Corps with 12th and 30th Divisions and Corps troops.
XXXXI Corps with 8th and 10th Panzer Divisions, 29th (Motorized) Division, the SS Leibstandarte Adolph Hitler and the Grossdeutschland Infantry Regiment.

(15)  The third wave will follow with:
IV Corps with 24th and 58th Divisions and Corps troops
XXXXII Corps with 45th and 164th Division and Corps troops.

(16)  Execution:
   (a) The course of the operation will depend upon a number of unforeseen factors. Preparations for the embarkation, crossing and first landings must be so flexible that any changes can be acted upon by the commanders without a loss of time. . . .
   (b) A pre-condition for the undertaking is that the Luftwaffe has gained superiority in the air; that the Luftwaffe has cleared channels through the minefields and that, in conjunction with the Luftwaffe, it is protecting the flanks of the assault. . . .

The Army's part in the operation begins with the
...ing....
...) Command during embarkation and crossing....

...) Organization and tasks of the Navy.

...8) The provisional time of landing is DAYBREAK. The
...eather conditions, the need to deceive the enemy; delays
...other reasons may make it necessary for the landings
...take place in full daylight.

(19) Shipping space.

(20) Times.... Moving up to embarkation areas....

(21) Defensive fire and use of smoke. In addition to the
fire support which the Navy will supply by special
'Artillery Carriers' (Naval ships with 15cm guns) all tugs
and ferries will be fitted out with weapons of calibres
between 4.7 and 7.5cm.

Fire support.
    During the crossing and the landing there will
possibly be support from:
    (a) During the crossing....
    (b) During the landings.
        Minimal support from artillery which has been
        landed.
        The guns of the minesweeping and artillery
        carriers.
        The 7.5cm guns of the tugs and ferries.
        From Stukas.
        Through the increasing firepower of successive
        waves of artillery.
        From the moment that the enemy on the coast
realizes our intentions he must be bombarded from every
available weapon and smothered with as much metal as
possible. Even if the supporting fire from the ships is not
accurate, the hail of projectiles will force the enemy to
take cover at the decisive time when the landings take
place....

    (22) Engineer tasks....

    (23) Anti-gas....

    (24) Railways....

    (25) The Luftwaffe.
      (a) Sixteenth Army will enjoy the collaboration of
Luftflotte 2. Under command of Luftflotte 2 are: II
Fliegerkorps, VIII Fliegerkorps, II FlaK Corps.
      (b) Air support during the initial landings is under the
command of VIII Fliegerkorps (General Freiherr von
Richthofen).
      (c) The tasks of II Fliegerkorps (Colonel General
Loerzer) are, in the first stages, to attack the enemy's
rear areas....
      (d) The employment of VIII Fliegerkorps (Stukas) will
be determined by the Army in conjunction with Corps....
      (e) ....
      (f) It is intended that the main bombing effort will be
against Dover and Folkestone....
      (g) FlaK units....

    (26) Headquarters in England....

    (27) Maps....

    (28) Location of Army HQ in France....

Appendices
1.   Enemy Forces.
2.   The defensive position Canterbury – Burwash.
3.   Organization and tasks of the Navy.
4.   Signals network.

# 'SEALION': 1940

## LUFTFLOTTE 2

| | | |
|---|---|---|
| Fliegerkorps I: | Kampfgeschwader I | (He III) |
| | Kampfgeschwader 76: | (Ju 88 and Do 17) |
| Fliegerkorps II: | Kampfgeschwader II | (Do 17) |
| | Kampfgeschwader III | (Do 17) |
| | Kampfgeschwader 53 | (He III and Ju 87) |
| Fliegerkorps IX: | Kampfgeschwader 4 | (He III and Ju 88) |
| | Kampfgeschwader 100 | (He III) |
| JAFU 2: | Jagdgeschwader 3 | (Me 109) |
| | Jagdgeschwader 26 | (Me 109) |
| | Jagdgeschwader 51 | (Me 109) |
| | Jagdgeschwader 52 | (Me 109) |
| | Jagdgeschwader 54 | (Me 109) |
| | Zerstörergeschwader 26 | (Me 110) |
| | Zerstörergeschwader 76 | (Me 110) |

# ORDERS

From Luftflotte 2 for the use of
7th Airborne Division (Fliegerdivision 7)
during Operation 'Sealion'.

18 September 1940

Secret
(1)   The 7th Fliegerdivision will take and occupy as
quickly as possible, the high ground to the north and
northwest of Folkestone, with the following intentions.
    (a) To open the crossings across the canal around and
to the west of Hythe, in front of 16th Army's right wing.
    (b) To secure the landings against enemy thrusts from
a north or northwesterly direction, particularly by
blocking the roads leading from Canterbury towards
Folkestone.
    (c) During the course of operations it is anticipated
that part of 7th Division may be used in support of the
capture of Dover.
(2)   Once it has landed in enemy territory the 7th
Fliegerdivision will come under the command of 16th
Army.
    Details of the time and place of missions to be
carried out will be issued by 16th Army.
(3)   Details of fighter cover.
(4)   The movement of 7th Division to 'lift off'
airfields....
(5)   Orders for the air transport groups to reassemble
after the drops have been made.

photographs showing shipping concentrations in the harbours of France, Belgium and Holland, would indicate troop numbers, would enable convoy speeds to be estimated and would locate those areas along the south-east coast where the invading troops might be likely to land. The German seaborne assault, whenever it was undertaken, would not have the important element of surprise.

Four days after Jodl had written his 'First thoughts . . .', Hitler produced Directive No. 16, entitled 'Regarding the preparations for a landing operation in England.' This accepted the Army High Command's operational plan and ordered the army to make a surprise assault upon the south-east coast of England, along an area extending from Ramsgate to a point west of the Isle of Wight. The Luftwaffe would operate as flying artillery and the navy would perform the tasks usually undertaken by army assault engineers; that of ferrymen to the first wave troops.

Army Group A would mount the operation with two armies, of which Sixteenth would form the right wing of the assault and Ninth the left wing. The Divisions of Army Group A were to establish a bridgehead and advance some distance inland and seize tactically important high ground.

Mention was made earlier of Generalmajor Jodl's estimate of nine weeks to plan, prepare and carry out the invasion of England. In this optimism Jodl was not alone; indeed the diary entries, reports and letters of most senior commanders express the same conviction. It is right and proper that commanders who are to lead enterprises of importance have faith in the ability of their army to gain victories and in themselves to lead their men towards that goal. There is, however, a difference between confidence and a refusal to draw proper conclusions from presented facts. It is not confidence but stupidity to consider that a battle has been won that has yet to be fought, or to base future strategic plans upon an, as yet, unattained victory. Nor ought an operation so complex as 'Sealion', be undertaken without the fighting services having planned each single move and having agreed every controversial factor. For commanders to ignore these things does not show confidence but contempt. Contempt for the enemy whose fighting ability they have underestimated and contempt for the lives of their men who would be killed because of their faulty appreciations.

In that connection let us, with the benefit of hindsight, consider what it was that the German Army intended to do. It planned to send its soldiers across the North Sea and the English Channel – stretches of water notorious for sudden squalls – in a miscellany of craft most of which would be unsuited for the strains of such a crossing. Very few of the barges would be powered and would have to be towed or pushed to the landing areas. Not only would the craft be poor in quality but they would be insufficient in number to carry the whole of the assault wave. Some troops might find themselves being conveyed on a raft kept afloat by empty petrol drums, wine barrels or kapok cushions. The fastest speed that the convoys would be able to maintain for any length of time was three knots – which meant that the shortest crossing, that between Calais and Dover, would take more than eight hours. The men of the assault wave making that crossing would be without reinforcement for a minimum of sixteen hours until the ships had returned to France, there to embark more troops and make the second slow journey back to the landing beaches.

Those units of the invasion force that would be conveyed in the large troop transports would have to leave these some distance from the shore and embark into barges for a very long run in because the seas around England were too shallow to allow deep-draught vessels to come close in. Until a port had been captured this slow method of unloading men, materials and heavy weapons would continue. The army's major priority, therefore, was to capture a harbour and the High Command hoped that the paratroop formations would achieve this. It was accepted that the paras in the initial assault wave were also unlikely to be reinforced quickly as there were too few transport aircraft to carry all the regiments in one single lift and a shuttle service would have to be operated. The great coastal guns of the Royal Artillery would be taken out by a detachment of the Abwehr's Brandenburg Regiment. Other Brandenburgers were to be landed near Dover to prevent the British from destroying the dock installations there.

The principal factor – the *sine qua non* for any cross-Channel assault – was air supremacy. No one disputed this. Indeed every report from that of November 1939 onwards had stressed that without it it was not possible to undertake the operation. Yet it was accepted, without question, by the German leaders that the Luftwaffe would gain and hold that supremacy with ease. As late as 29 July, Luftwaffe General Stapf described the RAF as numerically inferior to the Luftwaffe and went on to report that Fighter Command was badly trained and equipped. The defeat of the Royal Air Force was so inevitable that, according to the writer of the Luftwaffe War Diaries, the Air Force Commander-in-Chief, Hermann Goering, had lost interest in the cross-Channel parts of the plan. There would be no need for it. His Luftwaffe would achieve victory for the Führer.

According to the army's timetable the Luftwaffe would have won its easy victory and S-Day (the date of the invasion) would be named. The infantry divisions would by that time have marched to the ports and embarked. The troops would be packed into the holds of the transports. The convoys would set sail. Throughout the night the long columns of vessels would sail towards England, so completely 'blacked out' that not a glimmer of light could be seen. Not even signalling lamps were to be used. During the night crossings, for all practical purposes, the convoys sailing without lights and without wireless contact between ships would be blind, deaf and dumb. Another worry for the navy was that there were so few radios available for use in the convoy that the only method of communication between vessels would be by loud hailer. There may have been a shortage of essential equipment but there was no shortage of bureaucratic detail. Precise regulations had been issued detailing the type of flag each ship was to wear – either the Reichs War Banner or that of the Merchant Marine. In the operations zone and by day an ordinary swastika flag was to be spread out on the deck of each ship as a recognition signal to the Luftwaffe.

While still some way from the landing areas and still hidden under the cover of darkness, the vessels forming each column would reach a designated point at which they would make a 90° turn to starboard. With the formation now changed from line ahead to line abreast, the ships of the assault wave would wait for a smoke-screen to be laid. Just before S-Hour Ju 52s, carrying paratroops, would roar over the impatient line and with the first light of dawn the two-fold assault, from the air and from the sea, would begin. Then out of a rolling brown/grey bank of smoke the barges would be pushed forward. Infantry seated in motor-powered assault craft or perched on the gunwales and wielding paddles would race towards

the shore. Panzers would roll out of the sea under which they had been submerged. Others would swim ashore and those fitted with flamethrowers would burn out the opposition with gouts of fire. That was the theory. This was undoubtedly the picture that was in the minds of all the Staff planners.

The true picture might well have been different. Whether nine weeks' training would have made the army and airborne assault units a cohesive and proficient team, is unlikely. Whether the soldiers would still be proficient and ready for action after hours of sea-sick confinement in a vessel's hold, is open to doubt. Would the rafts, supported on empty petrol drums, stand the strain of being used as platforms for the 88mm guns, and if they capsized from where would supporting fire come? There were very few artillery pieces with the first wave troops except for the guns on board the warships and the weapons hastily fitted to the barge decks. Would there have been impatience, fear indeed, among the infantry soldiers waiting under fire for their turn to move down the barge ramps and on to British soil? And what about the horses? I can only assume that the beasts would have been stampeded over the sides of the ships and into the shallows there to wait, under fire, frightened and shivering until the gunners, sweating with exertion, dragged the heavy artillery pieces through the surf, on to dry land and hitched the teams to the traces.

The first paragraphs of this section of the book described the feelings of a German artillery officer who saw the Allied invasion fleet loom out of the dawn darkness on 6 June 1944. I wonder what would have been the first thoughts of a British observer on Britain's south-east coast had he seen, chugging out of the artificial fog, the ill-assorted collection of craft bringing in a German assault division.

The breadth and depth of the Allied D-Day fleet had covered the sea. By contrast the invasion convoy of each German spearhead division would have comprised a single wave of boats of varying sizes, speeds and designs. And yet, such was the confidence of the German Army's High Command that it had planned this major, seaborne assault as if the operation were no more than the crossing of an exceptionally wide and very calm river.

Although, in the opinion of Naval High Command, the cross-Channel assault was an operation of high and unnecessary risk, the admirals were

Above: Assault landing craft being prepared for Operation 'Sealion' in 1940. The German people were quite unaware of how inadequate were the preparations for a landing on the British coast.

prepared to discuss with their opposite numbers on the Army Staff the Directive which Hitler had issued and to carry out his orders to establish just how much shipping was available to carry through operation 'Sealion'. The census was to cover all craft from steamships, through trawlers and drifters down to the barges which had plied on inland water-ways. Naval teams were set up to establish how long it would take to convert requisitioned vessels to troop carriers or assault craft. Discussions at levels between officers of

the army and the navy were long and often fruitless. Each conference that passed without accord made the invasion plan that much more hazardous, and each day brought the discordant services nearer to that time when the assault must be undertaken; an assault for the success of which it was imperative that they work in harmony.

For its part the army, with Hitler's Directive to fire it, set its troops on strict training schedules. Those areas of the coast along which the divisions of the two assault armies were deployed, became the scene of mock assault landings, of training in cliff climbing and in large-scale field exercises.

Made aware that there were too few properly designed and constructed barges and of how little artillery support there was for the first wave, army teams were employed to construct rafts. They searched for any type of buoyant container. Wine barrels, oil drums – anything that would float was taken to support platforms on which 88mm guns or infantry detachments would be mounted. There were troops other than infantry that would be vital to the initial assault. These were the airborne regiments which had shown their effectiveness in the campaigns in the Low Countries, and the High Command intended to use them for the attack upon Britain. Both para and glider troops would be used. Promptly at two minutes past sun-rise the first wave of paras, Major Meindl's battalion, would jump over and around Hythe and as these men landed on Romney Marsh, elements from Oberst Brauer's regiment would jump over Paddlesworth and Etchinghill, and move towards their first objective, Sandgate. Then there would be a period of about an hour while the JUs flew back to France, refuelled, and took off again with other companies of paratroops. Around the villages of Sellinge and Postling, Stenzler's battalion would then be landed and the centre and eastern side of the German perimeter would be firm. There would be another wait for the next reinforcement wave before the western perimeter could be built. Then the whole area would be consolidated and an advance made to seize the airfield at Lympne as well as the high ground beyond this. On to that captured field the JU 52 transports would land, bringing in battalions of 22nd Air Landing Division to strengthen the perimeter and to exploit the gains made by the lightly armed paratroops. From Lympne, too, would fly off the first fighter squadrons of the Luftwaffe's Advanced Strike Force, to give local and immediate support.

There were certain factors regarding the airborne troops which the planners had to face. The manpower losses suffered by the battalions during Operation 'Gelb', the campaign in the West, had been made good, but the replacements, although fully trained, had not yet had time to work as part of a team. The advice from Luftwaffe headquarters was that the earliest date on which the Fallschirmjäger units could be ready was 15 August; only a month before the projected date of S-Day.

For the commanders of armoured units the different types of beach in the assault areas also presented problems and to overcome these orders were given for some panzers to be outfitted as submersibles and others sealed so that they swam on the surface of the sea. To co-ordinate this work and to check on the many, often unusual problems that would arise, a training and research establishment was set up under Reinhardt, a brilliant panzer General. Almost his first problem was that most of the Panzer III and IV on which he was to conduct his experiments were comandeered to take part in the Victory Parade in Paris. He could not experiment on tanks he did not have and when they were returned to him he was shocked to be given orders that Army High Command required 180 submersibles, a greater number than originally proposed, that these were to be upgunned to carry heavier main armament and that they must be capable of submerging to a depth of 15 metres – double that which Reinhardt and his teams had achieved.

In his first report to the Army Chief of Staff, Reinhardt wrote of the problems which were being encountered and of the conclusions to be drawn from the research. Chief among these was the problem of communication. There was a need for a wireless link between the submerged tanks and the mother ship which had carried them. Once the vehicles were under the water they were blind and needed to be guided to the shore. Then it was shown that in choppy water the panzers swimming on the surface could not use their main armament, nor could their gun be used as a howitzer to give high-angle fire. Both the submersibles and the swimmers performed well, but too much time was spent in stripping off the waterproof sealant before the machines could go into action. Reinhardt also wrote that landings from barges could only take place at low water. Tests had shown, he wrote, 'That landing craft . . . must be in assault position about half an hour after high tide so that landings take place as the tide begins to ebb. This leaves little time for the assault operation to be carried out . . . The first units will be carried on to the beach in infantry assault boats or barges . . . Unpowered barges, once these have been cast off by their tug, will be pushed towards the shore by a pair of motor boats and brought in so close to the shore that their landing ramps can be put out.' In addition to the tanks on which the research teams worked, they also carried out tests on other pieces of equipment, including concrete barges and Dr Fritz Todt's panzer-carrying ferries.

Discussions between Staff and regimental officers showed that there was among the latter general dissatisfaction with the assault barges. These were commercial vessels which had been taken out of civilian service and adapted for their role in 'Sealion'. They were not fitted with derricks so that the infantry storm craft which they carried could not be lowered into the sea nor had it proved practicable to push them bow first into the water. The method chosen was to cast them out from the barge and then to hold the storm boats alongside while the troops climbed in. The difficulties of such a procedure even in a smooth sea were obvious. How much harder, the regimental officers asked, would it be in choppy conditions and under enemy fire? This then produced the next problem. Once cast off from the mother ship the troops had to reach the shore which might be, depending upon a number of factors, as close as 40 metres or as distant as 100 metres. However close to the shore the boats were launched, the distance would still have to be covered by unprotected soldiers seated in rubber assault boats and being shot at. The standard method of propelling the assault boats was by paddles and the regimental officers asked whether the assault craft could be fitted with an outboard motor so as to reduce the time between launching-point and shore. A check in the Quartermaster General's Department showed that there were not sufficient motorized assault boats available and even if every suitable outboard motor were to be requisitioned and fitted to paddle craft, the numbers obtained would only be sufficient to make the craft of half the first wave mobile. The other assault boats would still have to paddle against a turning tide to gain the land.

The regimental commanders reported the troops to be in good heart, although there were grumbles at the high prices charged by local shopkeepers and restaurants. But most soldiers were anticipating the invasion with optimism, confident that the successful operation would bring peace again. They were undergoing the hard and unusual training, with a will.

Alexander Hofer, a rifleman in a mountain regiment, had been three years in the army and had fought in Poland. 'We were told that we had been selected to form the spearhead of our corps and although we were not told the precise area we were to attack, the training we underwent made it clear that it would be a cliff section, probably around Dover.

'You will understand, most of us were mountain men from the heartlands of Europe and that few of us had ever seen the ocean. None of us had ever been trained to make an assault landing from the sea on to a defended shore. Yet this was our task. Scaling the cliffs of England would be easy. We had all done that sort of thing in recruit training and, of course, it would be easier to make secure footholds in the hard dry chalk than on the slippery, freezing granite of a mountain. There was, however, more to it than that.

'The lectures we were given had the message we had all heard in past campaigns and which we would continue to hear all through the war. This was that the operation was going to be simply a mopping-up detail. The enemy was as good as defeated anyway; weak in numbers and in morale. The English, so we were told, were a badly armed army which had been shattered at Dunkirk. The Tommies would not be in position to interfere seriously with our landing. There would be fighting of course. The English were after all fighting in their own country. But we were superior in number, or would be once the supporting waves came in. Also we had better equipment. We even had submersible tanks. None of us believed that story until we saw a newsreel which showed a whole group of panzer which had been completely hidden under water, climb out of a river, then up a bank and halt there. Quick as a flash the crews were out of the turrets stripping off a sort of rubber covering and clearing the tank guns. In no time at all, or so it seemed, the panzer were in action. A Sonderführer who gave us a lecture on our part in the coming invasion, pointed out that our assault would be accompanied by such sub-

Right: German troops begin training for Operation 'Sealion' in barges hastily converted to landing craft. The improvised vessels and equipment compare badly with the sophisticated hardware developed by the Allies (over several years) for the invasion of Normandy in 1944.

mersible tanks. We were all reassured after that.

'What were the barges like? The upper works – a sort of low wall around the deck – had pieces cut out at the bow and the stern. Ramps were placed flat on the deck at each of these four places. The idea was that as soon as the barge ran on to the beach the ramps would be pushed through the four cut-out positions. We, the first infantry groups, would have climbed by ladder out of the hold in which we would sit throughout the crossing, and assemble on the deck. When the barge touched down, down would go the ramps we would race down them, across the beach and up the cliffs.

'Very few of the men were good sailors. Most of us were seasick at some time or another. Those barges had no stability in water and tossed about in a sickening motion even in the most moderate seas. So far as I can remember the trip across would have taken all night. We were to set off at last light to arrive in our attacking position just before dawn.

'We had been told that the Luftwaffe ruled the skies. Well maybe they did by day. After dark it was a different story. It seemed that almost from the first day that we arrived from Germany, the RAF came over. Night after night the alarm would sound and we would have to turn out in battle order. There were always fires in the docks after the bombing. The RAF tried to set fire to the barges, sometimes only hours after they had reached the area.

'Then the latrine rumours began. The English could set fire to the surface of the sea and would do this just before we landed. Not all the barges had engines. There were some as well as other vessels without any engines. These were to be towed in pairs behind a mother ship. On more than one occasion when we were out doing sea training barges collided and it was frightening to see how quickly they sank. My regiment did not lose anybody through drowning, for we put on life-jackets before we embarked and kept them on until we formed up to march back to the billeting area.

'I cannot remember whether I was pleased or sorry when we were told that the invasion had been postponed and that we were going to be trained for an attack against Gibraltar. I think I was glad because of being spared the misery of seasickness; the awful smell of vomit and damp salt air. We were being spared the misery of being wet and cold and, more than anything else, spared the awful motion of the barges. I suppose we felt regret because we did not make the attempt to invade England. How different would be the world now – had we tried and won.'

To summarize the position of the German Army in that summer of success. The Führer's Directive ordered preparations for 'Sealion', to be concluded by the middle of August. Operations and administration staffs of the army had gone immediately into action and from the reports they produced a comprehensive plan of action had been drawn up. Tasks were distributed to study teams in order to clarify certain difficult points, research groups set up to test equipment, training establishments formed to teach unusual skills and the whole mighty apparatus of the German Army had been put into action with just one purpose; the conquest of England.

Along the coasts of western Europe between Biscay and Rotterdam, German troops had begun training, setting out in assault boats, landing on beaches, scrambling up and down cliffs in preparation for the day when their training would become reality. For its part the German Navy had begun to organize the collection of the barges and tugs which would form part of the invasion fleet. At Abbeville and at other airfields immediately behind the French coast, pilots in the crack squadrons of the Luftwaffe, the arm of service most indoctrinated by National Socialist ethos, had already begun their part in 'Sealion'; the first to carry the war across the seas to England. Convinced of their own superiority as a result of two victorious campaigns, the pilots had drunk to the forthcoming battle for Britain.

Throughout Germany and in her armed forces a new song was being sung. It had a catchy tune with a simple lyric made up of rhyming couplets and a chorus which ran, 'Then give me your hand, your sweet, white hand, farewell my love, farewell, for we are sailing, we are sailing off to England; ahoy.'

Throughout July and August there were inter-service conferences and single service discussions aimed at finding solutions to the problems which divided the concepts of the army and the navy in relation to 'Sealion'. While those talks went on and on the Luftwaffe had begun its operations against the United Kingdom.

The role of the German Air Force in 'Sealion', was, as we have seen, not considered vital although it was accepted that the Service had three separate tasks to undertake. Two of these were strategic; important to the preparations for the actual invasion but, the third was purely tactical, connected with supporting the army in the post-landing, ground operations.

The first of the strategic duties was for the fighter Geschwader to gain air superiority in southern England. With that achieved the victorious Luftwaffe could then extend its radius of action into central and then northern England, establishing dominion over an RAF which would have, by that time, all but ceased to exist as a fighting force. Concurrent with the fighter aces gaining their victories, bomber squadrons would carry out the second of the Luftwaffe's strategic tasks, bombing airfields and factories and attacking convoys heading for British ports, thereby strangling the enemy's trade and industry. When both these offensives had been successfully carried out the Luftwaffe would hold air supremacy. The navy and the army could then undertake the sea crossing. Operational orders were issued to the Luftwaffe during July, but with the proviso that no target on the mainland of the United Kingdom was to be attacked although missions against shipping targets could be launched. Hitler did not intend that his speech offering peace should be prejudiced by a bombing campaign. The Führer's words were placatory. '. . . Conscience compels me to appeal to the British to listen to reason. I think I can do this since I come not as one defeated but as the victor hoping that reason will prevail. I do not see . . . why this war should continue . . .' Lord Halifax, the British Foreign Minister, rejected the appeal and that dismissal finally resolved the issue for the Führer. The war must now continue and Britain would be invaded.

On 6 August, Kesselring, commanding Luftflotte 2, was given verbal instructions by Goering. These were that the Luftwaffe was to undertake operations against mainland Britain. The intention was to destroy the British air defences and the Royal Air Force. 'Eagle Day', the day on which the air offensive would open, was 10 August.

The three Luftflotten, which were to take part in 'Sealion', had between them a total of 860 bombing aircraft, 250 Stukas, 650 single-seater fighters, 200 twin-engined fighters and 80 reconnaissance aircraft. The strength of Fighter Command was put at 500 fighters. To the German

commanders the Luftwaffe had not only quantitative superiority, but was also qualitatively superior for many of the German fighter pilots had fought in two successful campaigns and the force was equipped with better machines than those in service with the RAF. Small wonder then that there was a general confidence among the German High Commands. Much of this euphoria was based on the outcome of a war game played by the commanders of fighter and bomber squadrons from 2nd and 3rd Luftflotten. That war game, predicted on a Fighter Command strength of 500 machines and upon the projected reaction of the British Force, reached the conclusion that Fighter Command would be destroyed in a matter of a few days.

The war game had shown that the RAF would meet the Luftwaffe assaults with its squadrons massed for battle. The Luftwaffe would destroy the British in the air by individual combat, that is of plane against plane, as well as on the ground by a bombing campaign to attack headquarters and runways. It was a false appreciation; blindly false and yet there was evidence enough for correct conclusions to have been drawn. There had been skirmishes between the fighters of both sides during June and July. Had the Luftwaffe Intelligence officers debriefed their fighter pilots more thoroughly after those missions and collated and weighed up their common experiences, they would have learned that the British fighter squadrons were not reacting as the war game had forecast. British fighters were not rising to the bait of Stukas bombing the Channel convoys. Fighter Command Headquarters, made aware through radar that above the Stukas lurked massed fighter Geschwader, had not allowed its squadrons to accept the unequal challenge. The first part of the German Air Force plan, to destroy the RAF in the air, was not succeeding. The British were not taking the bait. It was not that the RAF would not fight; it would, but on its own terms and over its own territory.

In the event bad weather caused 'Eagle Day', to be postponed and not until three days later, at 07.30 hrs on 13 August, was the first bombing mission undertaken. The raid to destroy RAF airfields was a disaster. The Me 110 fighter escort, already airborne, was told by radio that the raid had been aborted. That information was not given to the bomber squadrons. These took off without fighter escort, were intercepted by the RAF and several were shot down. That afternoon the weather cleared and operations for 'Eagle Day' began in strength. The raids in the latter part of that first day were carried out by 485 Stuka and other bombers. The air offensive gained momentum and on 15 August 2,119 sorties were flown. But it was clear that the prime aim of the operation was not being gained. Four days had been projected for the destruction of Fighter Command; these had come and gone, but the RAF did not seem to be weakened and had certainly not been destroyed. In an effort to rejuvenate the squadrons with new blood, Goering replaced many unit commanders, then regrouped the whole fighter force and placed it under Kesselring's command. Neither change brought victory.

The continuing failure of his fighters to entice the RAF squadrons forced Goering to introduce a new tactic. Bomber raids would be launched in daylight and each would have a strong fighter escort. The British would have to accept this challenge or accept the destruction of their cities. And when the RAF aircraft did rise to intercept, battle would be joined and the British squadrons would be destroyed by his aces. On 31 August the major sortie of this new effort was flown.

During that day the German fighter Force flew 1,301 sorties to protect the 150 bombers which were attacking British cities. The tactic was not successful. The RAF was up in force and German losses were heavy. Furious at the failure of the Luftwaffe, his own creation, Goering then took over personal command and for nine days the air battle continued. The climax of that battle came on 15 September. Still the RAF was unbroken. Goering returned to his home, Karinhall, and summoned his Luftwaffe unit commanders. In a burst of anger he condemned them for having failed and all but accused the fighter pilots of cowardice. The Luftwaffe had failed the Führer. It had not brought about the preconditions for the safe sea crossing by the invasion fleet. It had lost a battle against a numerically inferior, badly trained and tactically inexperienced enemy.

From post-war records we know that during the Battle of Britain the RAF reached a crisis. Losses to aircraft and to men had bled Fighter Command white. It was Goering's intervention and his policy of switching Luftwaffe attacks from front-line airfields and on to bombing cities which gave the RAF a breathing-space during which it was reinforced massively ready to meet the Luftwaffe's anticipated new challenge. That new challenge did not come although the German Air Force had not achieved its primary task. It had not destroyed the RAF on the ground or in the air. Meanwhile, the army and navy High Commands had still not resolved their problems, the most important of which was the width of the assault area – whether this would be broad-fronted, as the generals demanded, or narrow-fronted as the admirals proposed.

With cold and sober realism the officers of the Directorate of Naval Operations and of the staff of the Commander-in-Chief, Navy had examined the army's proposals for Operation 'Sealion', and found them lacking. Small wonder that they sought to influence Hitler away from his own Directive No. 16, with its emphasis on the army's ideas and towards their own suggestions of how, where and when the operation should take place.

The navy High Command brought out again the same arguments against 'Sealion', that the Directorate had produced in 1939, for these were still valid and their conclusions inescapable. In the navy's view the whole of 'Sealion' was based on the faulty premises that Britain could not offer resistance, that the Luftwaffe would have an easy victory over the RAF, that the German convoys carrying troops between the European mainland and Britain would sail speedily and safely that that, finally, the British Army was defeated and unarmed. It was the navy's good fortune that relations between Grand Admiral Raeder, Admiral Doenitz and Hitler were better than those between the Führer and von Brauchitsch, the Commander-in-Chief of the army. Accordingly, he was more willing to accept the navy's points of view,

Right: Goering, with Kesselring (second from left) and other senior Luftwaffe officers, discusses plans for the air war against Great Britain. The German Air Force was seen to be taking the war to the enemy; the English warmongers would soon be reaping the just rewards of their ill deeds.

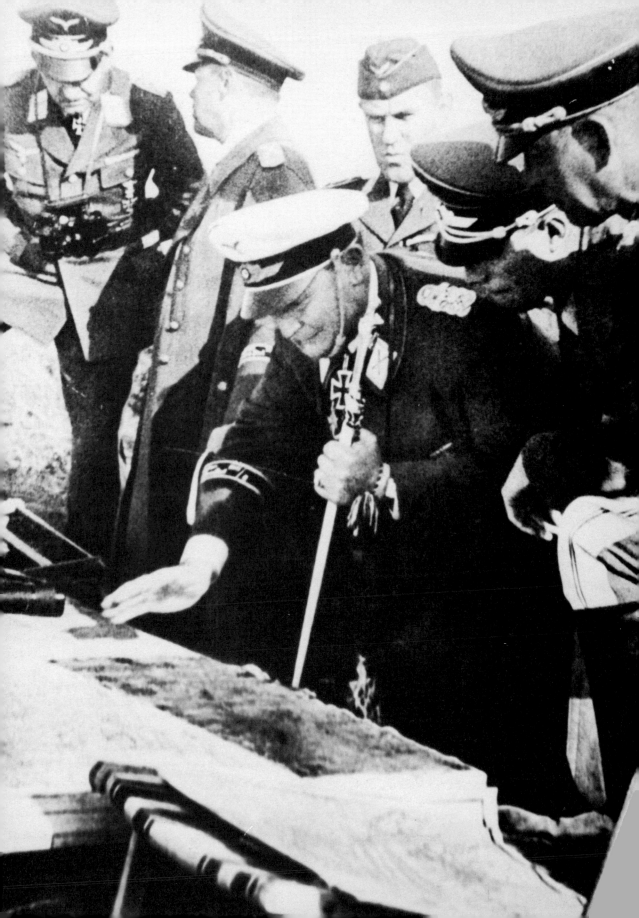

especially since their briefs contained the masses of statistics which he was able to quote in conferences and the technical details that he could reel off during a discussion.

Thus it was to naval voices, detailing the magnitude of the proposed operation, that Hitler began to listen. What they told him influenced his judgement and his decisions. Every discussion between the admirals and the Führer; every lecture by the Grand Admiral repeated the same bitter facts which were, in essence, that Germany was not industrially able to meet all the demands that were being made on her in relation to 'Sealion'. This led to the question of how long the navy would have to bear the burden of 'Sealion's' preparations, for in the opinion of the navy's commanders the absolute limit at which their service could be held in a top state of readiness for the invasion was mid-October?

The navy leaders' objections to the army's first requirement, a landing on a wide front, were that the whole width of the landing area could not be adequately protected by the forces available to the navy. There were no capital ships in commission. *Scharnhorst*, *Gneisenau* and *Scheer* were all in dry dock and *Prinz Eugen* would not be ready for another four months. There were only 48 U-boats in service and just four destroyers. The Royal Navy had nearly one hundred destroyers as well as cruisers, battleships and aircraft carriers and the British fleets were all within easy steaming range of the proposed landing areas.

Thus, as the naval commanders pointed out, a landing west of the Isle of Wight placed the convoys carrying Ninth Army at the mercy of British ships based on Portsmouth and Devonport. Likewise, the right wing of Sixteenth Army would be open to attack by Royal Navy destroyers which would have left the Firth of Forth by night and which would arrive in the assault areas before the first wave of German troops began their run in to the beaches.

The army idea that a corridor of water should be swept free of British mines and that a German minefield should be laid guarding both flanks of the assault area, was excellent – in principle. In practice, however, the two tasks; that of sweeping the British minefields and laying German ones, could not be carried out close to the English shore until aerial superiority had been gained.

Other facts and figures produced by the Kriegsmarine officers were equally negative. Their tasks, as the navy understood them, were to transport a succession of waves of soldiers, each wave made up of no fewer than 100,000 men together with their arms, vehicles and cattle. Each infantry division had 1,700 vehicles and 4,500 horses on its establishment and each motorized or panzer division had a minimum of 2,500 vehicles.

Even if it were possible for the navy to conscript and concentrate every available ship it would still not have the capacity to carry the seven assault divisions demanded by the army, together with all their vehicles and heavy weapons. There was just room enough in the transports for all the foot soldiers but only enough space for the equipment of three of the seven divisions. Even so, that equipment would have to be carried on the open, upper decks, because few of the ships had cranes to lift the material out of the holds.

Assault barges could only be built at the expense of U-Boat construction or the repairs and outfitting of capital ships, for there were just not enough dockyards or men to carry out all the projected plans. Still concerned with the economic burden of the operation, the navy stressed that the planned requisitions of coastal ships, trawlers and canal barges would place strain upon the German economy which would soon become an unendurable burden. The wholesale commandeering of ships would almost paralyse German industry and affect food production. There would be no ships to carry exports to the neutral countries of the Baltic or to move coal and iron. No fishing fleets would bring in their catch for the whole time that the emergency lasted. Then there was the problem of crewing those foreign ships requisitioned from the occupied countries, and any barges or assault craft that might be built. A minimum of 24,000 sailors would be required and the navy would not be able to meet that demand from its own resources. Even a partial conscription of shipping would have serious effect upon German industry. The navy proposal was that ships should be left in service until the decision had been taken to launch 'Sealion', although the Kriegsmarine officers stressed that the conversion of ships from their civilian role to combat readiness could not be carried out in less than four weeks.

A decision must soon be made for there was very little time remaining in 1940. Suitable tides and moonlight conditions coincided on only one or two days in any month. July was nearly spent and August was too near for 'Sealion' to be launched. September was notorious for its bad weather, and October, which might produce calmer conditions, also brought with it the problem of fog.

On the matter of weather, the Naval Directorate laid down that a period of not fewer than five days of very fine, calm conditions were essential for the Kriegsmarine to carry out the operation. It had to be considered that the flat-bottomed barges had been built for short-haul canal work and not for long voyages on the open sea. The barges were not seaworthy nor were they robust enough to withstand the rough conditions that might be met in the Channel. In that connection, the navy reported, it had to be accepted that most of the barges and ferries would be lost during the first assault and that there were, of course, no replacement vessels.

The navy's recommendation was to postpone 'Sealion' until May or June 1941, by which time a barge-building programe would be well in hand, more warships would have been commissioned, including a number of heavy units. The Luftwaffe would be stronger and would have destroyed British centres of production, and the U-boat campaign against Britain's shipping should be strangling her economy. In short, there was little to be gained from an autumn operation, but much that might be achieved by a postponement to the following spring. There was still no decision from the Führer and, lacking that central direction, both services continued to work to their original planning lines: the army for a wide-based landing, the navy for the narrow option. Documents still passed between the services on many vital matters, but the basic point of issue was never resolved.

Among the documents was one which confounded the Army High Command's plans. The Directorate of Naval Operations reported that, contrary to the army's belief, debarkation from large steamers could not be made from the open sea but had to be carried out in harbours. Thus the capture of a port of adequate size and with unloading facilities intact must be a principal objective. The navy could do nothing until a port had been captured. Then came a second blow; the Kriegsmarine could not spare anti-aircraft guns to protect the embarkation ports or the invasion convoys. It required all its guns to defend dockyards and construction centres from British air

raids. The Directorate also revised its estimate of crossing times and produced the figure of ten days as the minimum to ship across all the first echelons. This new figure horrified the army. It was absolutely unacceptable to leave so small an assault force isolated for so long without adequate reinforcement or replacements, and lacking all the requirements of a soldier in battle. The army would not agree to a build-up which would take ten days, while the navy, for its part, would not accept any shorter period as a responsible figure. It was an impasse.

As if all these factors were not sufficiently gloomy, the army was then confronted with the statement that the only extension of beachhead width which the Navy would consider northwards was from Folkestone to Ramsgate and then only if the defences in that area were first destroyed. This neutralization would have to be carried out by the Luftwaffe, but in view of that service's poor showing against the RAF it seemed unlikely that the task could be competently accomplished. That being the case the navy could not accept an extension of the right flank of Army Group A. And, since the Luftwaffe might not be competent to destroy by bombing static gun positions on the Ramsgate sector, would its squadrons be able to protect Army Group's left wing by sinking those ships of the Royal Navy which would come out of Portsmouth and Devonport to attack the German invasion fleets?

Nothing was said. No order was passed down, but perceptibly the sense of urgency which had formerly filled those who were planning the invasion began to diminish. There was no longer that tempo that had once filled every day. Indeed, the pace was casual, even leisurely and this may have been caused by delays in communication due to the distance which separated the various headquarters. Those of OKW and of the navy were both in Berlin. The OKH and Luftwaffe High Command Headquarters were in occupied Europe, and Karinhall, the home of the Commander-in-Chief of the Luftwaffe, was miles away in Prussia on the other side of Germany. The combat units were deployed along or immediately behind the Channel coast. Since most documents between commanders were both lengthy and secret, they could not be sent by telex but had to be carried by officer courier. A minimum of two days was thus wasted in travelling time and the reply which might take four or five days to formulate, would then have to be returned by another courier. This waste of effort was quite inexcusable in an operation where shortage of time was a crucial factor.

Another weakness was that at conferences at intermediate OKW level, where representatives of the army and navy put forward the points of view of their respective commanders, those junior officers did not have the power to reach binding agreements with their opposite numbers. Then, finally, there was Hitler's ambiguity. In his speech to his service commanders at the conference of 31 July, he had managed to give to the army commanders the idea that he supported their plan for the wide-based landing although the Commander-in-Chief, Navy, was convinced that the Führer had chosen the narrow-front option. Halder's notes contain the sentence 'Army; landing date 15.9. Broad front', and the OKW War Diary entry agrees with that received impression.

Halder's diary of 4 August, complained that two Naval Operations Staff documents show the navy to be still working on the narrow-front concept and he went on that the navy seemed to be finding excuses – the failure of the Luftwaffe and the weather – for its lack of initiative. The army's liaison officer with Naval Operations Section accused Raeder in a diary entry of having cold feet about 'Sealion' and of erecting a screen of 'technical difficulties'.

The continuing, unresolved basic differences needed to be settled at most senior level and the Chiefs of Staff of the army and navy met hoping to accomplish this. Their discussion, during the evening of 7 August, produced no solution to the issues which divided the two arms of service on the question of the size of the landing area. The three hours of talk only demonstrated that their respective views were still widely divergent. The army could not understand the navy's fears and the navy could not appreciate the army's need for the widest possible landing area.

The Chief of the Army General Staff pointed out that there was marshy terrain immediately behind the landing area proposed by the navy, between Folkestone and Beachy Head. Not only was this unsuitable for panzer operations, but the landing area was overlooked by high ground held in strength by twelve enemy divisions. There were, in addition, several other telling reasons to reject the navy's proposal. To summarize all the objections: the three divisions which might, or might not have landed intact in the areas selected by the navy, would be in an unsound tactical situation and, being inferior to the enemy both in numbers and supporting weapons, could be considered as little more than a sacrifice. 'I reject in the strongest possible terms', was Halder's bitter comment, 'the navy's proposals for a landing on a narrow front . . . From the army's point of view this could only be described as suicide. I might just as well put the troops through a mincing-machine.'

Army proposed a widening of the navy's suggested bridgehead to include the Brighton area where the more favourable terrain might allow a rapid advance and, in turn, threaten the enemy around Beachy Head. Navy rejected it, advancing the same reasons it had given when it rejected a landing in Lyme Bay, and went on to say that the Kriegsmarine saw a wide-based landing in the same morbid light as the army saw a narrow-based one.

It was a situation which could only be resolved by the Führer. The office of the Chief of the General Staff advised the Commander-in-Chief of the army, who wrote, on 10 August to the Chief of OKW stressing the irreconcilable differences of opinion between the army and navy. Hitler would have to make a decision on the extent of the landing area. His reply, dated 15 August, was not a clear-cut decision. The Führer ordered the preparations for a landing in Lyme Bay to be cancelled, but then, two paragraphs later used the phrase '. . . options remain open for a one-off operation in the Brighton area which would not be supplied with heavy weapons . . .' This satisfied neither service.

There are official documents and some diaries which cover that period of the war and which give an insight into contemporary thinking and planning. Some writers were very critical of the way in which decisions were reached at Supreme Command level, and Halder, Army Chief of Staff, expressed his dissatisfaction at the failure of OKW to produce a solution to the inter-service rivalry shown in the planning of 'Sealion'. In a diary entry dated 6 August, he wrote: 'Our impression (the army's) is that now that OKW is faced with the need to give a lead in an OKW matter, it plays dead . . .'

On 26 August, Hitler, in an obvious effort to settle the issue, produced a new Directive of which the most significant instruction was that the Army High Command must make its plans fit the existing situation. Further, those plans must take into account not only the amount of shipping space available but also the safety of the ships during the whole operation. That Directive showed that the navy's arguments on 'Sealion', had prevailed upon the Führer. The army had lost the battle of the bridgehead width.

A snowstorm of orders, schedules, instructions and landing tables which continued to flutter between the various service departments could not conceal the fact that the Führer, having conceded the navy's principal objection to 'Sealion', had also accepted in principle that the operation be postponed until the spring of 1941.

The army, not willing perhaps to admit its defeat, continued to produce Orders of the Day, commands from corps and directives from divisions concerning 'Sealion', but at senior level it was realized that these were redundant actions. The chance had passed; the opportunity to 'bounce' the Channel, to defeat the English and thus to end the war in the west, had not been taken.

As if to support the army's vain but untruthful stance that 'Sealion' would still be undertaken, Keitel's directive of 3 September reaffirmed the provisional dates for troop movements towards the embarkation ports as well as for S-Day itself. This remained as 15 September. The army Commander-in-Chief's own instructions dated 30 August, laid out army intentions and stressed that S-Day was only sixteen days away. The next military level of command, and the one concerned with the field operations in the invasion, was Army Group A. Orders were issued to its subordinate formations on 5 September and Sixteenth Army produced its version of those orders on the 9th. From the extracts of that Army's orders reproduced on pages 130 and 131, it can be seen that the provisional date of 15 September had now been changed and that S-Day had been postponed to 20 September.

This later date was confirmed by OKW on 14 September, whose directive ordered that active preparations should be continued and that existing counter-Intelligence activities and deception measures should continue. The British were to be kept under pressure and fully alive to the threat that an invasion might come at any time. To assist in this psychological warfare, OKW ordered the sailing of fake troop convoys appearing to be part of the invasion fleet. The intention was that enemy agents must see German troops embarking and observe German ship convoys sailing towards England, even though those convoys would then change course after dark and would put into a nearby port where the soldiers would be disembarked.

During a conference on 14 September, Hitler too, admitted that despite the Luftwaffe's first-class results, aerial supremacy had not been gained and that without it 'Sealion', could not be launched. Four days later, he made the final decision to postpone the operation and ordered the shipping in the embarkation harbours to be dispersed. He rationalized his instruction by claiming that dispersal made the ships less of a target to the RAF. Since he was aware that a minimum of ten days would be needed to concentrate the ships again, and that four weeks would be required to prepare them for their invasion role, his directive made it plain that no invasion would take place during 1940. Confirmation of that cancellation came with Keitel's directive of 12 October, which contained the telling sentence: '. . . should there be a new intention to undertake a landing in England in the spring or early summer of 1941, then preparations up to the required level of readiness will be put in hand . . .' The document then ordered that army units which had been selected for 'Sealion' were to be redeployed. The navy's preparations were to be halted and the shipping that had been gathered for 'Sealion', was to be returned to its previous deployment.

Operation 'Sealion', was not dead but dormant. From the British point of view the Germans had suffered a major, strategic defeat. The Luftwaffe had been driven from the skies of Britain in a succession of individual combats fought by the knights of the 20th century; the pilots of Fighter Command. It was not surprising that Churchill should say that never was so much owed to them, for the significance of their victory was that the German army and navy could not undertake an invasion during 1940. The earliest that a cross-Channel attack might again threaten was late spring. There were nine whole months during which Britain could prepare, grow stronger through the increase of her armed forces and by the recruiting of women into war work to produce the weapons for those new armies. Politically, too, there were indications that a dramatic change might come about. Germany's secrets; secret no longer thanks to our possession of 'Ultra', indicated that the Wehrmacht's future battle area would be the Eastern Front. Within a year, it might well be that Britain would no longer be alone in the fight for the freedom of the world, but that she might have been joined by the colossus of Soviet Russia. From the British point of view the air battle of Britain, prelude to the invasion, had been a strategic blow of wide-ranging consequence to the plans of the Third Reich.

Adolf Hitler and the OKW did not see it in so depressing a light. The German appreciation was that there had been a tactical reverse. The first phase of 'Sealion': the Luftwaffe's attempt to gain superiority in the air had been unsuccessful. This was a temporary reverse. By the spring of 1941, the projected U-boat blockade would be in full swing. Then, too, the Luftwaffe, equipped with more and better types of aircraft, would re-open the air battle and smash British centres of production. While that double offensive was destroying England, the new short campaign against Russia would have already opened, have been fought and have been victoriously concluded. A return would then be made to deal with the troublesome, offshore islands and to give them the *coup de grâce*.

In post-war years many German authors, historians and commanders have come to realize the significance of the Luftwaffe's strategic defeat in the skies over Britain, but contemporary letters, documents and reports seem to be unaware of its importance. Some writers ignore it altogether. So far as the leaders of Germany were concerned the fact that the Luftwaffe's efforts to destroy Fighter Command had come to naught, did not mean that the whole 'Sealion', operation had failed. Chagrin at a tactical setback and not despair at a strategic defeat, was the German perspective of the Luftwaffe's failure in the late summer of 1940.

The decision to postpone 'Sealion', until the following year begs the questions whether an invasion might have succeeded had it been launched immediately after Dunkirk or, alternatively, whether an operation mounted in September might have achieved its objective.

Hitler had hoped in July that Britain would sue for peace and it follows that he would not have permitted an invasion in June or July which would have prejudiced those hopes. And if we accept the hypothesis that the Führer had given the invasion order, could the operation have succeeded at that time? I doubt it. Even had the landing taken place on a narrow front it must have failed. The Royal Navy would have sacrificed itself to smash the German convoys. Bombing squadrons of the Royal Air Force and of the Fleet Air Arm would also have gone in against the Luftwaffe to smash enemy ships and those German soldiers who did land would have faced a British Army imbued with Churchill's self-sacrificing battle cry, 'Take one with you.'

Any attempt to cross the Channel might have had a better chance in September, except that Britain had had a couple of months to prepare and to bring in supplies to cover immediate losses. Then, too, 'Sealion', was based upon the certainty of the Luftwaffe beating the RAF and that had not happened.

The plan to invade Britain was not popular with the German Army, for the bases of success lay not under its aegis, but under those of the Luftwaffe and of the navy. Operation 'Sealion', was the first time that control of a battle in which the army had a principal role, was not under the direction of its officers. Small wonder, therefore, given the navy's obstruction and the failure of the Luftwaffe in the skies over Britain, that the Army High Command turned its attention away from a seaborne operation which it did not control and towards a land-based enemy against whom it could act. Planning began for a war against the Soviet Union. In the weeks following the signing of the French armistice Halder noted how Russia dominated discussion on foreign policy and, in later entries, he expressed the need to build up the German forces on the eastern front. From his diary notes one sees an officer, working hard in the planning of a successful invasion of Britain, while at the same time preparing a lightning blow to clear away the enemy in the east; the foe at Germany's back. To Halder the overthrow of England was the principal war aim. Russia, certainly to begin with, was the secondary objective.

Could 'Sealion', have been revitalized and brought into action during the spring of 1941? This is, I feel, unlikely for Operation 'Barbarossa' the attack upon the Soviet Union, had by that time become the greater priority. Had 'Barbarossa' succeeded, no doubt a return to the invasion plan would have been ordered. But then, 'Barbarossa', was based upon faulty Intelligence and overweening self-confidence as 'Sealion' had been, and it too was a flawed plan.

# GERMAN CONCERN ABOUT THE BALKANS

Italy, Germany's partner in the Axis, was led by Benito Mussolini, a man who aspired to imperial glory which the poverty of his nation could not allow him to achieve. Italy lacked the natural resources necessary for a war industry and was financially impoverished. She had misspent her wealth on grandiose projects and imperial wars and the Italian armed forces which, in the early 1930s, had been powerful and aggressive were by 1940 badly organized and equipped with obsolete aircraft and weapons.

Mussolini's declaration of war upon the Western Allies filled the leaders of the German Army's High Command with deep foreboding. Their army's recent successes against Britain and France had made the western seaboard from the Franco/Spanish border to northern Norway impregnable against attack by a Britain known to be militarily weak. But, by the entry of Italy into the war, British forces in Middle East Command, believed to be very strong, had been given a chance to strike at Germany's exposed southern flank in the Mediterranean. From the Grand Strategy perspective the entry of Italy into the war as Germany's ally was a disaster.

As if to prove the fears of the German High Command the first Italian offensive launched in Africa had been repelled by the British Western Desert Force. Wavell's army, outnumbered by more than ten to one, had struck back with such élan that only the arrival of a German Corps in February 1941, had stopped the British from capturing the Italian North African Empire.

The detachment of a corps to a minor theatre of operations like Africa was only one of the problems which faced OKW at the end of 1940. The Italian Army was also facing defeat at the hands of the Greeks and there was a need for the whole of south-eastern Europe to be strengthened. High Command plans for Operation 'Barbarossa' were well advanced, but those countries out of which Army Group South would strike towards the Black Sea had to be made secure against any attack by a hostile force. The Greeks, for example, might drive into the right flank of the Army Group, upset its timetable and jeopardize the whole operational plan of 'Barbarossa'.

That Greece might undertake such a hostile act could be blamed upon the Italians who had attacked her. As a consequence of Mussolini's action Great Britain had become the ally of the Greeks. In the German perspective the danger was that RAF squadrons might now move into northern Greece from which they could bomb Ploesti from whose oil fields Germany obtained six million of the twelve million tons which she needed to fuel her war effort.

Small wonder then that Paragraph 4 of Hitler's Directive No. 18, dated 12 November 1940, dealt with the threat posed by Greece. The Führer charged the army's Supreme Commander with the planning of an attack aimed at capturing the Greek territory north of the Aegean Sea. The success of that operation would afford bases to the Luftwaffe from which British targets in the eastern Mediterranean could be attacked. Simultaneously, the RAF would be deprived of bases from which it could strike at Ploesti.

Seen from the point of view of the German High Command, the whole of the territory between Gibraltar and Iran, much of which was the area of British Middle East Command, was a springboard from which strong forces could be launched against the soft underbelly of the Axis. Britain had one unsinkable aircraft carrier, Malta, in the central Mediterranean. Another British island possession, Cyprus, dominated the eastern part of that sea and the number of British advanced island bases was increased when she sent garrisons to Crete and to Lemnos, and followed this action by the dispatch of an expeditionary force to the Greek mainland. The fears of OKW had been realized. The British Army was back on the mainland of Europe.

To strengthen the southern area of Europe, Bulgaria was invited to become a partner in a Three Power Agreement. The attack which German High Command proposed upon Greece would have to be made out of Bulgarian territory. It was also necessary to enlist Yugoslavia in the German diplomatic moves. On 25 March the Regent of that country became a signatory to the pact, thus clearing the way for an invasion of Greece through Yugoslav territory. News of the signing of a pact with Hitler provoked riots in the streets of Belgrade, riots which the Germans were convinced were the work of British agents. The Regent was overthrown on 27 March, and the young King Peter took over the government of his country. To Hitler, this action, coming as it did just before the opening of Operation 'Marita', the campaign against Greece, was the direst perfidy. His anger was reflected in the intention to destroy the Yugoslav State, as expressed in Directive No. 25. He ordered an extension of 'Marita' to include a war against Yugoslavia. The new and extended operational plan was handed to the Führer by OKH within ten days.

According to the Intelligence Appreciation of XXXX Corps, there were weak British forces in Katerini and the bulk of the Imperial troops, reckoned to be 2 to 3 divisions in strength, was concentrated round Larissa. On 5 April, 'Leibstandarte SS Adolf Hitler' issued orders to its subordinate units. Paragraph 1 read: 'The development of the political situation makes it necessary to destroy the State of Yugoslavia, a product of the peace treaties of the World War. An attack upon Greece will occur simultaneously.'

The Balkan campaign opened at first light on 6 April, with attacks by Freiherr von Weich's Second Army and the Twelfth Army under Field Marshal Sigmund List. By the last day of April, operations on the Greek mainland had been completed. Southwards across the sea lay Crete, now a British advanced base and which must be captured if only to deny it to the enemy. But the Royal Navy controlled the seas and thus a shipborne invasion was out of the question. The problem was solved by an airborne assault which began on 20 May and soon developed into a land battle, brought to a successful conclusion on 31 May, by German airborne forces.

The German Supreme Command had overreacted to an unlikely British threat. The OKW was not aware of just how few troops there were in Middle East Command or of the demands that were being made upon them from a great many sources. British troops were fighting in Abyssinia, some were battling in other Italian colonies. There was an anti-British uprising in Iran and the Vichy French forces in Syria needed to be dealt with. These and other drains on the strength of Middle East Command would have made it unlikely that the British could gather sufficient forces to make an assault landing in strength at that time. It is surprising that OKW Intelligence sources seem not to have established the true strength of the British forces or that this information had not been gathered by Abwehr. Lacking such elementary details the planners at OKW convinced themselves that logically, Britain's main military effort would be made against the long and unfortified coastline of southern Europe. Their moves to counter this threat involved them in three campaigns: against Yugoslavia, against Greece and against Crete. High-quality troops had had to be employed; the Leibstandarte, several first class Panzer divisions and the crack Parachute Division. Losses had been suffered and now the divisions and corps which had fought in the Balkans would have to be rested, refreshed, regrouped and routed eastwards where the campain to destroy the Soviet Union was about to open. Operation 'Barbarossa' was now only days away and Hitler's Germany was at the pinnacle of its achievements. Proud of its new achievements there was now a new song. No longer 'Wir fahren gegen England' which had been sung during Operation 'Sealion', but the new 'We have swept the tommies from the Continent'. They were heady days.

Above right: A Greek bunker of the Metaxas Line destroyed during the campaign in the Balkans, April 1942. Right: The German flag flies above yet another conquered city – Athens.

Above: A German poster proclaims that victory over Russia will ensure Germany's standard of living. Quick work was necessary to adjust the German attitude toward the Soviet Union, which until the summer of 1941 had been a friend and ally. The war in the west, meanwhile, was seen as won – crosses depict the demise of the enemy. (Imperial War Museum)

# THE ATTACK UPON THE SOVIET UNION

The regimes of Nazi Germany and of Soviet Russia were politically hostile to each other. Racially, the two nations were enemies. Culturally, they were deeply divided. Given these and other factors, it was inevitable that in time war would break out between them.

The Teutons and the Slavs had been racial enemies for hundreds of years. The former, viewing the under-populated and agriculturally fertile lands in the east, had seen in them the chance to realize the Germanic dream of Lebensraum – living space. Space in which to expand. Space which they could colonize. In *Mein Kampf*, Hitler had expressed this age-old ambition in the words, 'If one needs space and territory in Europe then, by and large, this can only be gained at the expense of Russia.' There had always been, in Germany, this pressure to the east – *der Drang nach Osten* – and Hitler was in his time, only the most recent of those German leaders who sought to still their peoples' hunger for land at the expense of the eastern neighbour.

Culturally, the National Socialists considered the eastern lands to be populated by a race almost subhuman in social outlook and in culture. Russia had scarcely changed since Byzantium, according to some German political philosophers, and the terribly low living standard of the great mass of the people, was on a level more akin to an oriental state than to a major European nation. There was no doubt about it, so far as the Nazi politicians were concerned; the Slavs were a poor lot, fit only to carry out simple tasks under the direction of German masters.

Politically, Soviet Communism was the antithesis of German National Socialism, and the Nazi leaders were convinced that the Bolshevik grip on Russia was despotic and orientally cruel, intended to keep the peoples of the Soviet Union in permanent political subjection. The Communist butchery of hostages and prisoners during the Revolution had been on a scale not previously known among great nations. The deliberate starvation of millions of Ukrainians in government-directed famines, the purges of the military, of the intellectuals and of the Party faithful were further proof to the Nazis that Stalin was a bloody tyrant

holding together his tortured state only by repression and terror. The whole Soviet system was considered to be in decay. Hitler condemned the USSR as '. . . a ramshackle affair. One good kick at the front door will bring the whole rotten edifice crashing down.'

In the preparations he made to bring about war in Europe, the German leader sought to avoid the mistake of which the Imperial leadership had been guilty in the First World War. Political errors had forced Germany to fight on two fronts during that war. Hitler decided that if the Reich was to fight on one front at a time, he must neutralize the threat from the east. If he could achieve this, with his back shielded he could turn against the western enemies and destroy them. The racial and political enmity that divided Russia and Germany would certainly make it difficult to reach an understanding with the Soviets, but Hitler knew he could exploit the hostility that existed between the Capitalist West and the Communist East. This enmity was due not only to the antipathy of political systems, but owed more to the Russian fear that the Western powers were determined to overthrow the revolution. This they had attempted to do between 1918 and 1922 when expeditionary forces from western European and American armies had been sent to destroy the infant Bolshevik State. Determined to exploit this phobia of the Soviet government, *vis-à-vis* the Western democracies, Hitler made discreet approaches to the Soviets. The reward for these diplomatic efforts was the 1939 non-aggression pact between the two countries.

The principal outcome of the signing of that pact was that the full strength of the German war machine could be deployed against other enemies of the Reich particularly, against France and Great Britain. More than that. Not only did Germany not have to fear an attack from the east, but Russian oil fuelled the panzers during the first campaigns; Russian wheat fed German troops during their victorious advances; Russian petrol sped the bombers which raided the cities of the United Kingdom during the Battle of Britain, and Russian steel made the bombs which destroyed the houses of those cities. The non-aggression pact had given Germany not only a shield to her back but food and fuel for her economy. It was a good bargain for the Germans. The Russians also gained, but their benefits included other, less material advantages.

German exports to the USSR had not been as economically important as the Russian grain and oil imports from that country, but the Soviets achieved one important concession. They no longer had to waste effort infiltrating agents into arms factories to establish what was being produced. Officers from the Red Army were encouraged to visit German factories to see for themselves the efficient war production whose output, in the capable hands of the Wehrmacht, had laid low the Reich's enemies in the west. The intention to over-awe the simple Slavs with Teuton efficiency rebounded upon the Germans. Those Red Army officers were indeed astonished. Not, however, at the efficiency within the factories, but at the low production rates and the inferior types of machines that were being produced.

There was the case of a Red Army commission whose officers were shown round a factory in which the Panzer IV, described to them as Germany's heavy tank, were being constructed. The Red Army experts refused to believe that the Panzer IV represented Germany's principal armoured fighting vehicle and demanded to see the real, heavy machines. Still encountering what they thought to be deliberate obstruction they appealed to Hitler and were assured by him that what had been told them was true. The Panzer IV was Germany's main battle tank. The Russians were aware that in their own factories the KV I and the T-34 were already in full production and that these were, in every respect, superior machines to any being produced in Germany. Another commission was surprised, but hid that surprise well, when it learned that the German Army's principal anti-tank gun was the 5cm weapon which had proved impotent against Allied armour in the French campaign. Both in tank and anti-tank technology the Red Army would have the advantage if it came to war.

The 1939 pact had been a complete reversal and the former political foe, Soviet Russia, was now linked to Germany, however uneasily. But the feelings of hostility towards a racial enemy are less easy to submerge than are contemporary political compromises. It is, therefore, not surprising to learn that the professional soldier, Halder,

had begun to consider a military operation against the Soviet Union even before plans for Operation 'Sealion' had been formally committed to paper. As early as 30 June, his diary entry had expressed the necessity for Germany to prepare herself for a war in the east and, at the end of July, his diary entry recorded the conviction that war with Russia was inevitable.

Such thoughts had always been in the mind of the Führer and despite the advantages which the non-aggression pact had brought, he decided to give substance to his thoughts and invited the Army Commander-in-Chief, Field Marshal Walter von Brauchitsch, to the Chancellery. During the course of the discussion von Brauchitsch was ordered to attack the Soviet Union in the autumn of 1940. Although the Commander-in-Chief of the army was able to assure the Führer that some work had indeed started, he felt it his duty to point out that such an operation required detailed planning, preparation and a build-up of military strength. Troop movements, concentration of materials and strategic planning had only just begun. Reluctantly, Hitler was forced to concede that war against the Soviet Union could not be undertaken during what remained of 1940. For its part, the German military leadership, now aware of the Führer's intentions, acted with speed and within ten days OKW was able to lay down that May would be the month during which the new campaign would begin. Hitler then ordered the strength of the field army to be raised to 180 divisions, more than sufficient to meet the needs of the new campaign.

Discussions between von Brauchitsch and Halder, his Chief of Staff, considered the way in which the new war would be conducted. Lacking, as yet, Hitler's clear directive on grand strategy, the army leaders considered how the German Army was to engage and destroy the Russian forces in the 'Barbarossa' operation. The most favoured plan was for the mass of the army to advance towards Moscow with the armies of its left wing touching the Baltic thus forming a flank protection to the drive against Moscow, and for a strong right wing force to act against the great mass of Red Army divisions and corps which were believed to be concentrated in the Ukraine, and which would be attacked first and in strength.

The projected battle plan was textbook in its approach. In the south the powerful attack by the German right wing would smash a gap in the Red line through which would pour panzer columns heading relentlessly south-eastwards towards the Caspian Sea. The German armies would thus pass behind the Russian front, moving quickly so as to trap the enemy host inside the battle area. Within that trap the great mass of the Red Army grouped in the Ukraine, caught between German forces attacking from both west and east would be forced to fight on two fronts and would be destroyed. With the bulk of the Red Army smashed in the south, the attack against the Russian capital would then become the first priority.

Major-General Marcks, Chief of Staff of Eighteenth Army, was given the task of drawing up an operations plan for the war against the Soviet Union. His report proposed a strategy which differed in detail from that of Halder and von Brauchitsch although both plans did agree that, '. . . the purpose of the campaign is to smash the Russian armed forces and to destroy Russia's capacity to act aggressively against the Reich'. Marcks went farther than von Brauchitsch and laid down a final objective. '. . . in order to protect the German Homeland against attacks by Red Air Force bombers, a line must be reached extending from the lower Don – the middle Volga to north of Dvina. Russia's war industries, her food supplies and raw material deposits are in the Ukraine and in the basin of the Donets, as well as in the industrial complexes of Moscow and Leningrad. The eastern factory areas (the Urals) are not yet in full operation . . . Moscow must be considered as the industrial, political and spiritual centre of Russia. Its seizure would lead to the destruction of a coherent Russian State . . .'

Marcks proposed that to carry out the plan of operation two groups of German armies would be needed. These could not advance eastwards as a single united force for they would be separated at the very opening of the campaign by a vast terrain barrier, the Pripet Marshes. Not until those army groups had bypassed the marshes could they join up on its eastern side and resume a joint advance towards Moscow.

The destruction of the Red Army in the western regions of the Soviet Union should present no difficulty; Marcks advancing the proposition that the enemy would be forced to stand and fight in western Russia. 'They. . . (the Russian armies) cannot avoid a decision as they did in 1812 . . . A modern military force of more than a hundred divisions cannot simply abandon its supply source. It is, therefore, to be anticipated that the Red Army will stand and do battle in a defensive position protecting Great Russia and the Ukraine. . .'

Amendments to the Marcks plan by von Paulus, Deputy Chief of the General Staff, proposed three army groups to make the attack and not two as Marcks had proposed. The objective second in importance to the destruction of the Red Army was the capture of the Soviet capital, Moscow, and the battle plans drawn up by the Chiefs of Staff of each of the army groups agreed with those priorities.

The battle strategy had been decided. All three army groups would co-operate in the destruction of the Red Army and would then go on to other objectives. Army Group North would strike in a generally north-eastern direction, aiming to reach and to invest, but not to fight for, its final objective, Leningrad. Hitler saw little point in fighting inside a major city when it could be starved and bombarded into surrender. Finnish military units would co-operate with Army Group North in surrounding and cutting off the city of Lenin.

Army Group Centre would drive towards its objective, Moscow, which Hitler did not see as one of the major objectives of the campaign. He directed that the Soviet capital would only form a principal target when the objectives of Army Groups North and South had been accomplished.

Army Group South, in order to achieve its final objective, was to strike deep into the Ukraine to seize the agricultural prizes of that region as well as the coal and iron producing areas of the Donets basin. Hitler kept the final army group objectives deliberately vague, intending to switch forces from one army group to another as the military situation demanded it. This was what the Führer enjoyed; for his soldiers to move on the battlefield as he commanded. Not for him those limitations of time and space that inhibited conventional commanders.

During 'Barbarossa' he was, in fact, to move whole corps and armies from one sector to another to gain some tactical advantage. In pursuit of these limited objectives he lost sight of the strategic target. This switching of whole formations, this flexibility would have been time-consuming and difficult to achieve using the well-developed road and rail networks of western Europe. In an area as poor in those facilities as the Soviet Union, the German Army was to find it

ГІТЛЕР ВИЗВОЛИТЕЛЬ

Left: Hitler the Liberator – from the oppressive regime of the despised Communists. This sort of propaganda was intended to appeal to the subject nations and communities of the USSR – such as the Baltic states and Georgia, which had suffered badly at the hands of the Communists during the 1920s.

almost impossible to carry out the Führer's commands.

Hitler was not alone in his ignorance of the new enemy. The difficulties of terrain and of communications inside Russia had not been fully realized by the army planners because little was known positively of that country. That conditions were poor had been appreciated, but not the degree of primitiveness. Country roads were little more than pathways connecting villages. Second-class roads were the same sort of tracks only wider and with more potholes and with surfaces that washed away in wet weather to become mud slicks. The main highways, and they were few in number, had all-weather surfaces, but were poorly designed and constructed. Army Department (Foreign Armies East), had produced for the campaign a series of handbooks on the various regions of the Soviet Union. The principal book in the series dealt with the western regions of that huge country. Despite these handbooks the German Army was entering a land almost unknown to it. The western regions of the Soviet Union were not visited by tourists and the only recent memories

**Солдаты Гитлера – друзья народа**

Right: German troops as friends of the people. This propaganda sheet was aimed specifically against the Communist partisans – from whom, implicitly, nobody was safe without the protection of the German Army. Propaganda of this type did not appear in the west.

of that region were those of the German soldiers who had fought there during the First World War. Out of a mosaic of memories, old military maps dating from Tsarist days, some geological treatises and a few train journeys were constructed the volumes produced by Foreign Armies East and these were intended to be military guides to the new theatre of operations. The results of the reconnaissance flights over western Russia which the Luftwaffe had begun in October 1940, were apparently not passed to the Foreign Armies Sections of OKH, for contemporary aerial photo-graphs of the region are not shown in the regional volumes.

The huge, almost impassable, natural obstacle known as the Pripet Marshes is ignored altogether in the Central Russian volume of the series and that central region seems to have been considered by the High Command as a land bridge across which the troops would pass to the assault upon Moscow. This High Command perspective obviously considered the Pripet Marshes, 600km long and more than 200km wide, as a sort of desert – an obstacle which would be bypassed and not fought across. It was poor in any sort of road links, especially those on an east/west axis.

The German High Command's plan to destroy the Red Army west of the Dnieper depended upon speed. Therefore, the marsh could not be allowed to be a major barrier. Army Group South would have to cross the major portion of it very quickly, while Army Group North would have to fight through only part of the swamp before it gained the Smolensk land bridge and the crossings over four major Russian rivers. Although Army High Command accepted that Red Army detachments would withdraw into the marsh, that risk was calculated and it was accepted that those defeated elements would be in no position to interfere with the German eastward drive.

Army High Command had then to consider the strength of the new enemy, the quality of his equipment and his fighting ability. The battlefield strength of the Red Army was put at about 175 divisions but the great mass of its soldiers had had no experience of battle. The German commanders thought themselves competent to judge the quality of the Red Army, for in the years before Hitler's rise to power Soviet Russia had provided the Germany Army with training grounds in the USSR. On the vast steppe lands the future panzer Generals had learned the tactics and strategy of mechanized warfare and how to control armour in the mass. Reports made by those officers when they returned to Germany described the Red Army as being still the traditional Russian steam-roller, ponderous in movement; crushing the enemy rather by force of numbers than by skill, and unmoved by hardships or casualties. In 1939, German officers were able to re-evaluate the men, the training and equipment of the Red Army units, having met them in Poland when Russia invaded that country. Then as a final confirmation came reports on the Red Army which had attacked Finland during the winter of 1939/40. The sickening casualty rate, the shoddy equipment, the appallingly low standard of training and tactics had all served to convince those in authority in Germany that the Red Army was a mass of unthinking moujiks, almost animal in their acceptance of primitive conditions.

The war with Russia would be almost exclusively an army operation. The generals had been deprived of the chance of proving their skill in an invasion of Britain by the opposition of the admirals. This new campaign did not need the navy's support and that service could be excluded, as far as it was possible to do this, from any part of Operation 'Barbarossa'. The Army alone would win this war for the Führer and the Fatherland.

The navy was hardly involved and the Luftwaffe had only its usual role to play. During the opening hours of the new war its machines would destroy the Red Air Force on the ground. To render the Soviet air force impotent would take two or three days. Then the Luftwaffe could begin the second task – close support for the forces locked in the vast battle of annihilation on the ground.

Not all the German commanders viewed with enthusiasm the prospect of a war with Russia. Many, including Halder, were convinced that in relation to Germany's grand strategy there was nothing to be gained from a war with the USSR until Britain, the foe in the west, had been beaten. In the opinion of those officers, Russia, in 1940, posed no military threat to the Reich nor would she until military parity with Germany had been gained and that would not be for several years. During that time, if the grand strategy design were accepted and followed, Great Britain and her Middle East Empire would have been defeated and all the strategic, economic and political initiatives would be in German hands.

This grand strategy concept of the senior commanders was rejected by Hitler. In his opinion the Soviet State was in decay and therefore the Soviet armed forces, the military guardians of that state, must be poor in quality. To prove his thesis he could point to the débâcle in Finland and evidence of the Red Army's low fighting morale, poor equipment and bad leadership during that campaign. The most senior Russian commanders were, he concluded, the cowed, repressed survivors of the bloody purges of 1937, whose every action had to be approved by a political commissar. Such a command structure did not argue for dynamic leadership on the battlefield. Russia was ripe to be attacked.

The High Command, obedient to the Führer, saw only a ponderous, slow moving mass of the Red Army which, in Marcks' opinion, would not abandon its sources of supply and which, tied down economically in western Russia, would be annihilated by a blitzkrieg fought out to the west of the River Dnieper. That blitzkrieg would be fought with such fury that the campaign would be opened, fought and won before the onset of winter. So confident were the army commanders

Above: The dawn of war in the east. Guderian (right) was to lead his tanks at breathtaking speed through the Russian defences; the campaign would be short, sharp and triumphant. But few really understood how vast were the lands to the east.

of victory within five months that cold weather clothing had been ordered for only one fifth of the field army – sufficient to equip only those divisions which would form the army of occupation in Russia.

The timetable for the new war was a short one. From start line to final objective – five months. That is, from the first barrage to the sounding of the ceasefire, about twenty weeks. Within that short time the Red Army would have been destroyed in the field, the principal cities of western Russia would have been taken, the economic prizes of the Ukraine wheat and industries of the Donets basin would be in German hands and the Third Reich, extending from the North Sea to the Volga, would be powerful enough to challenge America. It was an intoxicating picture.

Small wonder then, that one of the most telling photographs of the Russo-German war, was that taken shortly before dawn on 22 June 1941. The scene is a hill overlooking a Polish river which marked the frontier between the Third Reich and the Soviet Union. The silhouettes of German generals can be seen. Field Marshal Fedor von Bock, Commanding Army Group Centre, stands, his face turned eastward toward the dawn. The stocky shape of Guderian, the Panzer commander, is easily identified. One of the group is drinking from a champagne flute. This scene was repeated at many places along the demarcation line between the two powers – German officers with glasses of champagne in their hands, drinking a toast to the war which they were so very soon to fight.

They were drinking to a war against a country of whose potential they were ignorant; against a force which was superior in number to their own but which they were confident they could defeat in five months. What would happen if that timetable were not kept to was one question that seemed not to have been asked. The German Army did not know it, but it was entering upon a war based on theses which were invalid. Their Supreme Commander, Adolf Hitler, did not have a fixed operational plan, but instead a pragmatic approach. Nor had strategic objectives been set, other than that the army was to reach a line from Archangelsk to the Caspian Sea, so that German factories could not be bombed by Russian aircraft. That alone seems to have been the intention.

It seems unbelievable that a war should come about on so flimsy a pretext as the need to protect German factories against bombing by the Red Air Force. Had Germany's leaders so desired, the Soviets could have been kept neutral for years by political and diplomatic means and, for as long as they were neutral, there was no likelihood of Red bombs falling on Silesian factories. As a defence against any aerial attack the build-up of an efficient night fighter arm or a greater density of anti-aircraft guns would have been a cheaper solution to the hypothetical problem than the unleashing of a major war. The battle line, along which seven thousand German guns were lined up, ran for 1,600km, from Memel in the north to the Black Sea. Along its length were poised Army Group North commanded by Field Marshal Ritter von Leeb; Army Group Centre under the command of Field Marshal Fedor von Bock; and finally, Army Group South, led by Field Marshal Gerd von Rundstedt. The establishment of Army Group South included two Roumanian armies, and Army Group North had the support of the small but efficient Finnish Army.

The maximum strength was with Army Group Centre which was considered by Hitler as a sort of reservoir of forces from which units could be taken to build up whatever plan was at that time in his mind. Army Group Centre's infantry armies were strengthened by two Panzer groups – later to be known as Panzer armies. On the left flank, 3rd (Colonel General Hoth), and 2nd (Colonel General Guderian), on the right. Army Groups South and North each had one Panzer army; the 4th (Colonel General Hoepner) with Army Group North and 1st (Colonel General von Kleist), with Army Group South. A total of 2,700 armoured fighting vehicles were in the four Panzer armies. The whole weight of the Luftwaffe, excepting only those few squadrons serving in other theatres, was deployed in support of the army in the east; a force of about 2,700 aircraft; principally bombers.

From the German point of view their army, the most battle tested force in Europe, victors of a succession of glittering campaigns; powerful, well-equipped and strongly supported by a very competent Luftwaffe, was ready to attack the ancient racial and political enemy in the east. The Germans were supremely confident. They could not be otherwise. There must be an absolute certainty of victory when a nation of eighty millions and having limited resources, goes to war with a nation whose territory comprises one-sixth of the earth's surface and which is possessed of almost unlimited resources in manpower and materials. During the early hours of the morning of 22 June 1941, the second-hands ticked away the last minutes of peace between the Third Reich and Soviet Russia, and the German Army, supremely confident, stood waiting for the new war to begin.

The Red Army, which would meet the fury of the German assault, was indeed an unknown factor. Hitler was correct, in one of his assessments of it.

It did lack dynamism because the Russian service had undergone a fearful blood-letting. In 1937 Stalin, fearing that the military leaders might feel themselves strong enough to challenge the political rule of the Communist Party, sought ways to reduce their power.

There had been rumblings of discontent from the military during the collectivization programme of the 1920s and 1930s. At that time millions of Russian farmers were being murdered or starved to death on Party orders, in an attempt to force the survivors to agree to the swindle of collectivization. Army leaders had warned that the peasants who made up much of the Red Army, might not obey orders to kill their own people. To question the Party's orders demanded that the military be punished but the opposition had not been sufficiently sinister for its leaders to be put on public show trial. A more plausible reason must be found before Stalin could unleash the terror. He found it by casting suspicion on the training facilities which had been made available to the Reichswehr before Hitler's accession to power. Stalin described these facilities as the cover for a plot between the Red Army commanders and the German High Command. Proof positive was still lacking to justify the action he was planning, but by a sinister coincidence it was soon to hand. What was the revelation which caused the terror to be unleashed upon the Soviet military commanders has never been proved, but it was widely believed, in German military circles, that the accusations made by the Communist prosecutors were based upon forged documents. What is known for certain is that SS General Heydrich, leader of the SD, the Sicherheitsdienst of the SS, had approached the leaders of Abwehr, the official Intelligence-gathering service of the Reich, and had asked for specimen signatures of leading Russian soldiers. Forged letters incriminating the Soviet military leaders in a plot with the German General Staff found their way to Moscow. Shortly thereafter, the blood-letting began and it ran unchecked almost until the German attack in June 1941.

The first soldiers to fall were Marshal Tuchachevsky, one of the founders of the Red Army, and with him seven other senior commanders. The 'bolshaya Chistka', the great purge of the officer corps had begun. Before it ended three of the five marshals of the Soviet Union had been shot, as well as thirteen of the fifteen army commanders and 220 out of 406 brigade commanders. Thirty-five thousand of the Red Army's most capable officers were murdered, including more than half the generals and eighty per cent of the colonels.

Great numbers of Red Army commanders of intermediate rank vanished into concentration camps and stayed there until, with the German invasion, their skills were suddenly needed and they were officers once again. Those men accepted, apparently without complaint, the falseness of the charges that imprisoned them, the humiliation of the concentration camps and their own cynical reinstatement as officers. This passive acceptance of Fate's blows is part of the Russian make-up and the 'nichevo' concept was reinforced by the Soviet ethos that the Party is always right and that, therefore, Comrade Stalin, must have acted correctly. This humiliating acceptance of injustice was seen by the Germans as another example of the inability of the Slavs to see justice and reason as moral precepts rather than instruments of Party policy.

A great many of the officers of the Red Army were members of the Communist Party who accepted that it might sacrifice without hesitation, not only comrades but even cherished principles to gain an advantage. Brought back from the stinking Gulags those men were put straight into uniform and took up the task of defending the

Below: The enemy. Soviet senior commanders at pre-war manoeuvres in Germany.

Party and the tyrant who had caused them to be imprisoned and tortured. One senior Red Army commander was famous for his set of stainless steel false teeth. His natural teeth had been bashed out of his head by enthusiastic agents of the NKVD; the forerunners of the KGB.

The pre-war purges broke the morale of the Red Army, not merely by killing its most experienced officers, but through the reimposition of the commissar system. During the Revolution, to ensure compliance to Party orders the system was introduced that any military decision had to be approved by a Communist commissar. This situation led, inevitably, to conflicts of opinion between the political and the military officers on a course of an action to be followed. The decision of the Party man almost invariably overrode that of the soldier. The rule that a political decided military policy was shown to be unsound and in the early 1930s there had been a move to reduce the influence of the commissar and to raise that of the military.

It had once been Soviet dogma that only workers and peasants could be considered as soldiers of the Red Army. When general conscription was introduced and all Soviet men of military age were recruited, commissars were considered unnecessary and were abolished. Such liberalization was short-lived. After 1937, following the purges, not only were the commissars reintroduced into the service but their power was increased. The influence of the military was thereby diminished because officers were reluctant to make decisions for fear of being denounced by the politicals. Officers either deferred making a decision, hoping in a fatalistic way that a problem would resolve itself, or else asked for a ruling from a higher authority. This situation, which reduced the professional soldier to impotence by the rule of the Party and the decisions of a commissar unfamiliar with military problems, did not, as Hitler correctly surmised, make for efficiency.

The concept of the infallibility of the leader permeated every strata of Soviet society – the army no less than the civilian. Stalin had only to hint, to suggest, to propose and his words were acted upon as if they were commandments. His idea that major tank formations should be broken up and distributed in small numbers in an infantry support role, was contrary to contemporary military thought. It was not only accepted by the Red Army High Command but was lauded by them

as a brilliant move. The Germans in their successful campaigns had shown that armour used in mass brought victory. Stalin thought otherwise and broke down seven armoured corps to brigade formations.

In essence then, the Red Army was a conscript mass led by officers frightened to make decisions and in many cases untrained for the task of commanding major formations in a modern war. In the small, pre-Hitler German Army, every NCO and officer had been trained to take over a post one or two ranks superior to his own. Thus, a divisional commander was capable of leading a corps and a battalion commander could lead a brigade. In the Red Army, and because of the purges, the reverse applied. A divisional commander was often only a battalion commander promoted because the post was vacant and not because he was competent. That situation, too, militated against the Red Army's being an effective fighting force in time of war.

Weakness at command level has the effect that officers lack initiative and act according to the book. It was written in Red Army regulations that in every situation the soldier must attack. Is an enemy position to be taken? then attack. Is ground lost? attack and recover it. And if the first assault fails, it is to be repeated at regular and precise intervals until the lost ground is recovered. Such a rigid policy, applied without consideration to the tactical situation, can only result in high casualties. Added to that the insistence of commanders upon using the Red Army infantry's standard assault tactic, that of the human wave – line after line of men marching almost shoulder to shoulder toward the enemy lines, resulted in even higher casualty returns. The tactics of fire and movement, although written into field service regulations and adopted, were in practice seldom used. Bolshevik dogma prevailed and because the psychological effect of the human wave had been successful in the Revolution's wars, it followed, so far as the Red Army's commanders were concerned, that that tactic, allied to Communist attitudes, would make the Red Army invincible in any war. Sadly for thousands of Russian infantrymen those headlong charges into machine-gun fire brought not victory but death.

In the matter of arms and equipment the Red Army was in many ways superior to the Germans. We have seen earlier in this chapter that the

Soviets had T-34 and the KV I tanks ready to bring into action. Russian anti-tank guns were superior in range and penetrative powers to those on standard issue to the German Army. The Shpagin machine pistols were on general issue and in the matter of clothing, Russian boots were first-class, completely waterproof – which the German jack-boots were not – and the Red Army had winter clothing – which the Germans had not.

This catalogue needs qualification. The actual number of T-34 and KV I with the field army was not more than 1,500. The greater proportion of AFVs were lightly armoured and undergunned models from the late 1920s. There were defects in the supply system which depended upon an over-worked rail system with insufficient tracks; on convoys of lorries driving on the terrible roads or else upon the ubiquitous *panje* wagons – light wooden carts drawn by horses. There was one sure Russian method of overcoming local short-ages. This was to load each foot soldier en route to the forward area with something extra to carry; a box of ammunition or a couple of shells. It was a simple solution which had proved itself during manoeuvres and would be sure to work under active service conditions. According to Red Army manuals, any enemy invasion of Soviet territory would be rebuffed and followed by an advance into that enemy's country. Thus there would be little need to provide rations for the advancing Soviet soldiers. The peasants of the enemy country, liberated from the yoke of landlords and capit-alists, would, in gratitude, shower food upon the Red Army men and, if the Fascist oppressors had driven away the generously disposed local civilian population, the Red Army would help itself and live off the land.

Western Russia was split into four military districts, the name of each of which was changed to 'Fronts' when war began. Given here are the names and orders of battle for just those Fronts which faced the Germans. Red Army formations which confronted the Finns are not listed.

The Baltic Military District/North-west Front, was commanded by Colonel-General Kusnetzov, who controlled 8th (Sobenikov) and 4th (Morosov) Armies. In reserve was 27th Army. The total strength of North-west Front, excluding the reserve army, was twenty infantry and the equivalent of six armoured divisions. That group was deployed along the border with East Prussia, extending northwards as far as Memel.

The Western Military District/West Front, the central group of armies, was in a tactically unsound situation. Much of the territory it held was a salient which followed the course of the River Bug, the frontier between the Reich and the Soviet Union. West Front was commanded by General Pavlov, with the right flank made up of 3rd Army (Lieutenant-General Kusnetzov). The 10th Army (Golubyev) stood in the salient out-flanked by a Panzer Group to the north and Kluge's Army to the south. The 4th Red Army, on the left wing, had at its back the northern reaches of the Pripet Marshes. West Front had under command 26 infantry and 10 armoured divisions. In reserve stood Flatov's 13th Army; a chiefly infantry grouping.

The Kiev Military District/South-west Front, under the command of Colonel-General Kirponos, formed the left wing of the Red armies confronting Army Group South. In the belief that the principal German thrust would be made to seize economic prizes, the Soviet High Command had concen-trated the greatest number of its armies in the south. The battle line of South-west Front was 5th Army (Potapov), 6th (Musechenko), 26th (Kostenko), 12th (Ponedelin) and 19th Army (Smirnov). The 19th Army was, until the outbreak of war, known as the Odessa Military District, but was incorporated into Kirponos' command at the outbreak of war. In reserve to South-west Front was the newly formed 28th Army. The strength of the front, excluding the Reserve Army, was fifty-two divisions of infantry and the equivalent of eighteen armoured divisions, and these were disposed along a line from the Black Sea, along the Carpathian mountains to the lower reaches of the Bug. At the back of Potapov's 5th Army ran a major area of the Pripet Marshes.

There were ten Red armies in the battle line with a further three in reserve. These (excluding the reserves) made up a force of 98 infantry or motorized divisions and the equivalent of 34 armoured divisions, together with a number of cavalry and security divisions.

But the Red Army was not deployed for war. Stalin was unwilling to believe that Germany would attack. He reasoned that such an action would open a two-front war for Germany and that on economic grounds, the dependence of the Third Reich upon supplies from Russia was so great, that war was out of the question. In order not to provide Hitler with an excuse for war, the

Red dictator gave strict orders that Russian anti-aircraft batteries were not to fire at any Luftwaffe machines which infringed Soviet air space along the common frontier. So unprepared was the Red Army for the coming conflict that in two of the military districts tractors, which were in use as prime movers for the army's heavy artillery, were taken away from the artillery and handed back to the farmers from whom they had been comandeered. Then, too, at the time of the German assault, 5th Army was on manoeuvres. On a number of other sectors Red Army divisions had been pulled back from the frontier lest their presence be considered provocative to the Germans.

On 13 June, to still the rumours of an impending war and in carefully chosen words, Tass Press Agency put out a Soviet Government statement that the Third Reich had made no demands upon the Soviet Union, that the mobilization of reserves and the military manoeuvres to train them was not in any way a threat to Germany.

In the concluding paragraph of that Tass report the Soviet authorities laid the blame for the spread of rumours very firmly upon the British Government's using crude propaganda tricks against both Germany and the Soviet Union. The Tass report was not even mentioned by German newspapers. They had begun to leak the story that the invasion of England would take place within three – at the latest five – weeks. All this activity was deception. The Germans spread rumours and speculated in newspapers about an invasion in order to deceive the Soviets about the build-up of the forces facing the Red Army. The hours passed. Then the code word 'Dortmund' was issued; the instruction that Operation 'Barbarossa', was definitely 'on'. German troops began to move towards their start lines.

In the Soviet Union, Stalin and the senior military commanders, not convinced despite the flow of reports of German activity, still forbade the Red Army to undertake any action which the Germans could claim as provocative. Even as late as 21 June, the day before the war began, Stalin refused to place the Red Army formations along the frontier on full alert. He underwent a change of mind during that evening and produced Directive No. 1, the instruction for the Army to go on to a war footing. The Directive was hedged about with conditions, the chief of which was that the troops were not to make any noise which would alarm the Germans and thereby provoke an attack. The Red Army's senior commanders were warned not to respond to German provocation and they were forbidden to undertake any sort of retaliatory action against German incursions without direct and specific orders from Stalin.

His refusal to accept the clear evidence of a German invasion condemned a great many Red Army soldiers to death or to captivity. The Red dictator had convinced himself that the build-up of German forces in Poland had been a manoeuvre to deceive the British. The Intelligence details he had received giving the exact date of the German assault, reports from Soviet agents within the Reichs Government, reports from German deserters; even British warnings of an attack were all discounted. The leader knew best. In his eyes the British needed Russia as an ally in her war against Germany and would use every means to bring this about. The Leader knew best, and refused to act. Thus, to a high degree unprepared,

Below and right: To begin with, the Germans were received as liberators. To the conquerors, the poverty of the peasants came as a shock, and an exhibition was mounted in Germany to demonstrate the reality of life in the east.

the Red Army came under attack. On the face of it, there was every possibility that the Red Army – ponderous in planning and in manoeuvre, might be overrun in the first great assault by the three German Army Groups. There were, however, certain factors to aid the Soviets of which Marcks had been unaware when he made his plans.

The assessment of Red Army strength was based on out-of-date figures obtained years before by German Intelligence sources and never updated. These figures seriously underestimated not only the field force, with which the Red Army would enter the war; or the reserves available to replace the losses which would be suffered, but more importantly, they ignored completely the partisan forces. A second factor concerned industry. According to Marcks, the Red Army would have to stand and fight because no modern army could afford to abandon its supply sources. The German General Staff Intelligence departments were obviously not aware that the movement of Soviet arms factories to areas east of the Urals had already begun and that these were already in production. The factories and mines of the Donets basin were certainly important to Russian arms production but they were not vital to the Soviet war plan. If they were to be lost to the German invader, arms and supplies could still be produced in sufficient numbers in the factories in the east. Marcks, who did not know of the relocation of Russian industry, still thought of the Donets as its heart. His whole strategy was based on the premise that the Red forces, low in number and poor in morale, would have to fight to defend those arms-producing areas in western Russia and being thus tied down could be destroyed west of the Dnieper. It was a miscalculation that was to play its part in causing Operation 'Barbarossa' to fail.

We now have both armies positioned. The Germans, their pragmatic plans based upon false premises, wait for X-Hour. The Führer's Order of the Day had been read out on every company parade during that last evening. 'The task is no longer the defence of individual countries but the security of Europe and thus the saving of them all . . .' Such sentiments proclaimed nothing less than a crusade.

In the godless empire across the Bug, men of the Red Army moved into field fortifications not knowing what lay ahead of them. Their leaders had told them, through the Tass Agency, that the Germans wanted peace. Shortly after midnight a Russian train loaded with wheat and the raw materials of war crossed the Bug river bridge and into German-held Poland. Only hours before the invasion began Stalin was still sending vital war supplies to the Reich.

Two world powers stood in confrontation. Seen from the perspective of one of those powers – Germany – the new war would be a five-month campaign. The Soviet perspective was that any attack would be countered and followed, within days, by their own counter-offensive. Communist élan would make the Red Army victorious and send it to cleanse those enemy lands of the fascists who had invaded the Soviet Union. Neither power was right in their forecast of how the war would develop, but eventually, and only after years of bitter conflict, the Russians did move into German territory. They came not as liberators, however, but as conquerers determined on revenge; by the time that the Red Army had smashed its way into Germany, twenty million Russians had been killed.

At 5.30 on the morning of Sunday, 22 June, the German Press Agency announced the declaration of war on the Soviet Union. That announcement was repeated throughout the day, always accompanied by a heroic fanfare, the choice of which had cost Josef Goebbels, the Reichs Propaganda Minister, a great many sleepless hours, for the fanfare had to have the right sound of authority but not be pompous. The fanfare was used to precede each High Command communiqué and in those early weeks they came fast and often; on some occasions several times in a single day.

'Barbarossa' had begun well for the Germans. Two hours before the Press Agency announced the declaration of war, the barrage had opened and under its cover seven infantry armies and four panzer groups had crossed the start lines. The greatest war in history had begun.

In matters of strategy and tactics considerable advantage accrues to the side which gains the element of surprise. This, the Germans were able to achieve. When, at long last, Stalin's Directive No. 1 was issued it was already too late for some front-line units. The German attack had begun before they had received the new orders.

The opening barrage, fired by 7,184 guns, crashed down upon the Russian front line and then marched eastwards searching out and destroying troop concentrations in the reserve areas. On some parts of the Russian line the bombardment's fury fell upon trenches that were empty. There the infantry divisions which should have manned the positions had been pulled back from the frontier because of Stalin's determination to avoid a confrontation. On other sectors the trenches were unmanned because the Directive to take up full alert status had not been received. But there was slaughter in other areas. There the shells killed Russian troops as they waited, cocooned within that torpor into which infantrymen fall after they have been wakened from sleep and marched into trenches there to wait through long, long hours for God knows what to happen, because nobody ever tells them anything.

Those sleepy soldiers saw at last, in the middle hours of the night, flickering white lights in the west followed within seconds by whirring, whistling sounds and then crashing detonations as shells exploded around them. The Germans; those people on the other side of the frontier, had opened fire. The duration of the bombardment was not everywhere the same. On some sectors a short but furious barrage was followed by a panzer thrust or a storming charge by infantry. The artillery fire lasted longer on those sectors where the local German commander was determined to smash all likelihood of opposition before he committed his own infantry to battle.

Nor did the barrage fall along the whole battle line between Memel and the Black Sea, for that was more than 1,600 kilometres long and the strength of the German artillery was just over 7,000 barrels. The gun density was thus, four guns for every kilometre of front. The battle line was too vast to be attacked along its entire length and there were great stretches on which not even the flicker of gunfire on a far horizon or the murmuring thunder of guns showed that a war had begun.

But on those sectors where the barrage went in with full force, it crushed the Red Army defenders. Hans-Detlev Resch, a German soldier who went into 'Barbarossa' and lost a leg in the great encirclement battle near Kiev, described the events of the opening day as seen by an infantryman. 'Even before the barrage finished we were already in assault readiness. We had been told that our guns would fire until the enemy was "sturm reif", that is to say that he was in a condition where he will offer only little resistance to our infantry assault. Our gunners were doing their work well. Then red flares went up along our regiment's front – all three battalions were in the line. It was the sign to prepare to storm. Our officers stood up. We also stood, bowed over our rifles – there were no machine pistols in those days – and waited.

'The enemy positions lay across a very small stream and their outposts were not more than 400 metres distant from our own. There was only stunted vegetation along the river bank, otherwise the terrain was quite open. On our side of the river we had a low rise and we had our slit trenches on the reverse slope of that ridge. The Ivans had no hill, and their positions, a series of continuous trench lines, were in full view from our look-out posts.

'As soon as the first shells went over we moved up to the crest of the ridge and lay on the reverse slope waiting for the artillery to complete its work. Surprisingly, the Russians did not return our shell fire. At least I didn't hear anything and it is always possible to tell the difference between outgoing shells and incoming ones.

'It began to get light and then came the order to advance. The Russian outpost positions were a mess – completely destroyed – but there were no signs of bodies, pieces of uniform or equipment. The positions had been unmanned. The main trenches were a different matter and our greatest difficulty was making our way through the barbed wire barricades. We had been told to expect minefields but our pioneers found nothing.

'The slaughter in the main trenches was sickening. It was clear that the Ivans had been standing almost shoulder to shoulder waiting for us when the guns caught them. There was some fighting along other company sectors but none on ours. At one place a Maxim machine-gun came into action. The two men firing it were both Asiatics and had both been wounded but had kept firing until a patrol wiped them out.

'Our advance took us across the Russian reserve positions and we followed closely behind our barrage. A shell had smashed the roof of one dugout and a number of Ivans came scrambling out. They were so covered in powdery dust that they looked millers. Some of them were wearing only shirts. They had been sleeping in the dormitory dugout and they were all wearing their side hats. It was an incongruous sight; flapping shirt tails and little side hats.

'Our section overran their position and I was able to use, for the first time in my life, words in a foreign language. Our company commander had taught us a few basic words of Russian and as those dusty figures scrambled through the broken timbers of their dugout, I shouted at them "Rooki verch". To my delight and surprise, they put their hands up.'

It was not everywhere so easy. On some sectors where the Red Army unit was a first-class one, the German infantry advance was quickly slowed down and then halted by a great many snipers who found, in those first days, that the Germans were easy targets. There were several reasons for this. The comparatively easy successes between 1939 and 1941, had made the Germans careless. They had not suffered from snipers too much in other campaigns and were quite unaware of how efficiently the Red Army trained its men or the pains that those soldiers took to select a perfect killing-ground. The snipers were also aided by the design of German uniform in which officers wore shoulder-boards of aluminium thread with collar patches of the same material, and non-commissioned officers had aluminium lace on collars and shoulders. Wound badges, Iron Crosses, proficiency badges, all of them metal, were worn on the outside of the tunic where they reflected the sun and indicated a target. One Russian sniper called the Germans 'Christmas trees', from the colour of their uniforms and the sparkling baubles they wore.

Across the flat and open countryside of eastern Poland, through the densely wooded, marshland of the north-eastern Baltic sectors and across the open steppe land of southern Poland and the Ukraine, panzer divisions thrust forward; steel fingers reaching out seeking to locate, encircle and destroy the Red Army. In certain regions the advance was fast and furious. In other places German armoured columns encountered and destroyed units which were moving up to the battle area unaware of how deeply the Germans had penetrated.

'I was serving during the opening stages of the Russian war in the reconnaissance battalion of a panzer division with Guderian's Panzer Group 2. We made good progress and by the second day of the campaign were well over the old Polish border. Our motorcycle company was leading the divisional advance, but we could not drive on roads for they did not exist in that part of eastern Poland

or in the western parts of the Soviet Union. There were so-called main highways, but they were reserved for supply columns. Country roads, the sort of roads that link one small town with another, were not up to German standard and were little more than rutted tracks in the sandy soil.

'Because of the dust clouds that were thrown up by motorcycle wheels our company was ordered to ride in open order and across country. This way we covered a wider front and those at the rear of the company were not blinded by the dust of those at its head. Since sun up we had neither heard nor seen any sign of the enemy and even on the opening day of the war all we had seen were only a few frightened prisoners. We halted just before midday to rest ourselves and our machines and to wait for the petrol trucks to come forward. Until they came and we had tanked up ready to resume the advance there was a chance to eat and to carry out running repairs on our bikes. With any luck there might even be time for a little sleep. The hours of driving were really very fatiguing. Suddenly, there was a great deal of shouting as contradictory orders were issued.

'Some sort of order was quickly restored. The cause of the excitement was that a sentry had reported a large vehicle column approaching. The trucks had not been identified but it was unlikely for them to be German because they were coming from the east, where the Russians were. Nor were there motorcycle outriders at the head of the column and we always had escorts for traffic control at the head and tail.

'We were given two tasks. Some platoons of our company were to dismount and take up ambush positions. Once they had opened fire with their machine-guns and had halted the Russian column, other platoons were to race up and down the line of vehicles machine-gunning them. We were soon ready for action although from first sighting the Russian column until the time when it came within range could not have taken more than twelve to fifteen minutes. Very soon the enemy trucks were clearly visible through binoculars. A convoy of fifty plus, open-topped, heavy trucks each loaded with standing men. If one reckons forty Red Army men in each truck then we are talking of more than 2,000 soldiers.

'Our ambush platoons opened fire. The Red drivers broke column very quickly, each moving off the track and driving fast to get into open

THE ATTACK UPON THE SOVIET UNION

country. So it was no longer a question of us driving down either side of the line of trucks and firing at them. They had to be hunted down. Some did not try to escape, or perhaps they could not. They stopped dead and the infantry jumped out and formed up as if on parade. It was an unbelievable sight. Those men, under fire from our machine-guns, formed ranks and began firing back at us in volleys. They didn't last long and while they were being sorted out, our motorcycle groups shot up the trucks driving off. Few got away. Most of the enemy surrendered. We had achieved total surprise and an easy victory.'

The Germans were not the only ones to achieve surprise. On 23 June, the second day of 'Barbarossa', 6th Panzer Division came under sudden and furious attack from a Soviet mechanized corps. This was the first real clash of armour in the campaign and that meeting was a shock for the panzer men.

Reinhardt's corps, to which 6th Panzer belonged, formed part of 4th Panzer Army advancing through Lithuania towards Leningrad. Late in the afternoon of the 23rd, the point unit came under fire and halted to allow the main of the Panzer division's armoured regiment, about a hundred vehicles, to close up to engage the enemy. The Red Army tank corps, until then carefully concealed, broke cover and moved forward in a massive counter-attack. And it was a massive counter-attack. Six hundred vehicles advancing in a single block making no attempt to deploy or to adopt any sort of tactical formation. The shock for the Germans lay less in the number of enemy machines roaring so menacingly towards them as in the size of many of them. The panzer men were seeing for the first time KV I tanks, 100 of them 'beefing up' the Russian attack.

The German battle plan was a standard tactic. The front would be held by a weak screen of lightly armoured vehicles while the 'heavies', 35 Panzer IV, deployed to form a corridor through which the Red Army machines would have to advance. The Panzer IV was at that time the main German battle tank and was armed with a 7.5cm gun. As the KVs rumbled past the waiting panzer, the Germans opened up with their main armament, aiming at what was the thinner and,

Below: Hundreds of thousands of Russians were captured by the Germans during the campaigns of 1941 and 1942. (Note that the surrendering Russians have not bothered to remove the bolts from their rifles.)

usually, more vulnerable side armour. The panzer commandants saw to their horror that the armour-piercing shells were not penetrating the Russian vehicles. The German commander ordered his vehicles to close with the enemy. By reducing the range it would give the shells a greater penetrating force, but even at 200 metres the projectiles struck and broke up in a mass of sparks but still did not penetrate the enemy's giant tanks.

Russian reaction to the German tactics and gunfire was slow and the panzer men soon appreciated why. The Soviets were not using wireless between vehicles. Only one voice was coming over the air, that of the commander. Only he had both a transmitter and a receiver. His subordinates had only a receiver. The commander alone could pass messages; the others could only receive them. They could not let him know the tactical situation as it developed in their vicinity. That lack of radio communication was probably responsible for the poor handling of the Russian armoured mass. This advantage, enjoyed by the Germans, was soon added to by the terrain factor. The ground was soft, in places little more than a marsh, and as a result of a quick reconnaissance of the ground, General Landgraf, commanding 6th Panzer, decided on a new tactic. His unit would pretend to be retreating in panic flight and would make for the marsh. When the Soviets pursued, as they almost certainly would, they would be bogged down in the swampy earth. With luck, German flexibility in command and the rapid passing of orders between vehicles, the Soviet advantages in armour and in numbers could be nullified.

The panzers broke formation and headed for the swamp. The Russians followed them and very soon 180 of their heavily armoured fighting vehicles were trapped and held fast. The other machines, the lightly armoured obsolete models fell victim to the guns of the panzers and lay blazing outside the village of Rossyenye. The surviving Red vehicles fled. The Germans had won the day, but the appearance of a Russian tank which could not be destroyed by German armour-piercing shells depressed the panzer men. A second depressing factor was that the Red Army could afford to put 600 machines into a battle for a village that had no strategic and little tactical value to either side. These factors were portents that the blitzkrieg had met the counters which

would destroy it, Russian superiority in the quality of their weapons and in the numbers they could field.

What had been the reaction of the Soviet commanders to the shock of the German attack? At all levels of command, from highest to lowest, the automatic response to an enemy strike had been to strike back. But under Stalin's Directive the authority to strike back had first to be obtained and this authority was slow in coming. Even when commanders in the field reported that German artillery had opened a bombardment, authority to respond was forbidden – in case it was a German provocation, and while Stalin hesitated his soldiers died in thousands. Once the Red leaders were assured that the German war had begun they ordered their forces to retaliate and the Directives show evidence of the panic which seized them. We shall go on, later in this chapter, to the orders given to ground force commanders. Let us at this point, deal with the roles of the German and Russian air forces during the opening stages of Operation 'Barbarossa'.

The German blitzkrieg depended for its success upon gaining and holding air superiority and this had been achieved in other campaigns by destroying the enemy air forces on the ground. Operation 'Barbarossa', was no exception and from X-Hour on the first day relays of Luftwaffe aircraft had raided the Russian airfields. In contrast to the army, whose Intelligence details were often out of date, the information obtained by the Air Force was very recent. As early as October 1940, Hitler had ordered the Luftwaffe to undertake high-altitude reconnaissance flights over the Soviet Union, and instructed the unit commander to fly the machines at so great a height that the Russians would not be aware of the incursions. The Red Air Force was indeed aware of them, but, under orders from Stalin, did not take off to intercept the specially outfitted He IIIs and Do 215 B2s which flew at heights well over 27,000 feet.

These reconnaissance flights by the Luftwaffe's specialist squadrons using the landing facilities of countries allied to Germany or under her control were able to photograph the whole of Russia west of Moscow paying special attention to airfields, depots and dumps.

Because the Luftwaffe's own main airfields were some distance from the frontier, those squadrons which would start the destruction of the Red Air Force, needed to take off long before X-Hour so as to be in the air ready to attack as soon as the army's barrage opened. Other specially trained bomber crews from Kampfgeschwader 2, 3 and 53 took off from fields in Poland and arrived over Red Air Force airfields in time for the bombardment to open. The machines of Zerstörergruppe 26 took off shortly after the main bomber force had left. That Gruppe had the task of attacking Russian fighter airfields. At first light the fighter arm of the Luftwaffe was put into the air to intercept Red machines in the air and to complete the destruction of aircraft on the ground.

The first German victory in the air was achieved at 03.40 hrs by Oberfeldwebel Oljenik of Jagdgeschwader 53 who shot down an I 16 fighter aircraft, but during the same air battle a Red Air Force airman showed with what devotion to duty his service was prepared to fight. His own machine-guns failed and in order to destroy his enemy he rammed the German machine. On that first day of 'Barbarossa' Hauptmann Wilcke of Jagdgeschwader 3 shot down three Rata aircraft within twenty minutes and his squadron scored thirty-six kills in the air and destroyed 28 aircraft on the ground.

The warning to the Red Air Force squadrons which would have brought them to a war footing was not received in time and most squadrons still had their machines drawn up in peacetime fashion, in neat rows on the grass. Because of High Command orders to anti-aircraft regiments not to fire upon German machines violating Soviet air space, no shot was fired as the shining points of light in the dawn sky suddenly plunged and were revealed to be Ju 87s, whose bombs exploded among the neat rows of Russian fighters on the ground.

The first waves of Stukas flew away and were replaced by others who created more and more destruction. Still there was no authority from Moscow for the Red Air Force to take up the challenge nor did this come until the Soviet air arm had been crippled, Those few Red Air Force machines which went into action to intercept the first waves of German bombers had taken off without orders from Moscow, their commanders preferring to risk the wrath of the Russian leader rather than see their units destroyed without any counter-action being taken.

When the Air Force High Command did issue orders these demanded that the fighter squadrons intercept and destroy the Luftwaffe. But as a result of the High Command's ineptitude there was no longer a Red Fighter Command in the western regions capable of such a massive response. Those few machines which in the late afternoon of 22 June, did manage to take off from their cratered airfields in obedience to orders were picked off by the Luftwaffe's aces, whose skills had been sharpened by battle with the RAF.

One unit which reacted quickly to the German aggression was that on the North-west Front. As early as 07.15 hrs Red Army's VIII Corps ordered the bomber squadrons under its command to attack German airfields. The Red Air Force was at that time, not an independent command but was subordinate to the army, few of whose leaders appreciated air force problems. The orders from VIII Corps Command read 'Strong blows will be used to destroy the bomber and fighter squadrons of the German Luftwaffe on their airfields. The major groupings of the German ground forces are to be destroyed by bombing. These raids will penetrate inside enemy territory to a depth of 150km. Königsberg and Memel are to be destroyed by bombing.' The General commanding the Soviet bomber squadrons of the North-west Front region did in fact, order his units into action although he knew that there were no fighters to defend them. Wave after wave of bombers took off, not always without accidents, which left a great many machines wrecked or burning in bomb-craters. Once the old-fashioned, slow Russian machines had taken off, they formed up to fly westwards to carry out the lunatic orders which they had been given. Above the formating Soviet squadrons waited the German fighter aces and they struck without mercy. It was a slaughter of the innocents and in such circumstances it is no wonder that German fighter pilots claimed a vast number of kills during those first days of 'Barbarossa'.

There was, indeed, doubt among a great many senior Luftwaffe officers at the validity of these claims, but proof existed in post-operation aerial reconnaissance photographs of Soviet airfields. These showed that the Luftwaffe had destroyed hundreds of aircraft on the ground as well as putting out of action 31 airfields, three special-purposes bunkers, two barracks, two artillery positions, an underground bunker system and a petrol supply dump. Up to 29 June, German pilots had destroyed 4,017 Russian aircraft on the ground or in the air. Admitted German losses during that period amounted to fifteen aircraft. There is no mistaking the sense of satisfaction with which General von Waldau, Luftwaffe Chief of the General Staff, made his diary entry at the end of the first day of 'Barbarossa'. 'The timing of the air attack against Russian airfields was an absolute success. Those attacks opened the way for operations against the whole Red Air Force.'

Just as the Russian armoured counter-attack against 6th Panzer Division had been a portent for the future of land operations, so were the reports of the losses suffered by the Red Air Force an indication of just how badly the German leaders had underestimated the size of the Soviet forces. Luftwaffe experts had predicted the strength of the Red Air Force as about 6,000 machines. Luftwaffe High Command had always accepted that the Russians had more aircraft in service than the Luftwaffe had, but it was felt that that imbalance could be corrected many of the Russian machines were old-fashioned and slow and were piloted by men with no experience of aerial combat. Despite being outnumbered the Luftwaffe was still considered by the German leaders to be superior in every way to the Russian force.

In view of the high number of kills gained in the opening stages of 'Barbarossa', the Luftwaffe leaders were forced to re-evaluate their estimates of the strength of the Red Air Force. The German pilots had destroyed more than 4,000 enemy machines in one week but the Red Air Force was still flying sorties in strength. The conclusion drawn was that the true strength of the Russian service was higher than the 6,000 machines which the Luftwaffe experts had predicted. Those estimates must have been out by as much as 50 per cent. Thus, even though the Soviet force had suffered heavy losses, it was still numerically superior to the Luftwaffe by 2 to 1. Despite the Luftwaffe's achievements during those few first days, the Red Air Force had not been totally destroyed and thus the Luftwaffe's first task had not been completed. Nevertheless, the German High Command considered the death of the Red Air Force as a foregone conclusion. Tied to the army's timetable and with the first of its tasks as yet uncompleted, the Luftwaffe was then taken from the task of maintaining air superiority and put to the second of its tasks in 'Barbarossa' – close support of the Army; in other words its bombers were to act as long-range artillery.

The reaction of the Red Army High Command and the orders it issued to its subordinate formations were no less ridiculous than those which had been given to the airmen. From initial reluctance to accept that the Germans had invaded, the next progression was to forbid any retaliatory fire by Russian artillery, even though the German barrage was continuing. Many Front commanders, repeating Stalin's words, considered that the German moves were intended to provoke a Russian response that could justify war between the nations. The Red Army's guns thus stayed silent for some hours. When, at long last, the Soviet High Command was forced to accept the fact of the German invasion and was prepared to act against it, its immediate reaction was to declare that Communist ethics would triumph over the criminal fascist act. High Command ordered counter-attacks which were not just to recapture the ground that had been lost, but were intended to initiate a grand manoeuvre which would sweep into the lands of the Capitalist aggressors.

On that sector of the Soviet West-front which projected as a salient into German-held territory, the Red Army's military position was soon little short of disastrous. Panzers of Army Group North struck south-eastwards and others from Army Group Centre drove north-eastwards, aiming to trap the Russian divisions concentrated around Bialystok. Holding that particular sector was Major-General Bolubyev's 10th Army, whose front-line divisions, subjected to order and to counter-order in the last weeks and days of peace had dissolved into disorder when the German panzers drove through them. Those Red Army units had had a testing time. Quite unprepared for the German armour thrusts and the screaming dive-bombers, badly commanded and inefficiently organized, many units broke, fragmented and disappeared.

Into the chaos of the disintegrating 10th Army there then arrived at Army Field Headquarters near Bialystok, the Deputy Commander of West-front with demands for information about the military situation and for the measures which Golubyev was taking to destroy the Germans. The commander of 10th Army tried to explain that he could barely hold his units together and that a general counter-offensive was out of the question. The Deputy Commander was in no mood to listen. He adopted the policy common to all who had survived Stalin's terror purges of 1937 and passed the decision to his superior to resolve. He telephoned Front Commander, General Pavlov, from 10th Army HQ. Pavlov, in turn, referred the problem to his higher authority. After he had received their orders he telephoned Golubyev. 'Can you hear me clearly?' was his first question. 'You can? This is the order as given to me from Supreme Command. The enemy is to be destroyed by counter-attacks launched by 10th Army. General Golubyev is to be directed to recapture . . .' and Pavlov named a string of cities now well behind German lines. 'The counter-attack', Pavlov went on, 'is to take place and the objectives gained by this evening.' In vain Golubyev tried to explain to his superior that the orders had no sense in view of the situation as it really was on the ground. Pavlov merely repeated the instructions – waited – and then said 'You have been given the order. Carry it out.'

In the south, too, the same impossible demands were made and appeals to Kirponos, the Front Commander, by the leaders of his field armies, were brusquely rejected. He again, true to the fashion of the survivors of the 1937 purges, did not make that decision for himself, but asked the political commissar for advice. The answer from the political officer was the same as that of Pavlov. 'You have been given an order. Carry it out.'

High Command was so out of touch with the true situation that it gave orders for South-west Front not just to drive back the invading Germans and to capture a few cities, but for its troops to mount an attack which would take them to Lublin, nearly 200km behind the German front line. Lublin was to be recaptured during the second day of the counter-offensive. The regiments and divisions of Potapov's 5th Army, the formation which High Command had ordered to undertake that operation, no longer existed as a fighting force. They had been shattered in the first day's battle. Facing them were the armoured units of Guderian's 2nd Panzer Army and the infantry corps of Reichenau's 6th Army. The German

The factor not considered by the planners of the OKW was the Soviet partisan organization. Guerrilla warfare starved the German battle line of combat units and contributed to the victories of the Red Army. But to the Germans the guerrillas were not soldiers but bandits.

Army of those heady days had a number of force-ful, aggressive commanders and both Guderian and Reichenau had those characteristics in full measure. The shattered divisions of Potapov's army had no hope of even holding a line in the face of the storming German assault. That they were under orders to drive back the Germans for a distance of more than 200km was a fantasy.

But Potapov had received the order and he passed it to his subordinate units for action, over-riding their protests by referring them to the political commissar at South-west Front Head-quarters. For many, the command by a Party man had the authority of Stalin himself and submerg-ing their own doubts in the dogma that 'the chief knows best', they ordered the futile assaults to be launched. Those officers who managed to talk to the political commissar and who sought to con-vince him that the orders were suicidal were soon made aware of the implacable nature of the Party. The West-front commissar passed down to his political subordinates directives to arrest and to execute summarily those who wavered in their adherence to the Party's beliefs. Divisional com-manders, brigadiers, junior officers, NCOs and men; the NKVD squads shot them all. In the South, a Ukrainian division which refused to go up the Line to certain death, was surrounded by a corps of political troops and destroyed by shellfire, by tanks and by execution squads.

Those commanders who tried to carry out the orders to attack, knew that there could be no proper, co-ordination between the various arms of service. Any barrage fired to support the advanc-ing infantry would be brief, because many of the dumps from which the artillery should obtain their supplies of shells were now behind German lines, and confusion in the Russian rear areas had stopped supplies reaching the front. Many tanks were without fuel or ammunition. The Red Air Force could give little support in a ground role. The chief burden of battle fell, as it had in former days, upon the bravery of the infantry and the élan of the cavalry regiments. To their undying glory they attacked time after time, seeking to halt the invaders. Their assaults were exercises in futility, but they did have a psychological effect upon many German units facing them.

'I can never forget the first mass atack by Russian infantry . . . I could not believe that in the Second World War the tactics of the First Great War could still be used by any one of the major combatants. The whole assault was so ineptly handled that I found it difficult to believe that it was being carried out by a professional army. That incompetence reinforced the belief held at the time by many German officers, that the Red Army was being handled no differently to the Tsarist army. It was the same old steam-roller.

'The Soviet assaults were carried out by masses of men who made no attempt at concealment but trusted in sheer weight of numbers to overwhelm us . . . quite a long distance from our positions there were lines of brown-uniformed men tramp-ing forward. The first of these . . . was followed at about 200 metres distance by a second line. Then there rose out of the grass a third wave, then a fourth and then a fifth. The lines of men stretched to the right and left of our regimental front over-lapping it completely and the whole mass of Russian troops came trampling stolidly and relent-lessly forward. It was an unbelievable sight, a machine-gunner's dream target . . . At 600 metres we opened fire and whole sections of the first wave just vanished, leaving here and there an odd survivor still walking stolidly forward. The second wave had also taken losses but closed up towards the centre, marched round and across the bodies of their comrades who had fallen. Then as if on a signal the lines of men began running forward. As they advanced there was a low rumbling "Hoooooraaaay" . . .

'The first three waves had been destroyed by our fire but not all of the men in them had been killed. Some who dropped were snipers who worked their way forward through the grass to open fire upon our officers and machine-gun posts. The rush by the fourth wave came on more slowly for the men had to pick their way through a great carpet of bodies . . . The great mass of Soviet troops was now storming up the slope towards us but our fire was too great and they broke. About an hour later a further five lines of men came on in a second attack. We smashed this and then crushed a third and fourth assault. The numbers of the enemy seemed endless and the new waves of men advanced across their own dead without hesitation . . . The Ivans kept up their attacks for three days and even during the nights . . . The number and fury of those attacks exhausted and numbed us . . . not to hide the truth, they had frightened us . . . I think that on that day in 1941, some of us began to realize for the first time that the war against the Soviet Union was going to be bigger than we had thought it would be and a sense of depression, brought about by a fear of the unknown, settled upon us. That we would win we had no doubt, but what we were now engaged in would be a long, bitter and hard-fought war.'

The rigid and uninspired handling of the Red Army by its senior commanders was responsible for the dramatic events which marked the early weeks and months of 'Barbarossa'. These were the great encirclements of whole Russian armies by fast-moving panzer columns and their destruction by a double encirclement of German infantry and panzer forces.

The counter-offensive ordered by the Soviet High Command, or Supreme Stavka, as it was titled on 23 June, did nothing but assist the Germans in these encircling operations. Halder noted the Red Army's resistance with satisfaction and commented that the longer the Russians stood in defence of the western regions the easier it would be to destroy them west of the Dnieper. And as if to fulfill the intention of the German battle plan the Red armies stood and fought and by so doing were encircled. It would be both boring and repetitious to describe these battles individually, but a short list of the major engagements of 1941, serves to show not merely the swift efficiency of the German military machine, or even the obstinacy of the Red Army and its leaders, but also Russia's tremendous reserves of manpower and supplies.

In the Bialystok-Minsk encirclement 304,000 men, 3,332 tanks and 1,809 guns were lost. In the Smolensk pocket, 310,000 men, 3,205 tanks and 3,120 guns. The encirclement around Vyasma and Briansk, cost the Russians 663,000 men, 1,242 tanks and 5,452 guns. In the great Kiev operation 665,000 men, 884 tanks and 3,178 guns. At Uman 103,000 men, 317 tanks and 1,100 guns. These were the most important encirclements. There were a great many others where the number of prisoners taken were only 14–15,000. The totals of Red Army men captured in the operations listed above, exceeds two million. To that total must be added those who had been taken in the lesser encirclements, those who had been killed in action and those who had been wounded. The total exceeded four million men and must have given the German leaders reason to believe that the Red Army had indeed been destroyed.

But it was not to be as easy as that. The OKW had calculated that the Red Army might have an active service strength of 175 divisions and that with the bringing in of reserves perhaps 250 divisions could be put into action. Halder's querulous complaint, 'Until now we have identified 348 Red Army divisions', is the cry of a man who realizes with terrible clarity that the actual numbers of the enemy conflict with the figures on which the whole plan of battle had been based. It was that sober, frightening revelation which led to a re-evaluation of the successes which had been gained. Hitler's Directive No. 34, dated 30 July 1941, accepted that not one of the strategic intentions behind 'Barbarossa' had been achieved and seemed determined that none should. Bock's Army Group Centre had achieved great success but now under Hitler's Directive, it was to go over to the defensive while the main offensive efforts were to be made by von Leeb in the North and von Rundstedt in the South.

Less than a month later, on 26 August, OKW produced a memorandum accepting that the war against Russia could not be won during 1941. As if to underline the terrible prediction implied in that memorandum autumn rains began early and continued for days. Road surfaces were washed away and the highways became stretches of mud, in places 2 to 3 feet deep. Such weather and such roads were unknown to the Germans. The clinging mud halted their advance, but the Red Army overcame the conditions and near Yelnya, forced the 4th Army of Army Group Centre, to retreat; the first time that such a move had been made by a major German formation during the Second World War. The war in Russia had been lost.

In the weeks which followed the production of the OKW memorandum the greatest number of the encirclements given above were carried through successfully. Then, at long last, Army Group Centre was ordered to move against Moscow, but the decision had come too late. Stalin and the STAVKA had had weeks to prepare its defence. Weeks in which workers' militias had been formed, weeks during which the Soviet partisan organization was activated; weeks in which new Red Army divisions were raised and others on the strategic reserve in far-away Siberia were equipped and prepared for the winter campaign.

Dr Goebbels, made aware of the OKW memorandum, offered to start a collection of woollen garments to clothe the army in the field, but this suggestion was turned down. Such a move, the Supreme Command said, would shock the army and the nation in its implication that the war in Russia would not be ended before the onset of winter.

Winter came early, lasted long and was terrible in ferocity. When the battle for Moscow ended in December 1941, more than half a million German soldiers had become casualties. Another 100,000 had to be taken out of the line suffering from frost bite.

The German planners had underestimated the size of the Red Army, had been ignorant of the strategic reserve armies that could be put fresh into battle and whose numbers turned the tide. German Intelligence had been unaware of the relocation of Russian industry and the Nazi authorities had rejected contemptuously the offers of help in the fight against the Soviets which had been made by the peoples of the Baltic republics, the Ukrainians and by the nations of southern Russia. The political perspective of the Slav as an Untermensch – less than human – was a part of the Party philosophy. It was into the hands of men who believed fervently in that dogma that the administration of occupied Russia was placed and the brutality of the regimes they set up alienated the ordinary Russian and made him an enemy instead of the ally against the Soviets that he might have become.

In 1942, a new German summer offensive opened and thrust in a blitzkrieg campaign southwards into the Caucasus and eastwards to Stalingrad. These were offensives without purpose. By 1942 there were no circumstances under which the Germans could defeat the Red Army and win the war in Russia. German formations might still win encirclement victories, they might still conquer vast areas of steppe land – but the decisive victory could no longer be gained.

It is unlikely that the Germans could ever have won the war against Russia – a country which Hitler and his Generals had declared could be defeated within five months. The million German soldiers who fell between 22 June and 31 December 1941, proved that the perspective of the German Führer and his military subordinates had been a tragically distorted one.

Left: The shortage of warm clothing on the Eastern Front resulted in charity drives by the WHW to collect clothes from German civilians. This collection van bears the inscription 'From Berlin to Smolensk wool supplies'. The response to such appeals was generous; but Army obstruction, in view of the failure that such recourse admitted, prevented the clothing effort until almost too late.

# 'BASTOGNE MUST SURRENDER!'

At about 05.30 hrs on the morning of 16 December 1944, the last major military offensive to be launched by the German Army in the west, opened in the thunder of a short but fierce barrage. The objectives of that operation were, admittedly, ambitious and the soldiers were keen to gain them, but less than a month later and the columns, which had set out with high hopes of victory, were pulling back into the Reich, a defeated army. During the course of that short-lived offensive, one small town in the Ardennes was surrounded but held out, rejecting German military demands for its surrender. That town was Bastogne and the garrison which held it was drawn, principally, from 101st US Airborne Division. The Ardennes offensive, which has passed into history as the Battle of the Bulge, is of interest, not only for the American refusal at Bastogne to acede to a German surrender demand, but rather more for the strategic aims which caused it to be launched.

To set the scene we must go back to the late autumn of 1944, and to the swift Allied advances of that time. American units in the heart of France had right-wheeled and were striking towards Germany. On the left flank of the US armies British, Polish and Canadian formations were driving northwards through Belgium and into Holland, preparatory to swinging into the North German Plain. Under pressure from that Allied force, the German Army in the west was being forced back. A similar situation obtained in the east where Army Group Centre had collapsed and had opened the way into Germany for the divisions of the Red Army. Germany was everywhere on the defensive, a situation which Hitler found intolerable. It was, however, a situation which could not improve, unless Germany was able to halt the retreats and herself go over to the counter-attack.

The Führer demanded offensive operations. Germany's hope lay in her armies, either those in the east or those in the west, frustrating future Allied offensives by launcing a pre-emptive blow on one of the two major battle fronts. That blow, must be hard enough to paralyze the forces of the chosen enemy for some considerable time. With

them confounded and in disarray the German formations, encouraged by their victory, could be transported to the other front. There those new arrivals could regroup and deal the other enemy a savage blow.

The first strike, as the Führer saw it, would be made in the west. The supply situation of the Allied armies was not in good order. The Anglo-Americans in North-West Europe had no major ports near the battle line through which their armies could be nourished. The ports in Britanny were hundreds of miles away from the front and many of those on the Channel coast, which might have been used, were either garrisoned by Germans who refused to surrender or had had their dock installations so seriously damaged that they were unusable. The bulk of Allied war matériel had to be brought up by road convoy from Normandy and Brittany. The spearheads of the Allied military forces were at the end of a long and fragile supply route. To cut that would destroy the spearheads. And if, in addition, the British/Canadian armies could be sundered from the Americans, and each force defeated separately, a paralyzing blow would have been struck and disaster brough to some thirty Allied divisions. Hitler, convinced of the fragility of the alliance between the Russians and the Anglo-Americans, further convinced himself that the massive defeat which his new operations would produce, must lead to such bitter recriminations between the Allies that that alliance would be smashed.

In August Hitler ordered Jodl to produce a battle plan and soon the Führer had a choice of five offensive routes. Hitler selected the one which had first appealed to him; a panzer thrust through the lightly held US front in the Ardennes, between Monschau and Eternach. With the Americans flung aside, German armoured columns would race across Belgium, would 'bounce' the Maas and drive on to Antwerp. Hitler was acutely aware of the risks which the operation entailed of which Allied air superiority was the most crucial. To help overcome that problem he first chose a winter month when bad weather could be expected to reduce the scale of RAF and USAAF operations. The he gave orders that 1,500 Luftwaffe fighters, including 100 jets, were to support the offensive so that over the battlefield and for the duration of the attack the Germans would have air superiority. Not only in the air but in ground forces, too, there was to be a build-up of men and matériels. Twelve panzer and/or panzer grenadier divisions would be taken from the battle line for the coming offensive. Twenty Volksgrenadier divisions, whose National Socialist élan was expected to produce startling military results, would come on to the battle establishment by 10 December. Then there were two Para divisions and four standard infantry divisions which would be taken from the line, and which would be rested so that they could take part in Operation 'Watch on the Rhine'. Thus, 26 German divisions and a great number of heavy artillery and armoured formations would be ready for the assault. That mass of men, guns and tanks was assembled into three armies: 6th SS Panzer on the right wing, 5th Panzer in the centre and 7th Army on the left.

Army Group B laid out its battle plan on 29 November. In essence this stated that 6th SS Panzer Army was to break through the US front to the north of the Schnee Eifel and to force crossings of the Maas between Liège and Huy. Following the link up with parachute group 'Stoesser', the Army's panzer forces would make for the Albert Canal between Maastricht and Antwerp.

The 5th Panzer Army was to strike through the enemy front and by following a line Marche–Namur–Bastogne–Dinant was to cross the Maas between Andenne and Givet. The 7th Army was to form the left flank of 5th Panzer Army and would not only form a defensive front to the south and south-west, but was to drop troops off to secure the left flank of 5th Panzer Army as this advanced to the final objective; Antwerp.

The operational plans went into peculiar detail. Appendix 3 of 6th SS Panzer Army orders stated that the German infantry was to move so close to the enemy's forward positions that immediately after the last shell of the barrage had exploded, the foot troops could make their charge crying 'Hurrah'. Hitler interfered with the plan by laying out the routes to be followed by the spearhead group of 1st SS Panzer Division 'Leibstandarte'. He personally decreed which roads the columns were to follow and forbade any deviation from those routes. He, perhaps, neither knew nor cared that the roads were unsuitable for the Tigers and Panthers of Peiper's assault group. He had issued the orders. Peiper must obey them. If everybody did what they were told to do success was almost guaranteed. The task was not an impossible one.

The attack was intended to tear a 100km gap in the front of First US Army. This was known to be inexperienced in combat and as an added incentive to the attacking troops Foreign Armies (West) reissued its critique on the fighting abilities of the US and British soldiers. These were said to be poor. The Allied infantry were accused in the report of being slow in attack and weak in defence. The tank forces were not aggressive. Allied troops chose to give ground under German fire and had to be supported by aircraft or artillery. In view of these reported weaknesses the attack must be a successful one, stiffened as it would be by the politically inspired Volksgrenadier divisions.

At about 05.30 hrs on the morning of 16 December – several war diaries report the opening of the barrage to be later timed than that – the guns opened fire and continued firing for half an hour. Not quite the thunderous preparation that had been expected and in some areas the shells caused no damage for they fell on empty positions. The 'After Action' report of 393rd US Infantry Regiment claimed, by contrast, 'a concentration of artillery fire. That fire, together with mortar and six-barrelled rocket fire covered practically the whole front of regiment's 1st battalion . . .' Five minutes after the barrage opened rows of German searchlights threw their beams on to the low-lying clouds. They were creating artificial moonlight in which the infantry would advance. Whether or not the cries of 'Hurrah' were shouted by the storming troops is not stated in the war diaries.

One diary did record the spirit which animated the men of its panzer company. 'We knew that the hour had struck. The Order of the Day (issued by Gerd von Rundstedt, Supreme Commander West) was like one of those issued in the old days. One could sense that this was a decisive operation – that this was a unique chance to bring about a change in our fortunes . . .' That sense of destiny took the first attacking troops storming across the US trench lines. Some US units were overrun and lost every man. But others defended themselves well causing the Germans heavy losses. The speedy and aggressive American reaction was an indication that the appreciation by Foreign Armies (West) had underestimated the combat willingness of the US soldiers.

It is my intention to sketch just the outline of the Battle for Bastogne; suffice to say that German 47th Panzer Corps, commanded by von Luettwitz, was the formation which had the town as an objective. The first attacks by von Luettwitz's corps struck part of the line manned by US 28th Infantry Division, and specifically the area between Dasburg and Gemund. Through the gap which had been created poured elements of 2nd Panzer and 26th Volksgrenadier Divisions. Engineers from the latter unit then established bridgeheads across the River Clerf through which the Panzer Lehr Division passed. The US response was to order a Combat Command of 9th Armoured Division to block the roads leading to Bastogne.

The importance of that town in the Ardennes operation cannot be over-estimated. Through it passed several main roads; from Eternach to Namur; from Luxemburg to Liège and from Florenville to Liège. Whoever held Bastogne controlled the most important road communications in an area otherwise poorly served. Small wonder then that 47th Panzer Corps had Bastogne as an objective to be taken in the opening assault. The place had to be taken if 5th Panzer Army was to keep pace with 6th SS Panzer Army as it drove towards Antwerp.

By 18 December, General Bayerlein's Panzer Lehr Division together with 2nd Panzer Division had reached Mageret, some 4km and Noville some 7km from the town. Between the armoured spearheads of those two divisions stood Combat Command R of 9th US Armoured Division. Against so great a mass of tanks as the Germans had put in on that sector, a single combat command would have had small chance of holding the Germans to the east of Bastogne. To thicken the defensive line in that sector, 8th US Corps brought forward Combat Command B of 10th Armoured Division, combat team 'Cherry' and, during the morning of 19 December, 101st Airborne Division. These formations occupied villages to the east and to the north-east of the town, dug in and waited.

Throughout the morning of 20 December, German units closed up to Bastogne and in the afternoon Oberst von Lauchert of 2nd Panzer Division, asked permission for his unit to drive into the town. That request was denied. Instead, he was ordered to bypass it and make for the River Maas. The opportunity for a quick thrust by a veteran panzer unit to gain the objective was lost. In the succeeding days and weeks that fatal decision by German 47th Corps must have caused bitterness and recrimination at every level of command. Meanwhile, around the north-eastern and eastern suburbs of Bastogne part of a German ring had been created. To the south, 26th Volksgrenadier and Panzer Lehr Divisions had formed another segment of the ring. Leaving only a light

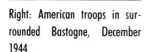

Right: American troops in surrounded Bastogne, December 1944.

screen of troops to contain the Americans, Panzer Lehr pushed on west and as it advanced past the town dropped off units to seal the western and south-western sides. Bastogne was encircled.

A situation had been created and to the Germans the outcome was a matter of military logic; inescapable logic. The town was surrounded and the battles of the past days must have reduced considerably, if not exhausted totally, the stocks of ammunition and supplies immediately available to the US defenders. In addition, the numbers of wounded must have increased enormously, so that medical supplies would be running short. True, there had been attempts at airdrops, but bad weather, flak and the Luftwaffe, had prevented those from being a success. No! It was quite clear. The town was quite cut off, the garrison was running short of matériel and was without hope of relief. Military logic demanded that the Americans surrender.

The US forces in and around Bastogne, however, were not convinced of the soundness of that logic. They knew that they had been cut off since the 20th, and Colonel Kinnard, G 3 of 101st Airborne, explained as much, although in a guarded way. Fearing that the excellent German intercept service might pick up information from his radio-telephone talk with the G 3 of 16th Corps, Kinnard explained the situation of 101st Airborne by asking, 'You know what a doughnut is? Well, we're the hole in the doughnut.' From Kinnard's confident manner it was clear that he was assured of the outcome of the siege and two days later the optimism he shared with the whole of the garrison was given a boost.

The 21st had passed in short, sharp battles, reconnaissance patrols and other encounters. On either side of Bastogne German columns were still heading westward, but the timetable for the offensive – 4 days to the Maas – was already running late. The determination of the US forces in the Bulge and in the town of Bastogne had destroyed the Führer's plan. The German corps commander resolved to point out to the surrounded garrison the situation in which they were placed. Consequently, at 11.30 hrs in the morning of 22 December, four Germans: a major, a captain and two other ranks, were seen on the Remoifosse to Bastogne road. The German group was carrying a large white flag. They were met by men from 327th Glider Infantry Regiment, one of whom spoke German. The German captain, who could speak English, opened the discussion by saying 'We are parlementaires'. The US Para soldiers took the Germans first to their own platoon headquarters where the two other ranks were left while the officers, now blindfolded, were led over the hill to company headquarters. The regiment's 2nd battalion was advised that a German surrender delegation had come in. That message was passed to regiment and then to division, but in the transmission the sense was misunderstood. The rumour which swept the Bastogne garrison was that the Germans had come in wishing to surrender. Suddenly all firing in the area died away.

The officer commanding F Company of 2nd battalion arrived at the headquarters of 101st Airborne and handed over the document which the Germans had brought. It called for the surrender of the Bastogne garrison and threatened, if the demand was not met, destruction by a furious bombardment. The surrender call appealed to the 'well-known American humanity', to save the civil population of the town from further suffering. Two hours were allowed for the Americans to consider the demand and the two German officers were to be released by 14.00 hrs. In the event of the surrender demand being rejected the threatened barrage would come in an hour after the release of the German delegation.

Colonel Harper, commanding 327th Glider Infantry Regiment, arrived at divisional headquarters to be told that the divisional staff was with General McAuliffe. The General asked what the paper contained and when told it demanded the surrender of the US force laughed and said, 'Aw, nuts'. It seemed odd that the Germans should make such a demand when his men were giving them 'one hell of a beating'. The ultimatum did not correspond to the existing situation. McAuliffe sat for a while to consider his reply. Pencil in hand he pondered and then remarked at last, 'Well, I don't know what to tell them.' He sought advice from his staff and Colonel Kinnard, the G 3, replied that the General's first remark could hardly be bettered.

McAuliffe could not recall what he had said so Kinnard reminded him. 'You said, "Nuts".' That drew applause from the staff and responding to their enthusiasm McAuliffe decided that that single word would be his rejection. The commanding officer of 327th Regiment was called in and McAuliffe asked him how he would respond to the demand. Giving Colonel Harper little time for

Above: SS armoured troops of Battle Group Peiper advance as American prisoners look on.
(Imperial War Museum)

reply McAuliffe handed him the surrender demand upon which he had written his one-word reply. He asked the Colonel to see that it was delivered. 'I'll deliver it myself,' Harper assured him. 'It will be a lot of fun.' Back at the headquarters of F Company the German officers, still blindfolded, were under guard. Colonel Harper told them, 'I have the American commander's reply.' 'Is it written or verbal?' he was asked. Harper replied that it was written and placed the document in the German major's hand.

The German captain was then told the text of the message but he could not understand the meaning, forcing the major to ask 'Is the reply negative or affirmative? If it is the latter then I shall negotiate further.' The attitude of the German officers was patronizing and it annoyed the Para Colonel. He replied, 'The answer is definitely not in the affirmative,' and went on, 'If

you continue your foolish attack your losses will be tremendous.' Harper took the two officers in his jeep back to the main road where the German other ranks were waiting. The blindfolds were removed and addressing the Captain directly Harper said, 'If you do not understand what Nuts means, then in plain English it means the same as Go to Hell. And I will tell you something else. If you continue to attack we will kill every goddam German that tries to break into this city.'

The two German officers held themselves erect and saluted stiffly. The Captain replied, 'We will kill many Americans. This is war.' The Colonel had the last word. 'On your way Bud.' The time was 13.50 hrs. The threatened bombardment did not come in and what remained of the winter day was comparatively quiet. A German infantry attack was launched over the ground across which the German mediators had come in the forenoon.

Company F broke it up as well as another small assault which came in later in the afternoon.

The chief event of the day was summed-up in the G 2 Periodic Report No. 4. 'The Commanding General's answer was, with a sarcastic air of humorous tolerance, emphatically negative. The catastrophic carnage of human lives resulting from the artillery barrage of astronomic proportions, which was to be the fate of the defending troops, failed to materialize. The well-known American humanity was considerate of the threatened possible civilian losses by firing artillery concentrations directed at the enemy impudence.'

German attacks against Bastogne continued to be pressed home and eventually not just 5th Panzer Army but also elements of 7th Army were drawn into the battle. The US High Command, aware of the significance of the town, poured in fresh troops and then broke the besieging ring of troops so that the beleaguered garrison could be nourished. The fortune of battle turned against the German troops and in the second week of January 1945, their armies which had advanced so confidently to battle, were in retreat. The last, major German offensive in the west had died.

Below: Two young soldiers of the Hitler Youth Division captured by American armoured troops during the Battle of the Bulge. The Nazi indoctrination had worked: there is still defiance in their eyes.

# DELUSION: BELIEF IN THE EAST-WEST CLASH

In the final weeks of the war Army Group South had a heavy duty laid upon it. Its terrible task was to hold the Eastern Front while behind the defensive shield which it constituted the mass of Army Group E retreated out of Yugoslavia. Let us consider why Army Group South was called upon to make such a sacrifice.

At that late stage of the war there was no cohesive battle front in northern or central Germany. Red Armies from 1st White Russian Front were fighting inside Berlin while 1st Ukrainian Front had swept past the dying capital and had reached the River Elbe where its troops had linked up with the Americans. Where German Army Group North had once stood a few shattered corps sought to contain the assaults of the Soviet Baltic Fronts and to maintain bridgeheads around the principal ports of Prussia and Kurland from which refugees were being evacuated to the western Baltic or Denmark.

Held distant from and, therefore, unable to influence the fighting in central Germany, Field Marshal Schoerner's powerful Army Group held the western regions of Czechoslovakia. To his south stood another major German military force holding a line in eastern Austria from the Semmering mountains to Radkersburg. That force was the remnants of Army Group South which had been driven back out of Russia, across Hungary and into Austria. Neither Army Group Schoerner nor Rendulic's Army Group South could support the other for a salient created by Malinovsky's 2nd Ukrainian Front held them apart. Nor were those German groups strong enough, individually or collectively, to destroy the Russian salient.

In Yugoslavia, to the south of Rendulic's Army Group, was Loehr's Army Group E. This force, which had held the Balkans, was conducting a fighting withdrawal out of Yugoslavia, a task made difficult through a combination of factors. First, there was now such close co-operation between the Soviet armies and JANL, the Yugoslav National Liberation Army, that they struck Army Group 'E' with co-ordinated, rapid and crushing blows. Secondly, Loehr felt a moral obligation to the Croat and Slovene peoples through whose lands he was retreating. His withdrawal would leave those populations undefended and at the mercy of the JANL which would exact a terrible revenge when it re-occupied Croatia and Slovenia. Not only were the peoples of those nations racial enemies of the Serbs who dominated the JANL, but they had demonstrated this racial hostility by fighting as Germany's allies. In addition both nations had declared themselves to be free states and independent of Yugoslavia. Tito was determined to bring them back into the federation and would use the standard brutal, Bolshevik methods to achieve that goal.

For fear of the wrath to come, the mass of the Croat and Slovene peoples joined Loehr's Army Group in its retreat. The great trek sought to reach and to cross the River Mur which marked the frontier between Austria and Yugoslavia. The Germans and their allies shared a naïve belief that once inside Austrian territory they would be safe. That Tito would cross the Mur in pursuit of his enemies seems, somehow, to have gone unconsidered.

The third factor working against Loehr was that Army Group C in Italy had signed an armistice with the Americans and the British. Through the gap which now yawned on Army Group E's right flank, poured crack units of British Eighth Army heading towards Trieste and the Austrian province of Carinthia.

From the situation maps in his headquarters, Field Marshal Kesselring, Supreme Commander South, could appreciate the situation facing the armies of his Command. Army Group E was isolated, but the gap on the right flank although serious was not critical. The British were not yet in sufficient strength to affect the withdrawal of Loehr's right wing, but seemed to be content to hold a containing line behind which the bulk of their forces advanced into Austria.

Viewing the situation facing Army Group South, Kesselring could see that in the Semmering mountains in northern Styria, 6th Army was withstanding the Soviet assaults. In its sector 2nd Panzer Army, forming the extreme right wing of Army Group South, was containing the Red Army along a line from Bad Gleichenberg to Radkersburg. The eastern wall was still holding, but

Kesselring asked himself for how long? Intelligence had forecast that Tolbhukin's 3rd Ukrainian Front would open an offensive strongly supported by a major effort by the JANL. Were 6th Army and 2nd Panzer to collapse under those combined assaults, nothing could halt the enemy's sweep across southern Styria and Loehr's armies would be trapped between Tolbhukin in the north and the JANL to the south.

If Army Group E was to be saved, the eastern wall in Styria had to be held until the formations, at present in Yugoslavia, were safe inside Austria. The task for the German commanders was to ensure that the troops manning the line between the Semmering and Radkersburg did hold fast. This would be difficult for it was obvious to the humblest private soldier that the end of the war could only be a matter of days. At that low military level the signs of dissolution were becoming more apparent. Food supplies were no longer reaching the front-line units. Rations had been cut and were cut again. Very little ammunition was coming forward. There were no new men to replace those who had been killed, who had been wounded, who had been taken prisoner – or who had deserted to the Reds. High Command was keenly aware of the unbearable pressures upon the soldiers to desert and to make an end to their sufferings. The commanders knew of the depression brought about by battle losses, short rations, the lack of news from home, the bitterly cold wet spring in the mountains, the unremitting strain of combat and the general hopelessness of the situation. Against all these negative factors could only be set the soldiers' traditional loyalties to Fatherland, Führer, the regiment and their comrades.

Rumour, ever-present on the battlefield, has the power to affect morale for good or for bad. The bitter rumours which swept through the embattled battalions in the first days of May were soon confirmed. The Führer was dead. He had fallen in battle. Berlin, the Reichs capital, was in Russian hands. The Reds and the 'Amis' had joined forces on the Elbe and US armies were overrunning southern Germany. These were days of mental anguish.

Clearly the war was ending and at this time of fear and doubt many must have asked themselves what was the point in their holding on? Where was the sense in staying wet through, hungry and cold in a slit trench facing certain death when, in the darkness of the night, a short walk into the Soviet lines could bring release. With any luck the first Ivans would not be too trigger-happy. Old soldiers said that if you survived the first five minutes; if the Red Army infantry didn't kill you on the spot, you were safe and then there would be warmth, food, rest and the certainty of surviving the war.

The senior military commanders, aware of the physical and emotional problems which beset their men, pondered whether they could keep their troops fighting until Loehr and his men had been brought out of the land of Yugoslavia. Suddenly, new rumours ensured that the soldiers would stand fast; firm as rocks against all the assaults of the enemy. The euphoria produced by the new rumour reached the trenches and the depression caused by the bad news of the first days of May was lifted immediately. The rumour was that the Anglo-Americans had formed an alliance with Germany. Hitler was dead and the Western Allies had made peace with the new German government. That these wild stories circulated and were believed as strongly at senior Army Group level as at the level of the ordinary grenadier shows that they were not the product of the military but that they had come from a source very close to the centre of power. 'The evil that men do lives after them,' declared Mark Antony. Even after Goebbels' half-incinerated body had been removed from the Reichskanzlei for autopsy, one of his most successful propaganda ploys, based upon a political conviction which he shared with Hitler, was circulating and was being believed. The Goebbels propaganda story was nothing less than that America and Britain would break their alliance with Russia and would then ally themselves with Germany. The three nations would then turn against the Soviet Union.

Earlier chapters of this book have shown the reasoning behind the confidence on the part of Germany's political leaders that such a clash must occur. It was, they declared, politically inevitable and lo, according to rumour, it had come to pass. As early as 28 April, OKW had ordered the number of German units to be reduced in those areas where US troops were no longer advancing or in which the Americans had given ground. The supernumerary German formations were then to be dispatched to the Eastern Front. Two days later, on 30 April, the orders from OKW were that the war was to be continued until the outcome of political moves had been resolved. Germany was playing for time. The understood inference was that hostilities would continue until the inevitable conflict between Russia and the Western Allies broke out.

The conviction of Hitler and Goebbels had been accepted at the most senior command level and repeated by the normally cautious OKW. Small wonder then that its words were more optimistically interpreted as they reached each subordinate echelon in the military hierarchy. The German armies had only to hold on and soon the Americans would be in the Line beside them. The next step, that of driving back the Soviet forces, would be easy. The field commanders were supremely confident of that. They were aware of the terrible war-weariness that infected the Red Army. The German Generals knew that the Red Army's battle line was made up of tired, exhausted and dispirited soldiers at the end of a poor and unreliable supply line. Soon the German forces would be properly equipped from the abundant resources of their Anglo-American allies. Then, together with those forces, the revitalized German armies would go over to a general attack, would thrust aside the low-moraled Soviets and would set out, once again, and this time would achieve the ambition of carving out an Empire in the East.

Following on from that basic rumour came others each more bizarre than the preceding one. One that was believed to the end was that in the west of Austria – in the high Alps – had been constructed an Alpine Fortress system inside which the German Army would gather new strength and would hold out until new secret weapons could be deployed. Underground factories within that Alpine Redoubt would construct aircraft and rockets to equip the men who would form the garrison. Other factories would turn out standard weapons, such as tanks and guns.

'We all hoped that the Alpine Fortress would be more substantial than the Reichsschützstellung (the national defence system) which was little more than an anti-tank ditch topped with barbed wire. It was well-known that at some places in Austria the Ivans had crossed the Reichsschützstellung before work on it had been completed.

'From my reading after the war I have learned that there was a conference in Graz in the first week of May. Kesselring realized that the East Front had to be held and so, although the capitulation was about to be signed in Reims, he issued orders that we in Austria were to carry on fighting.

The imminent capitulation was to apply only to the armies fighting in the west.'

Thus, up in the hills and mountains of northern Styria, fighting was carried on by soldiers unaware that the war was about to end. Their warrior spirit was bolstered by the belief that the 'Amis' were coming. Wireless reports seemed to confirm the rumour, for these told of an advance by troops of Patton's Third Army into Sudetenland, the western provinces of Czechoslovakia. It was known that other US armies, pouring through Germany, had altered the direction of their advance from east to south-eastward. Obviously, those formations were hurrying to the eastern wall in Styria. It was only a matter of holding on for a few more days and then the advance-guard of the 'Ami' army would roar up. As if to confirm these rumours the Red Army began a strong offensive on the Semmering. The truth was that the Soviets intended to break through the Muerz valley and to reach the River Enns, the halt line between the American and the Russian forces. If the Red Army could be in strength on that river line it would have trapped both German Army Groups; Loehr's and Reundulic's. More than that the Russians would have gained vast and important economic resources. Under the terms on which they intended to insist in their surrender document, it was not only the soldiers, their weapons and equipment which must be surrendered, but also all the factories and machines which had worked for the Third Reich. That was the true perspective.

The ordinary German soldiers, shivering in their sodden slit trenches on the Semmering, had a different perspective. They saw in the furious assaults of the Red Army proof that the Ivans were hoping to smash Army Group South before the Americans could arrive. The fiercer the assaults by the Russian infantry, cavalry and tank units, the more strong was the conviction of the German Landser that the 'Amis' were getting close. The rank and file of an army – of any army – are not privy to the details of military plans. Little information and few details are given to them. Their lives, their mental attitudes are determined not so much by accurate information imparted by their officers as by wild rumour and subjective reasoning. Thus, it was all too easy for them to accept without reserve, the rumours which swept through the battalions and companies like wildfire and it is easy for us to see and to understand the hopes that were entertained by these lowly men.

It is less easy for us to comprehend how OKW could have so misread the situation or have been so duped by propaganda as to accept the myth of an American-British-German alliance as if it were a fact. It was the conviction of many senior commanders that a common hated of the Nazi leadership was the only bond that held the Allies together. When that bond broke, as it must do with the Führer's death, there would be no impediment to an alliance with the conservative elements of the German nation. That the Allied hatred was not confined to Hitlerism but extended to include those conservative elements – to the army in particular – was just not understood by the Generals. Such a concept was unthinkable.

The wish is father to the deed and the wishes of the military commanders of Army Group South were expressed in deeds of such naïvety as to be almost unbelievable. Major-General Gaedke, Chief of Staff of Sixth Army, was directed by his commander to open discussions with General Patton, GOC Third US Army. The purpose of these discussions was to obtain passage for German troops through Third Army front and across Austria. There, those newly arrived reinforcements would thicken Sixth Army's battle line. When that offer was rejected by Patton's staff – the General refused to meet the German officer – Gaedke then requested medical supplies for the German units on the Eastern Front. That request, too, was turned down and the Chief of Staff returned to Sixth Army, obviously baffled by the, to him, incomprehensible attitude of the Americans.

Certainly the senior officers of 1st Panzer Division, holding the ground at Army Group's southern end, were of the opinion that some arrangement existed. Their conviction was based on the fact that reinforcements to the division had arrived from Germany, had been allowed to pass freely through the American lines and had not been taken prisoner. That unusual fact, taken in conjunction with the orders then issued by General Balck, commanding Sixth Army, for his units to head westward, fuelled the belief that 1st Panzer Division was to make for the Alpine Redoubt where, obviously, it would meet up with the Americans.

On just a slightly less absurd level was the attempt by General Ringel to influence the speed of the American advance through Austria. Ringel set out for the Enns under orders to offer the US Command an unopposed advance through the German-held areas of central and eastern Austria, in order that they would form a bulwark against the Red Army. Presumably, in view of the anticipated allied-German alliance, behind that American wall the mass of German forces in eastern Austria would be able to withdraw into the Alpine Redoubt.

The efforts of Balck's Chief of Staff, Gaedke, to allow reinforcements to stiffen the eastern wall, Ringel's attempt to speed the American advance and 1st Panzer's belief of a regrouping in the Redoubt, seen from our perspective, were ludicrous projects; the unrealizable dreams of men unwilling to face facts. The German perspective was, as we have seen, based on the certainty that Capitalism and Communism are incompatible; that the voracious Russian Empire must fight against the Imperial commitments of Great Britain and the interests of the neo-Colonial Empire of America. Within days of the war's end, Soviet acts in Europe, her increasingly threatening attitude and her support of Yugoslavia's territorial demands for the Austrian province of Carinthia, were the first signs of things to come. The reactions of the Anglo-Americans was not long in coming. A telegram to Eighth Army contained the dire order that with immediate effect the Soviet military forces were to be considered as hostile.

Within two years of the end of hostilities the nations of eastern Europe were under Soviet domination. Within three years the Berlin air-lift had to be mounted to keep the population of that city free of Soviet control. Within five years the Anglo-Americans were at war with Korean and Chinese Communist forces in Korea.

It was an historical inevitability, Goebbels had declared, that the two opposed political systems must clash. Events had shown that the prophecy born of his perspective had not been false – merely premature.

Above: Defendants at the Nuremberg trials after the war. Front row, from left to right: Goering, Hess, Ribbentrop, Keitel, Kaltenbrunner, Rosenberg, Frank, Frick, Streicher, Funk and Schacht. Back row, left to right: Doenitz, Raeder, von Schirach, Sauckel, Jodl, von Papen, Seyss-Inquart, Speer, Neurath and Krupp. News of the verdict and sentences of hanging shocked the German people deeply.

# BIBLIOGRAPHY

**German Home Front**

Bleuel, H. P. *Das saubere Reich. Eros und Sexualitat im 3ten Reich.* Munich, 1972.

Blum, John. *Deutschland ein Ackerland?* — *Aus den Morgenthau-Tagebucher.*

Boberach, Heinz (ed.). *Meldungen aus dem Reich. Geheime Lageberichten.* Herrsching, 1985.

Boddecker, G. *Der Untergang des 3ten Reich.*

Conway, J.S. *The Nazi Persecution of the Churches.* Lonn, 1968.

Doenitz, K. *Zehn Jahre u Zwanzig Tage.* Bonn, 1958.

Gersdorff, U. von. *Frauen im Kriegsdienst, 1914–1945.* Stuttgart, 1961.

Grunberger, R. *A Social History of the Third Reich.* London, 1971.

Kardorff, U. *Diary of a Nightmare.* London, 1965.

Kesselring, A. *Soldat bis zum letzten Tag.* Bonn, 1953; translated, London, 1953.

Kissell, H. *Der deutsche Volkssturm, 1944–45.* Frankfurt am Main, 1962.

Koch, H. W. *The Hitler Youth.* London, 1975.

Schonfeld, Sybil. *Sonderappell.*

Seidler, F. *Blitzmadchen.* Koblenz, 1979.

Seydewitz, M. *Civil Life in Wartime Germany.* New York, 1945.

Shirer, William L. *Berlin Diary.* London, 1941.

Speer, A. *Der Sklavenstaat.* Stuttgart, 1981.

Stephenson, J. *Women in Nazi Society.* London, 1975.

Studnitz, H. G. *While Berlin Burns.* Stuttgart, 1963; London 1963.

Thalmann, R. *Frauen im Dritten Reich.*

Tippelskirch, K. von. *Geschichte des 2tebn Weltkrieges.* Bonn, 1951.

Zeman, Z. *Nazi Propaganda.* London, 1964.

**Operation 'Sealion'**

German Preparations for war in 1935 (AL 2553 IWM).

Hossbach Memorandum. November 1937/(AL 2662 IWM).

'Seelöwe' The Planned Invasion of Great Britain. 1940.

Studie Nordwest. Voruberlegungen uber die Moglichkeiten einer Truppenlandung an der Kuste der britischen Inseln. Winter 1939/40.

Befehle: 'Unternehmen Seelöwe', Luftflotte 2 and Luftflotte 3.

Heeresgruppe A. Kriegstagebuch West. Teil III. 25.6.40. – 17.10.40.

Fremde Heere West. Chefsachen. 30.9.40. – 14.12.41.

OKH and OKM. Anweisungen an Oberbefehlshaber Heeresgruppen A:B:C: Versuchseinheiten – Seelöwe.

16te Armee. Kriegstagebuch.

XXXXI Korps. Versuchsstab R. (Reinhardt) Bericht. 30.7.40.

Jodl, Generalmajor Alfred. Denskschrift uber die Weiterfuhrung des Krieges gegen England. 30.6.40.

Jodl, Generalmajor Alfred. Denkschrift uber eine Landung in England. 12.7.40.

Hitler, A. Weisung Nr. 16. Uber die Vorbereitungen einer Landungsoperation gegen England. 16.7.40.

Falkenstein, Major von. Schreiben an Oberst von Waldau. 25.6.40. Appendix. 'Luftwaffenseitige Grundlagen fur eine Landung in England'.

Deichmann, General Paul. The struggle for air superiority during Phase 1 of the Battle of Britain.

OKW. Nord Afrika, Balkan und Russland.

OKW. Planning for Russia and the Balkans.

**Operation 'Barbarossa'**

Appreciation by Hitler of the situation in the area of Panzergruppe 1.

Armoured Breakthrough. The War Diary of Panzergruppe 1.

Raus, Generaloberst. Vorbereitung and Durchfuhrung des Grenzuberfalles sudlich Taurogen.

OKH Op. Abt. II. Barbarossa. Chefsachen. Band III.

Lutz, Generaleutnant H. Einsatz; 11te Panzer Division in der Nahe von Gornostaypol.

Xte Armee Korps. Sovietische Plane fur ein Uberfall auf Deutschland.

Gosztony, Dr. P. Uber die Vorgeschichte des deutschen Angriffs auf die Sovietunion im Juni 1941.

Handakte OKH. Fremke Heere Ost. Deutsche Unternehmungen: Ostfront 22/6/41 30.8.43.

Notice of a conference on 'Barbarossa' to be held on 14 June 1941 in the Reichskanzlei.

# APPENDIX

## PRINCIPAL DATES OF THE THIRD REICH

| | |
|---|---|
| 9 Nov 1918 | Declaration of the republic. |
| 28 June 1919 | Signing of the Treaty of Versailles. |
| 11 Aug 1919 | Announcement of the Weimar Constitution. |
| 11 Jan 1923 | Occupation of the Ruhr by French troops. |
| 13 Jan 1923 | Announcement of passive resistance in the Ruhr. |
| 9 Nov 1923 | Hitler putsch in Munich. |
| 10 Sept 1926 | Germany enters the League of Nations. |
| 20 May 1928 | General election gives the Nazi Party 3 per cent of the vote. |
| 14 Sept 1930 | Nazi landslide in the Reichstag elections. The Party gains 18 per cent of the vote and is second to the Social Democrats. |
| 10 April 1932 | Re-election of von Hindenburg as President. |

Under the terms of the Constitution the office of Chancellor of Germany could be offered to any politician at the discretion of the President. Brüning, Papen and von Schleicher had all been presidential appointees to the post. When, in January 1933, no government of Right Wing parties could be formed without the support of the Nazis, Hindenburg was forced to appoint Hitler to the Chancellorship.

| | |
|---|---|
| 30 May 1932 | Resignation of the Brüning government. |
| 1 June 1932 | Right-wing government formed by von Papen. |
| 31 July 1932 | NSDAP becomes the strongest party after the Reichstag elections with 37 per cent of the vote. |
| 6 Nov 1932 | Loss of support for Nazis in new elections. They gain 33 per cent of the vote. |
| 17 Nov 1932 | Resignation of von Papen's cabinet. |
| 3 Dec 1932 | Von Schleicher appointed Reichs Chancellor. |
| 28 Jan 1933 | Von Schleicher resigns. |
| 30 Jan 1933 | Hitler appointed Chancellor. |
| 27 Feb 1933 | Reichstag in flames. |
| 5 March 1933 | In new elections Nazis win majority. |
| 23 March 1933 | Reichstag passes the 'Enabling Act'. |
| 1 April 1933 | Organized boycott of Jewish businesses, doctors, lawyers, etc. |
| 7 April 1933 | Laws governing the expulsion of Jews from the Civil Service. |
| 2 May 1933 | Trades Unions disbanded. |
| June/July 1933 | All political parties, except the NSDAP, disbanded. |
| 14 Oct 1933 | Germany quits the League of Nations. |
| 26 Jan 1933 | German–Polish non-aggression Pact. |
| 30 June 1934 | The alleged Röhm putsch put down. |
| 25 July 1934 | Nazis attempt a putsch in Austria. |
| 2 Aug 1934 | Death of von Hindenburg. The armed forces swear an oath of allegiance to Hitler. |
| 13 Jan 1935 | Plebiscite in the Saarland on the issue of its return to the Reich. |
| 16 March 1935 | Military conscription reintroduced. |
| 18 June 1935 | Anglo-German Naval Agreement. |
| 15 Sept 1935 | The Nuremberg Laws passed. Under these Jews are deprived of citizenship, and marriage between Jews and German citizens are forbidden. |
| 7 March 1936 | German troops re-enter the demilitarized Rhineland in defiance of the Treaty of Locarno. |

| | | | |
|---|---|---|---|
| 25 Oct 1936 | Berlin-Rome Axis formed. | | confiscation of the property of Jews |
| 12 March 1938 | The Anschluss with Austria. | | who are deported. |
| 17 Aug 1938 | Introduction of special passports for | 11 Dec 1941 | Gemany declares war on the USA. |
| | Jews, who are compelled to carry the | 20 Jan 1942 | The conference at Wannsee deals |
| | name Israel or Sarah in those | | with the 'Final Solution of the Jewish |
| | documents. | | problem'. |
| 29 Sept 1938 | Under the terms of the Munich | 24 April 1942 | Jews forbidden to use public |
| | Agreement the Sudentenland is | | transport. |
| | ceded to Germany. | June 1942 | Mass gassing begins in Auschwitz. |
| 9 Nov 1938 | Following the murder of a German | Summer 1942 | The German summer offensive |
| | diplomat in Paris by a young Jew, | | opens. Its objectives are the Caucasus |
| | organized riots take place throughout | | and the Volga city of Stalingrad. |
| | Germany in the so-called | 23 Oct 1942 | The battle of El Alamein opens. |
| | Reichskristallnacht. | Nov 1942 | The battle for Stalingrad, reaches its |
| 12 Nov 1938 | German Jews have to pay a collective | | climax with the encirclement of |
| | fine of one billion marks for the | | German Sixth Army. |
| | murder of the German diplomat and | 9 Nov 1942 | Anglo-American invasion of French |
| | for the damage caused during the | | North Africa. |
| | Reichskristallnacht. | Feb 1943 | The battle for Stalingrad ends. |
| | Jews excluded from German | 13 May 1943 | Axis forces in Africa surrender. |
| | economic life and forbidden to visit | July 1943 | Operation 'Citadel', the battle for |
| | cultural establishments. | | Kursk, fought and ends with a |
| 14 Nov 1938 | Jews forbidden to visit German | | German defeat. |
| | schools. | Sept 1943 | The Anglo-Americans invade Italy. |
| 28 Nov 1938 | Restriction of freedom of movement | 6 June 1944 | 'D-Day', the invasion of North-West |
| | for Jews. | | Europe. |
| 3 Dec 1938 | Removal of driving licences from | July 1944 | The Red Army overruns the |
| | Jews. | | extermination camp at Maidenek in |
| 15 March 1939 | German troops invade | | Poland. The world becomes aware of |
| | Czechoslovakia. The | | the policy of racial extermination. |
| | Reichsprotektorat of Bohemia- | 16 Dec 1944 | Operation 'Watch on the Rhine', later |
| | Moravia established. | | code-named 'Autumn Fog', and |
| 23 March 1939 | Memel given back to the Reich. | | known to the Allies as the battle of |
| 23 August 1939 | German-Russian pact signed. | | the Bulge, opens. |
| | Confiscation of radios belonging to | March 1945 | Allies cross the Rhine. |
| | Jews. | 19 March 1945 | Hitler orders the 'scorched earth' |
| 1 Sept 1939 | German forces attack Poland. | | policy to begin. Speer prevents the |
| 3 Sept 1939 | Great Britain and France declare war | | full implementation of the Führer's |
| | on Germany. | | order. |
| 1939/1940 | Beginning of deportation of Jews in | 27 March 1945 | The last V2 rockets fall on London. |
| | Polish ghettos and camps. | 29 March 1945 | The Red Army enters Austria. |
| 9 April 1940 | Germany attacks Denmark and | April 1945 | The US First and Ninth Armies |
| | Norway. | | encircle the Ruhr; Model, |
| 10 May 1940 | Germany attacks in the west. | | commander of the encircled German |
| May/June 1940 | Evacuation of the Allied armies | | armies, commits suicide. |
| | through Dunkirk. | 20 April 1945 | First Russian shells fall on Berlin. |
| July/Sept 1940 | German plans for the invasion of | 21 April 1945 | British troops of Eighth Army, |
| | Great Britain, code-named Operation | | capture Bologna. |
| | 'Sealion' and the air battle over | 25 April 1945 | The battle for Berlin opens. |
| | Britain to destroy the RAF. | 30 April 1945 | Hitler commits suicide. |
| 22 June 1941 | Operation 'Barbarossa', the German | 2 May 1945 | Berlin falls to the Red Army. |
| | invasion of Russia opens. | 7 May 1945 | Surrender of the German forces in |
| 1 Sept 1941 | Regulations issued concerning the | | Reims. |
| | wearing of the Star of David. | 9 May 1945 | The final surrender to take effect |
| 1 Oct 1941 | Jews forbidden to emigrate. | | after the signing of the capitulation |
| 25 Nov 1941 | Regulations concerning the | | document in Berlin. |

# INDEX